I Think Our Son Is Gay

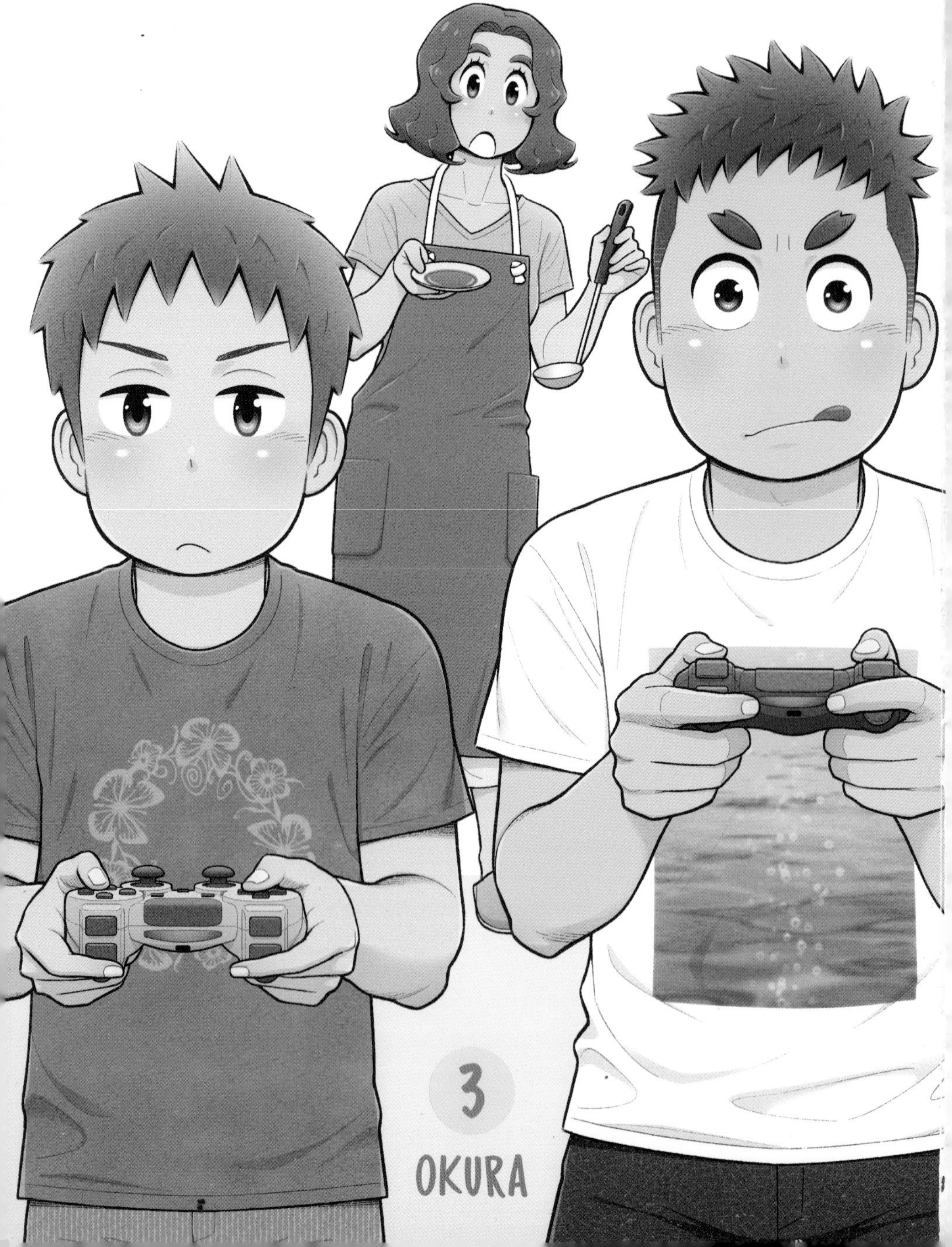

3

OKURA

I Think Our Son Is Gay

CONTENTS

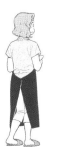

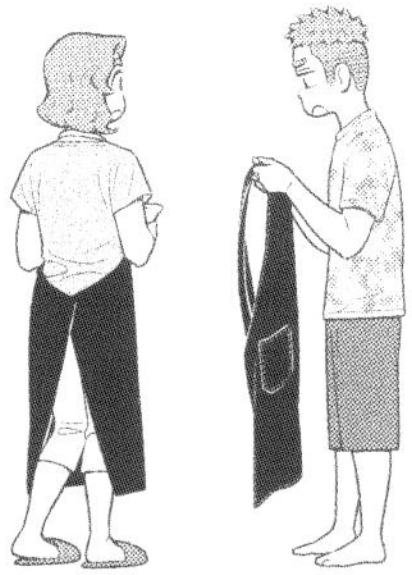

CHAPTER 43: IDOLS

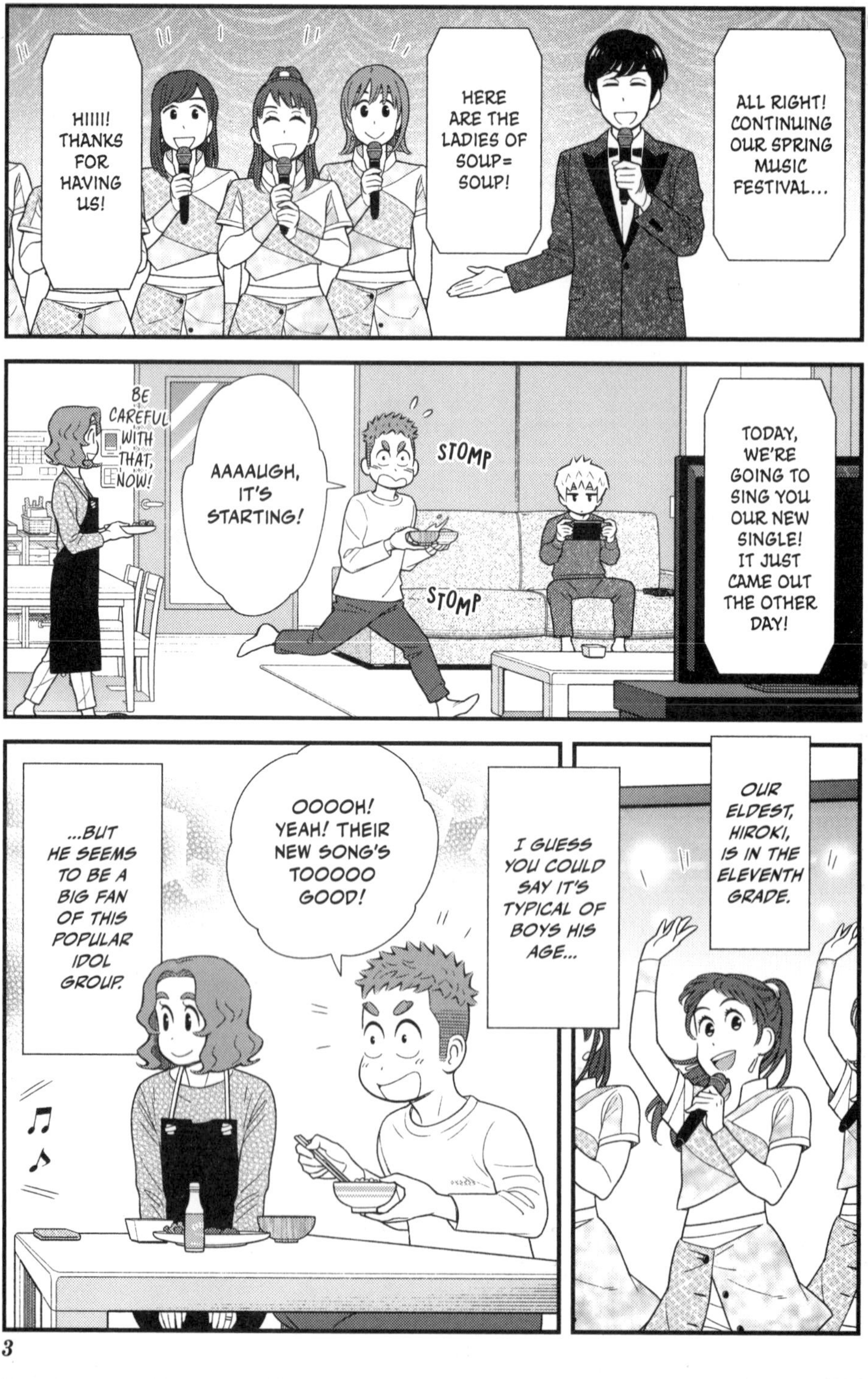

ALL RIGHT! CONTINUING OUR SPRING MUSIC FESTIVAL...
HERE ARE THE LADIES OF SOUP= SOUP!
HIIII! THANKS FOR HAVING US!
TODAY, WE'RE GOING TO SING YOU OUR NEW SINGLE! IT JUST CAME OUT THE OTHER DAY!
STOMP
STOMP
AAAAUGH, IT'S STARTING!
BE CAREFUL WITH THAT, NOW!
OUR ELDEST, HIROKI, IS IN THE ELEVENTH GRADE.
I GUESS YOU COULD SAY IT'S TYPICAL OF BOYS HIS AGE...
OOOOH! YEAH! THEIR NEW SONG'S TOOOOO GOOD!
...BUT HE SEEMS TO BE A BIG FAN OF THIS POPULAR IDOL GROUP.

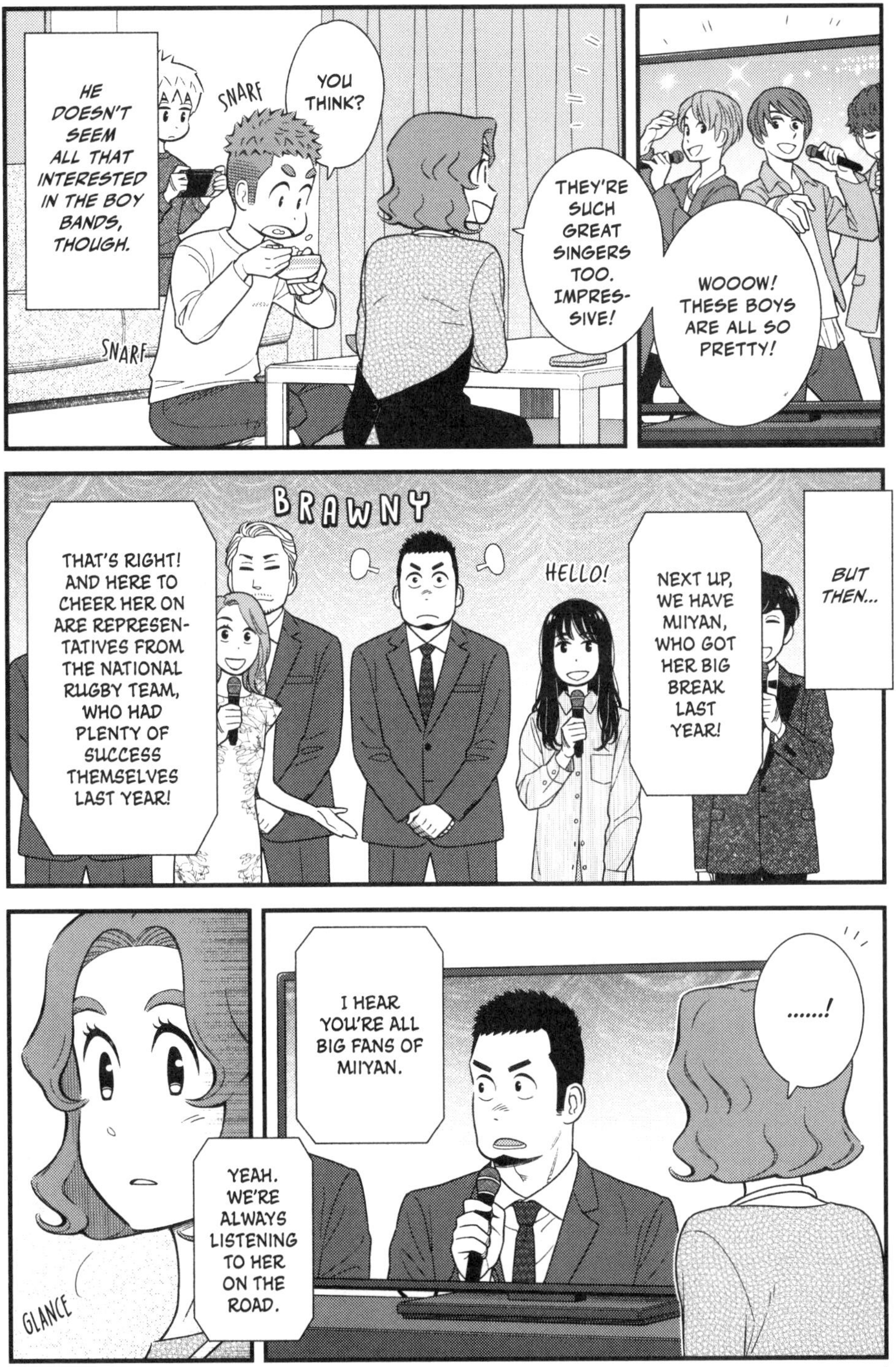
WOOOW! THESE BOYS ARE ALL SO PRETTY!
THEY'RE SUCH GREAT SINGERS TOO. IMPRESSIVE!
YOU THINK?
SNARF
HE DOESN'T SEEM ALL THAT INTERESTED IN THE BOY BANDS, THOUGH.
SNARF
BUT THEN...
NEXT UP, WE HAVE MIIYAN, WHO GOT HER BIG BREAK LAST YEAR!
HELLO!
BRAWNY
THAT'S RIGHT! AND HERE TO CHEER HER ON ARE REPRESENTATIVES FROM THE NATIONAL RUGBY TEAM, WHO HAD PLENTY OF SUCCESS THEMSELVES LAST YEAR!
......!
I HEAR YOU'RE ALL BIG FANS OF MIIYAN.
YEAH. WE'RE ALWAYS LISTENING TO HER ON THE ROAD.
GLANCE

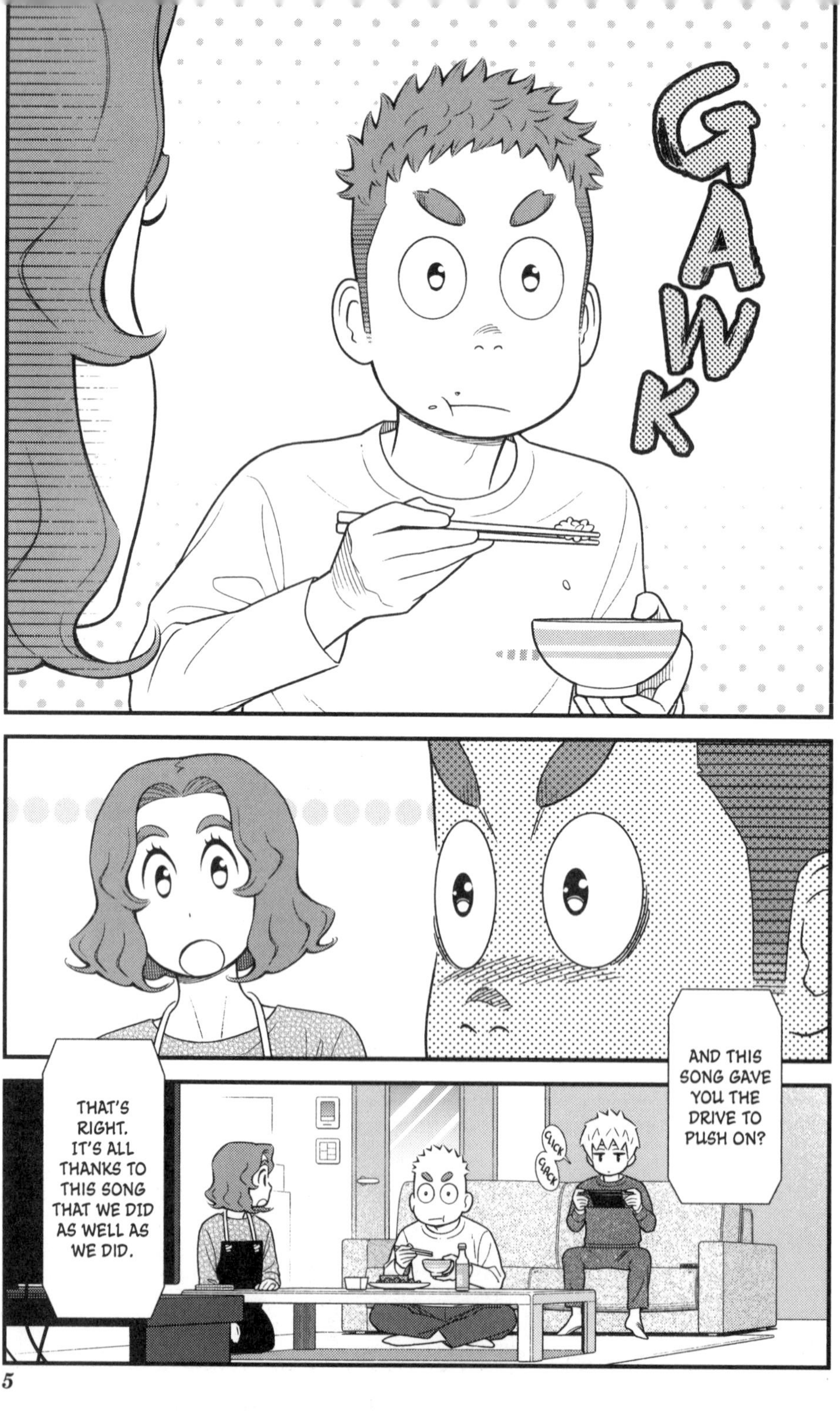
GAWK
AND THIS SONG GAVE YOU THE DRIVE TO PUSH ON?
CLICK CLACK
THAT'S RIGHT. IT'S ALL THANKS TO THIS SONG THAT WE DID AS WELL AS WE DID.

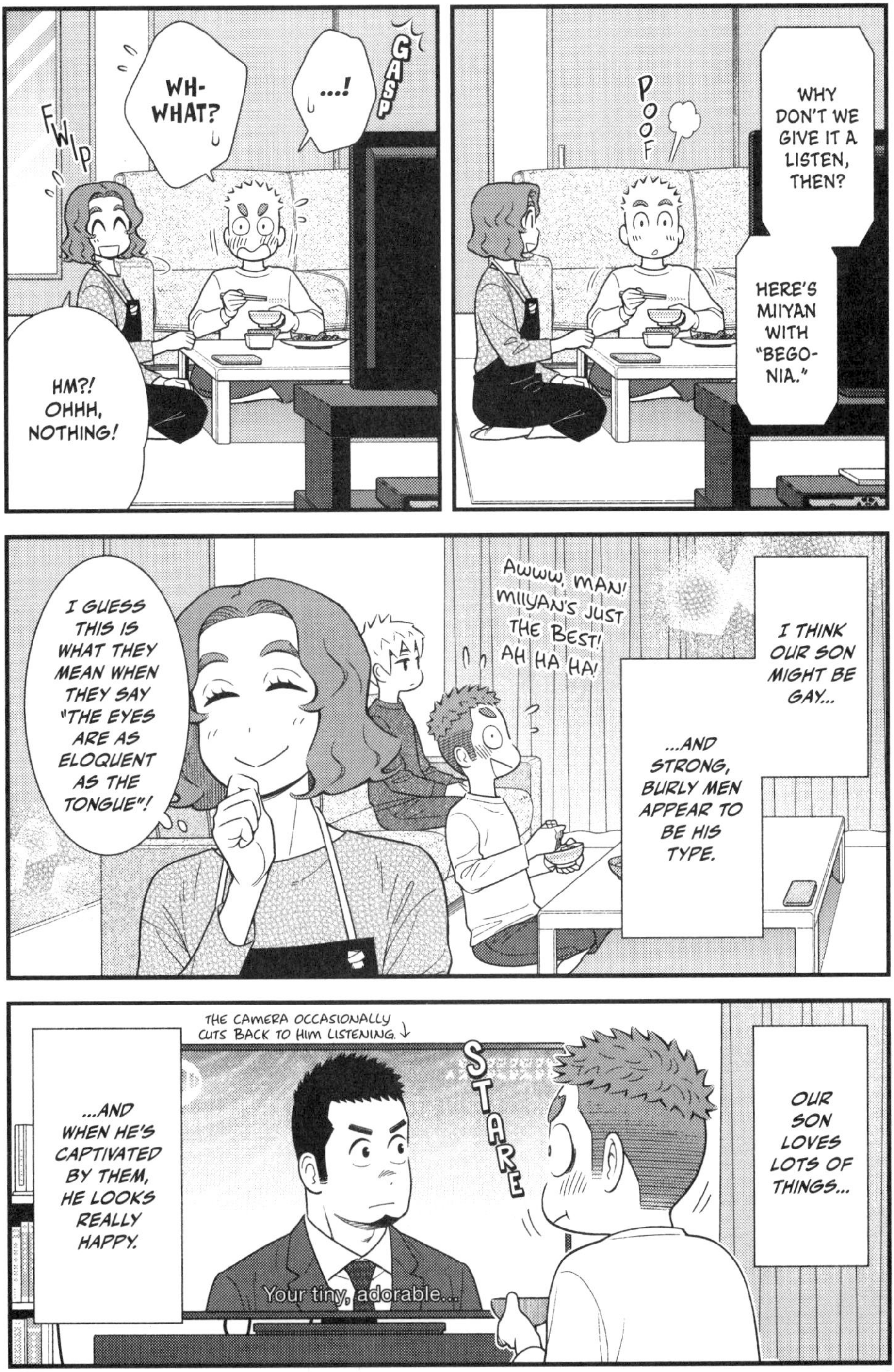
WHY DON'T WE GIVE IT A LISTEN, THEN?
HERE'S MIIYAN WITH "BEGONIA."
POOF
GASP
...!
WH-WHAT?
FWIP
HM?! OHHH, NOTHING!
I THINK OUR SON MIGHT BE GAY...
...AND STRONG, BURLY MEN APPEAR TO BE HIS TYPE.
AWWW, MAN! MIIYAN'S JUST THE BEST! AH HA HA!
I GUESS THIS IS WHAT THEY MEAN WHEN THEY SAY "THE EYES ARE AS ELOQUENT AS THE TONGUE"!
OUR SON LOVES LOTS OF THINGS...
STARE
THE CAMERA OCCASIONALLY CUTS BACK TO HIM LISTENING.
Your tiny, adorable...
...AND WHEN HE'S CAPTIVATED BY THEM, HE LOOKS REALLY HAPPY.

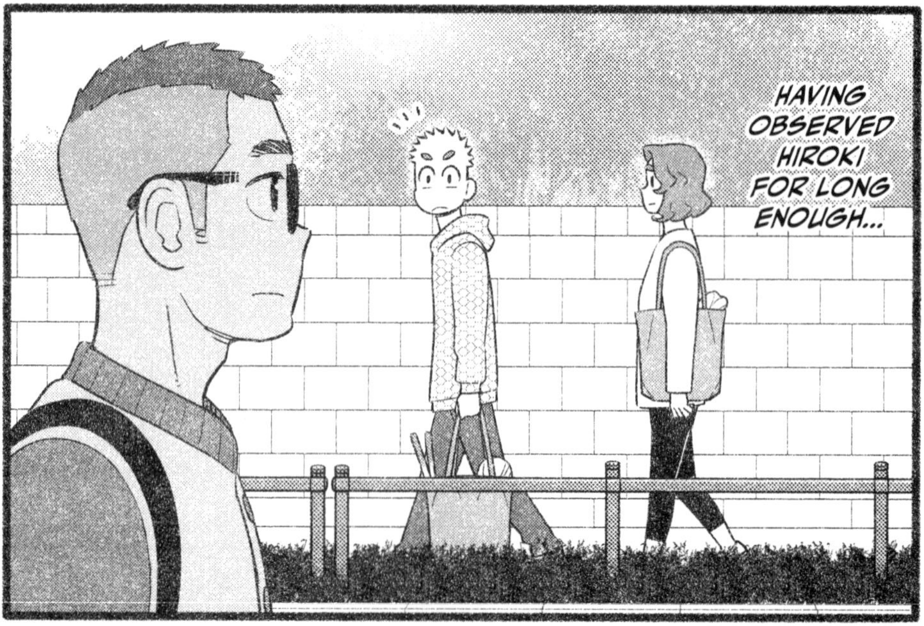
HAVING OBSERVED HIROKI FOR LONG ENOUGH...

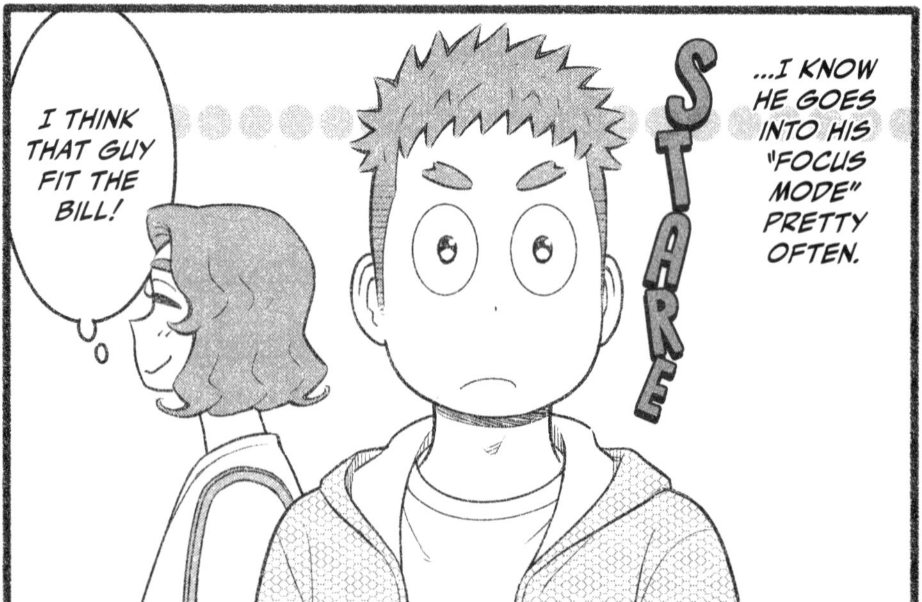
...I KNOW HE GOES INTO HIS "FOCUS MODE" PRETTY OFTEN.
STARE
I THINK THAT GUY FIT THE BILL!

I Think
Our Son
Is Gay

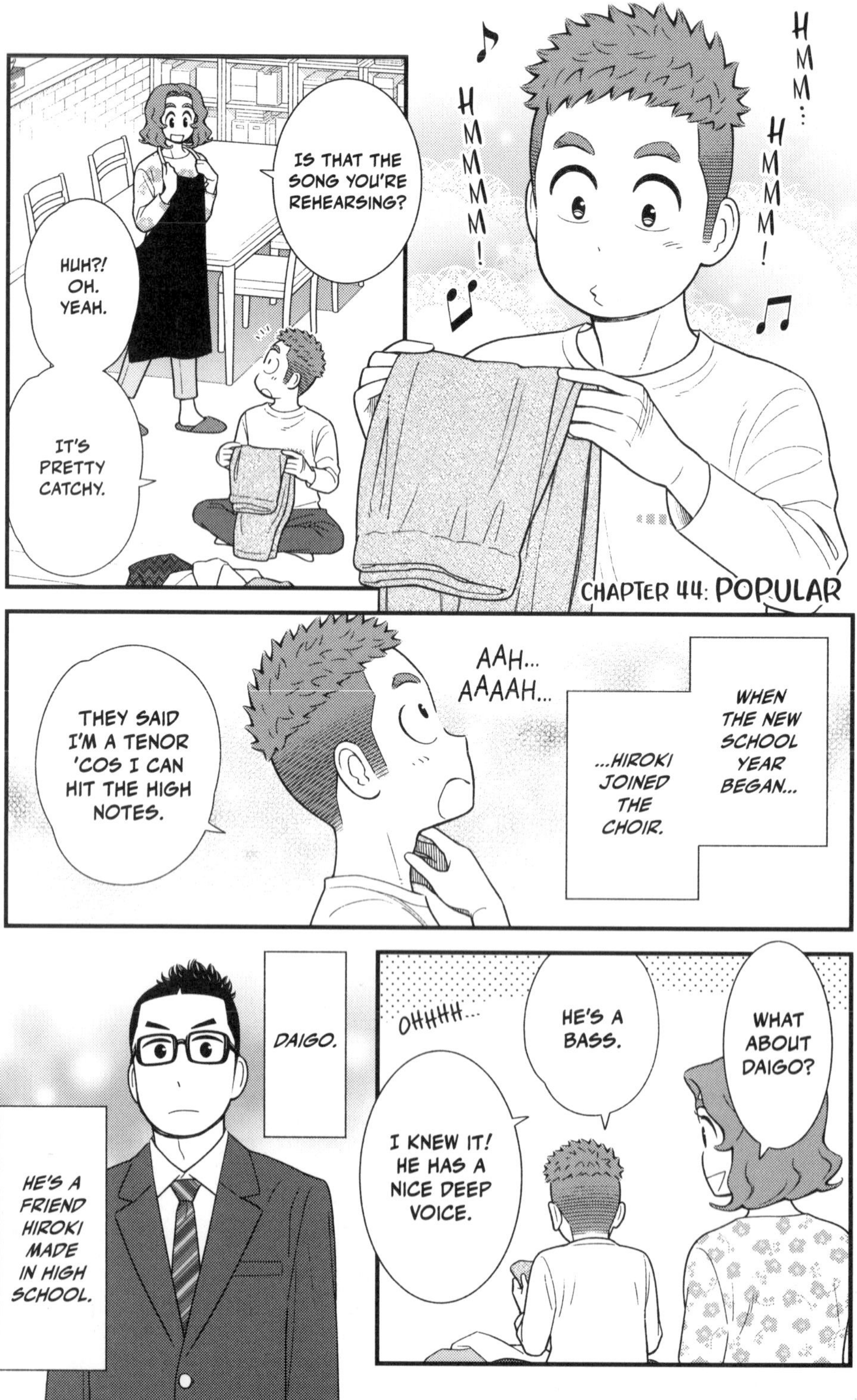
HMM...
HMMM!
HMMMM!
CHAPTER 44: POPULAR
IS THAT THE SONG YOU'RE REHEARSING?
HUH?! OH. YEAH.
IT'S PRETTY CATCHY.
WHEN THE NEW SCHOOL YEAR BEGAN...
...HIROKI JOINED THE CHOIR.
AAH... AAAAH...
THEY SAID I'M A TENOR 'COS I CAN HIT THE HIGH NOTES.
WHAT ABOUT DAIGO?
HE'S A BASS.
OHHHH...
I KNEW IT! HE HAS A NICE DEEP VOICE.
DAIGO.
HE'S A FRIEND HIROKI MADE IN HIGH SCHOOL.

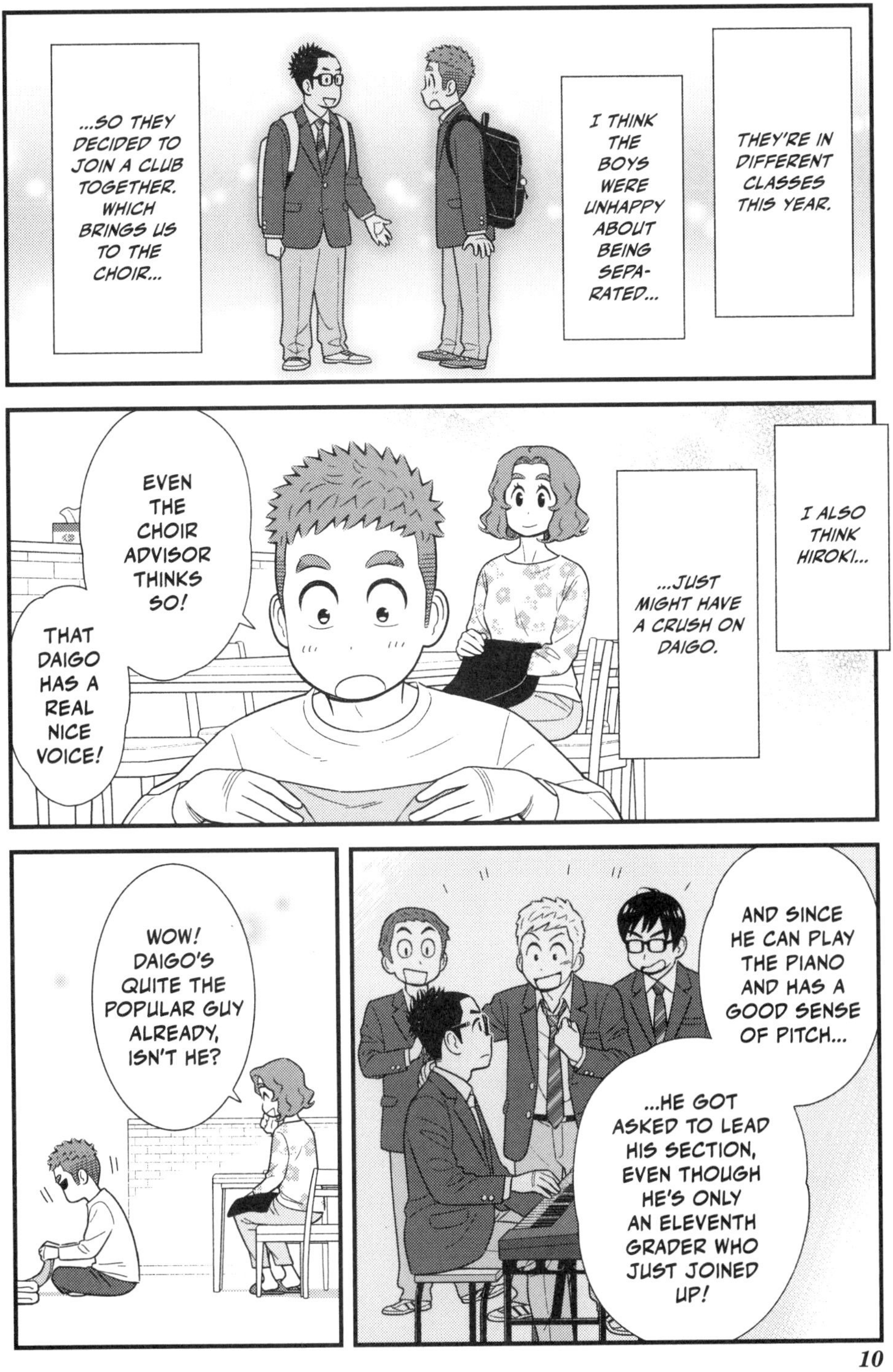
THEY'RE IN DIFFERENT CLASSES THIS YEAR.
I THINK THE BOYS WERE UNHAPPY ABOUT BEING SEPA-RATED...
...SO THEY DECIDED TO JOIN A CLUB TOGETHER. WHICH BRINGS US TO THE CHOIR...
I ALSO THINK HIROKI...
...JUST MIGHT HAVE A CRUSH ON DAIGO.
EVEN THE CHOIR ADVISOR THINKS SO!
THAT DAIGO HAS A REAL NICE VOICE!
AND SINCE HE CAN PLAY THE PIANO AND HAS A GOOD SENSE OF PITCH...
...HE GOT ASKED TO LEAD HIS SECTION, EVEN THOUGH HE'S ONLY AN ELEVENTH GRADER WHO JUST JOINED UP!
WOW! DAIGO'S QUITE THE POPULAR GUY ALREADY, ISN'T HE?

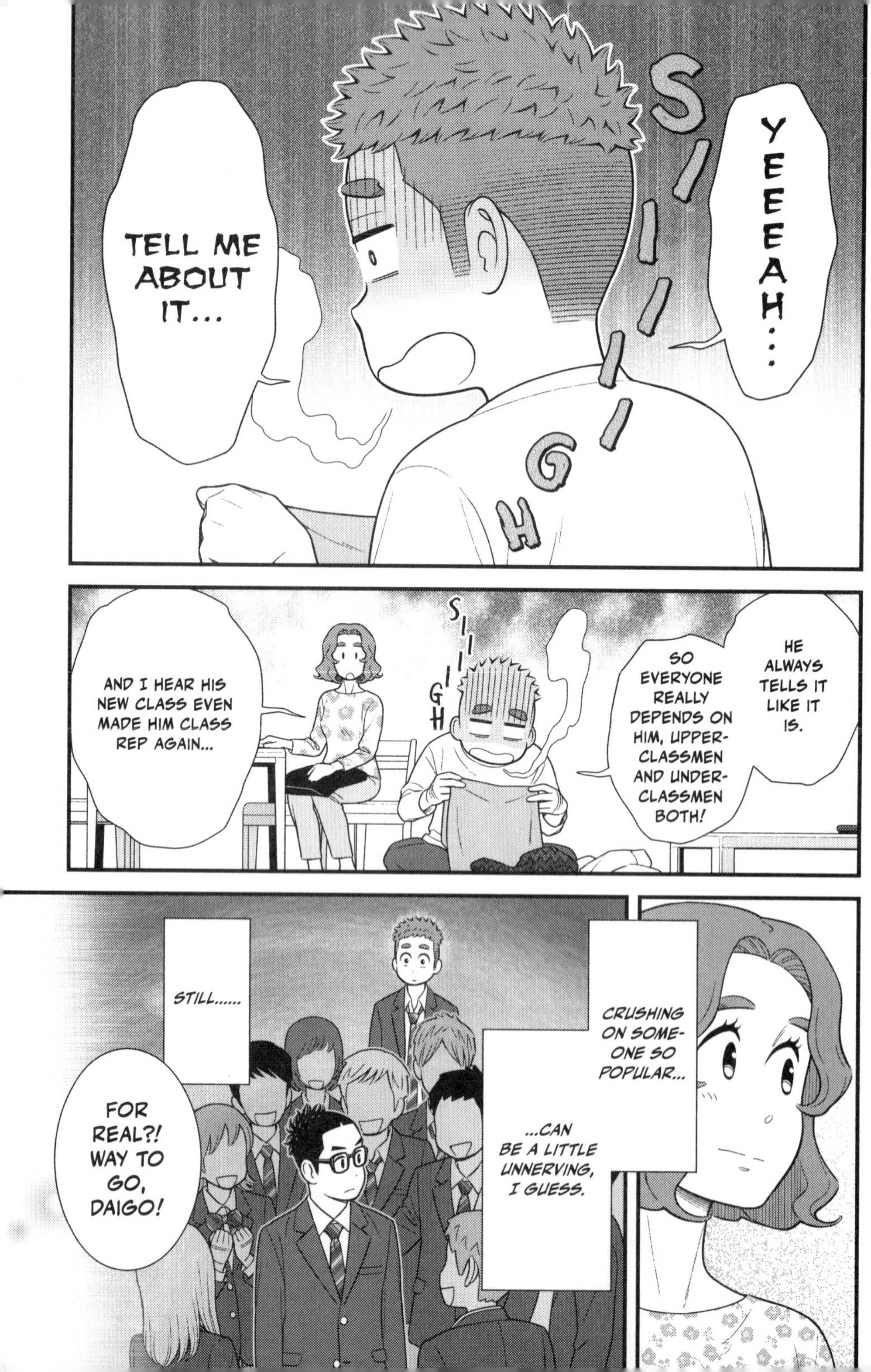
YEEEAH...
SIIIIIIGH
TELL ME ABOUT IT...
HE ALWAYS TELLS IT LIKE IT IS.
SO EVERYONE REALLY DEPENDS ON HIM, UPPER-CLASSMEN AND UNDER-CLASSMEN BOTH!
SIIIIGH
AND I HEAR HIS NEW CLASS EVEN MADE HIM CLASS REP AGAIN...
FOR REAL?! WAY TO GO, DAIGO!
STILL......
CRUSHING ON SOME-ONE SO POPULAR...
...CAN BE A LITTLE UNNERVING, I GUESS.

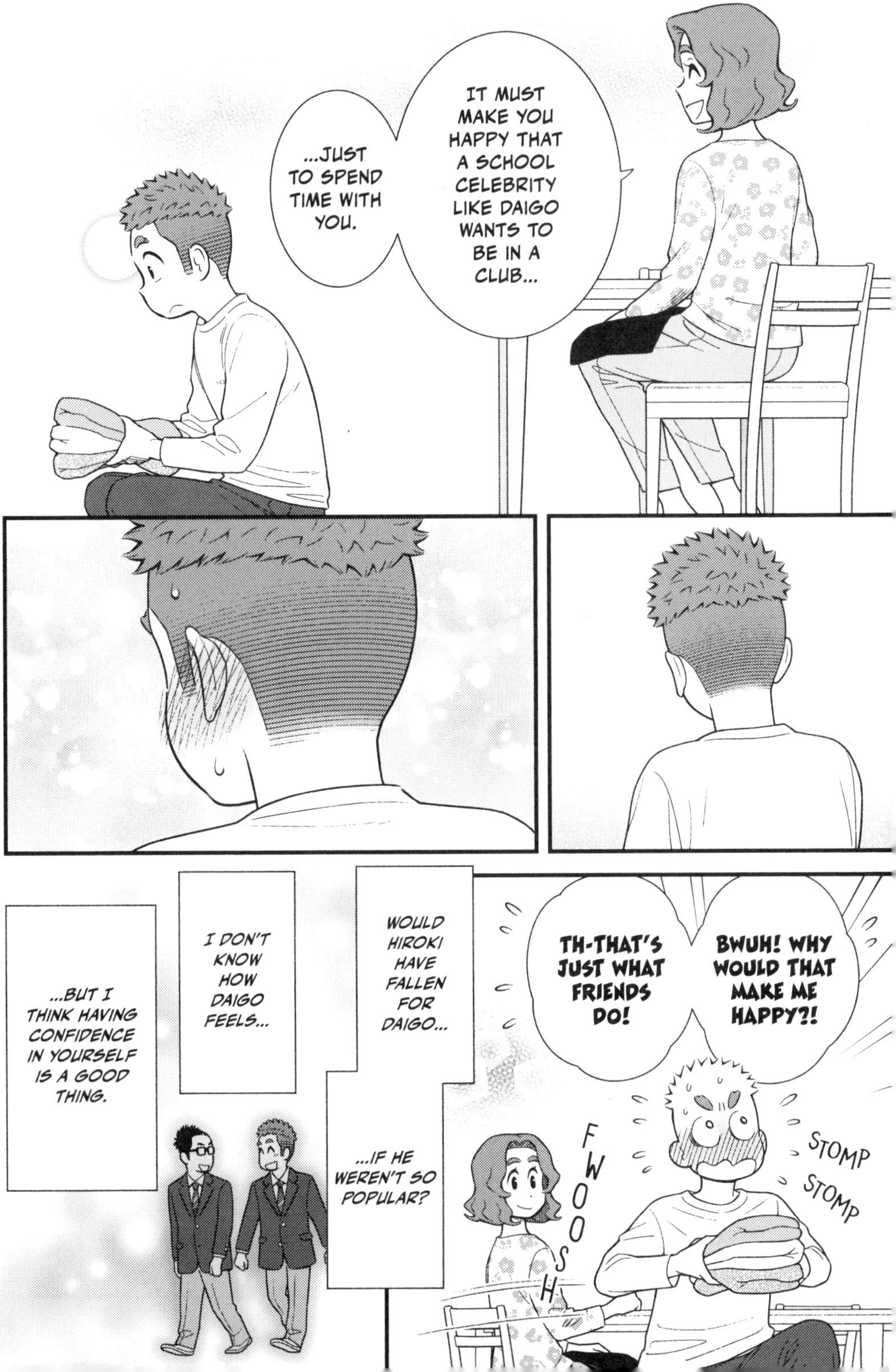
IT MUST MAKE YOU HAPPY THAT A SCHOOL CELEBRITY LIKE DAIGO WANTS TO BE IN A CLUB...
...JUST TO SPEND TIME WITH YOU.
BWUH! WHY WOULD THAT MAKE ME HAPPY?!
TH-THAT'S JUST WHAT FRIENDS DO!
STOMP
STOMP
FWOOSH
WOULD HIROKI HAVE FALLEN FOR DAIGO...
...IF HE WEREN'T SO POPULAR?
I DON'T KNOW HOW DAIGO FEELS...
...BUT I THINK HAVING CONFIDENCE IN YOURSELF IS A GOOD THING.

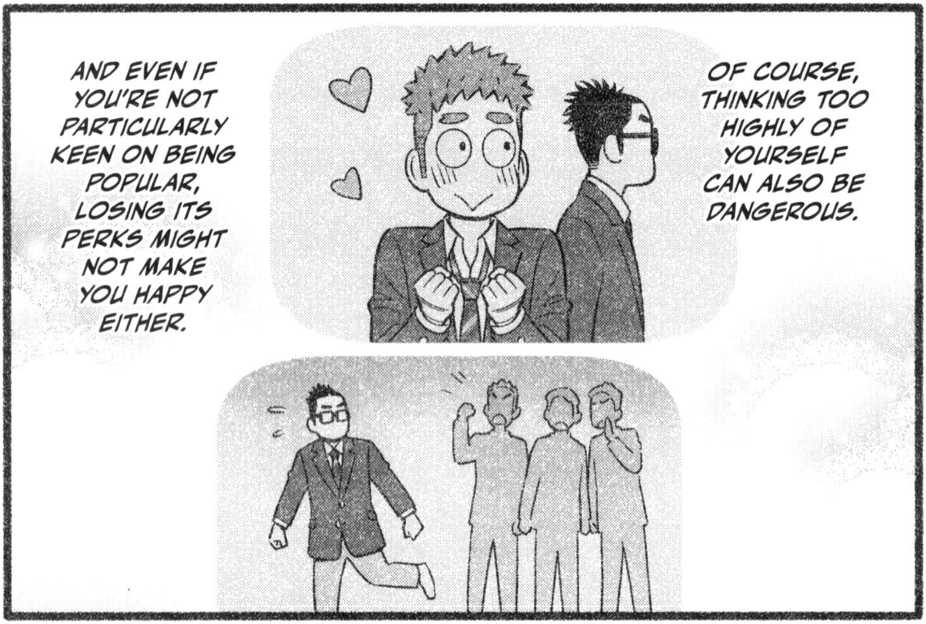
OF COURSE, THINKING TOO HIGHLY OF YOURSELF CAN ALSO BE DANGEROUS.
AND EVEN IF YOU'RE NOT PARTICULARLY KEEN ON BEING POPULAR, LOSING ITS PERKS MIGHT NOT MAKE YOU HAPPY EITHER.

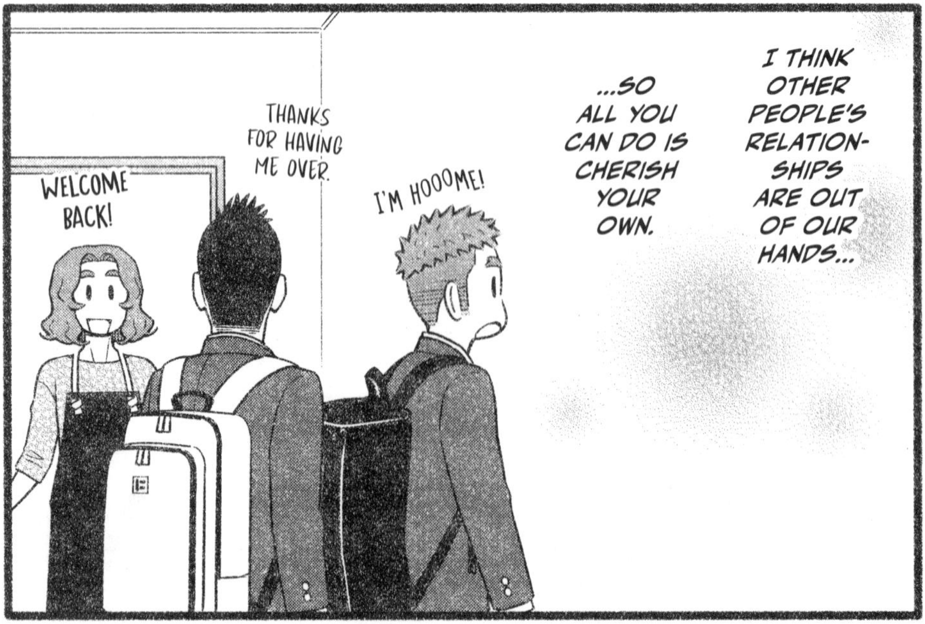
I THINK OTHER PEOPLE'S RELATION-SHIPS ARE OUT OF OUR HANDS...
...SO ALL YOU CAN DO IS CHERISH YOUR OWN.
I'M HOOOME!
THANKS FOR HAVING ME OVER.
WELCOME BACK!

I Think
Our Son
Is Gay

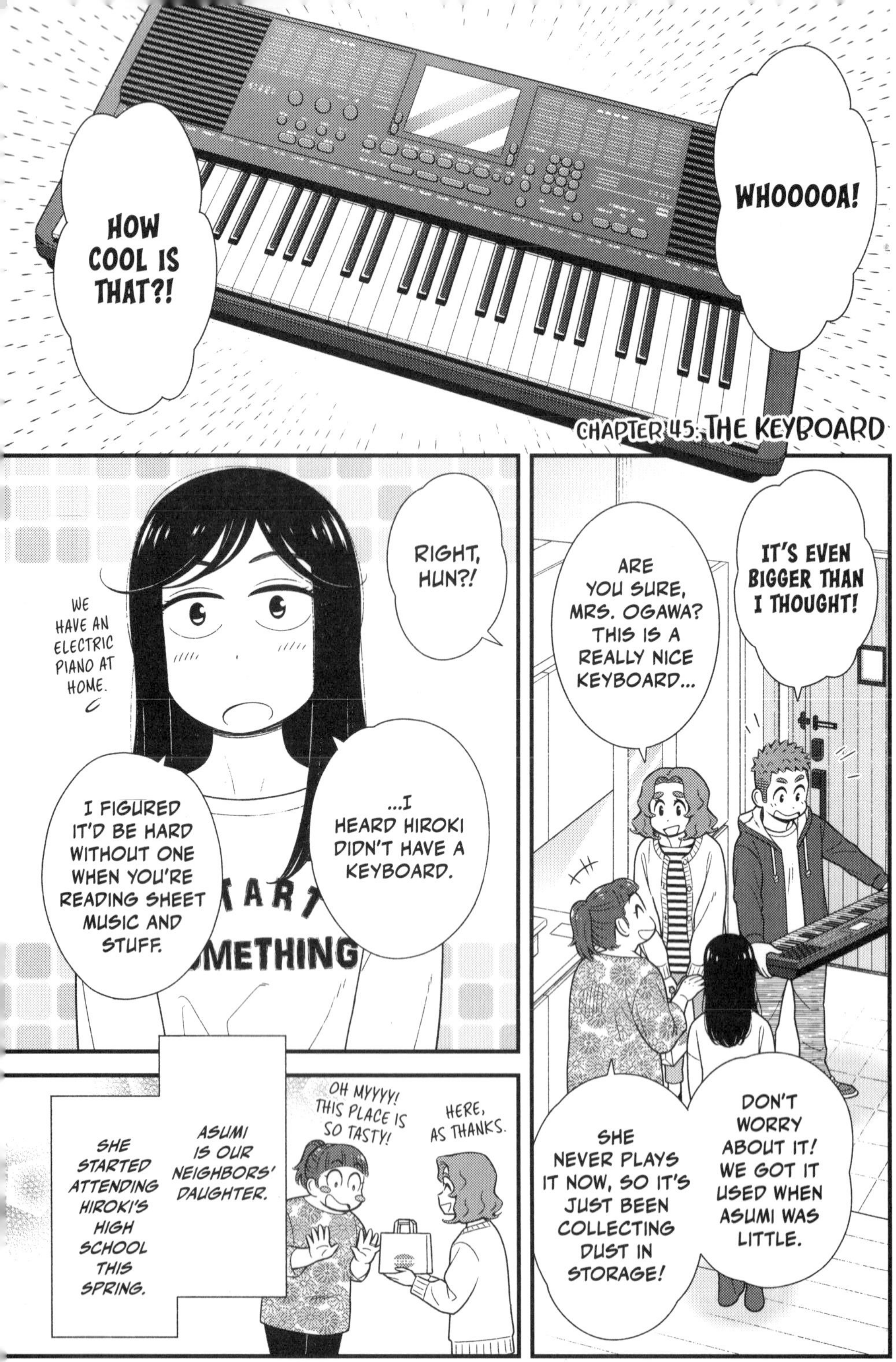
WHOOOOA!
HOW COOL IS THAT?!
CHAPTER 45: THE KEYBOARD
IT'S EVEN BIGGER THAN I THOUGHT!
ARE YOU SURE, MRS. OGAWA? THIS IS A REALLY NICE KEYBOARD...
DON'T WORRY ABOUT IT! WE GOT IT USED WHEN ASUMI WAS LITTLE.
SHE NEVER PLAYS IT NOW, SO IT'S JUST BEEN COLLECTING DUST IN STORAGE!
RIGHT, HUN?!
WE HAVE AN ELECTRIC PIANO AT HOME.
...I HEARD HIROKI DIDN'T HAVE A KEYBOARD.
I FIGURED IT'D BE HARD WITHOUT ONE WHEN YOU'RE READING SHEET MUSIC AND STUFF.
START SOMETHING
HERE, AS THANKS.
OH MYYYY! THIS PLACE IS SO TASTY!
ASUMI IS OUR NEIGHBORS' DAUGHTER.
SHE STARTED ATTENDING HIROKI'S HIGH SCHOOL THIS SPRING.

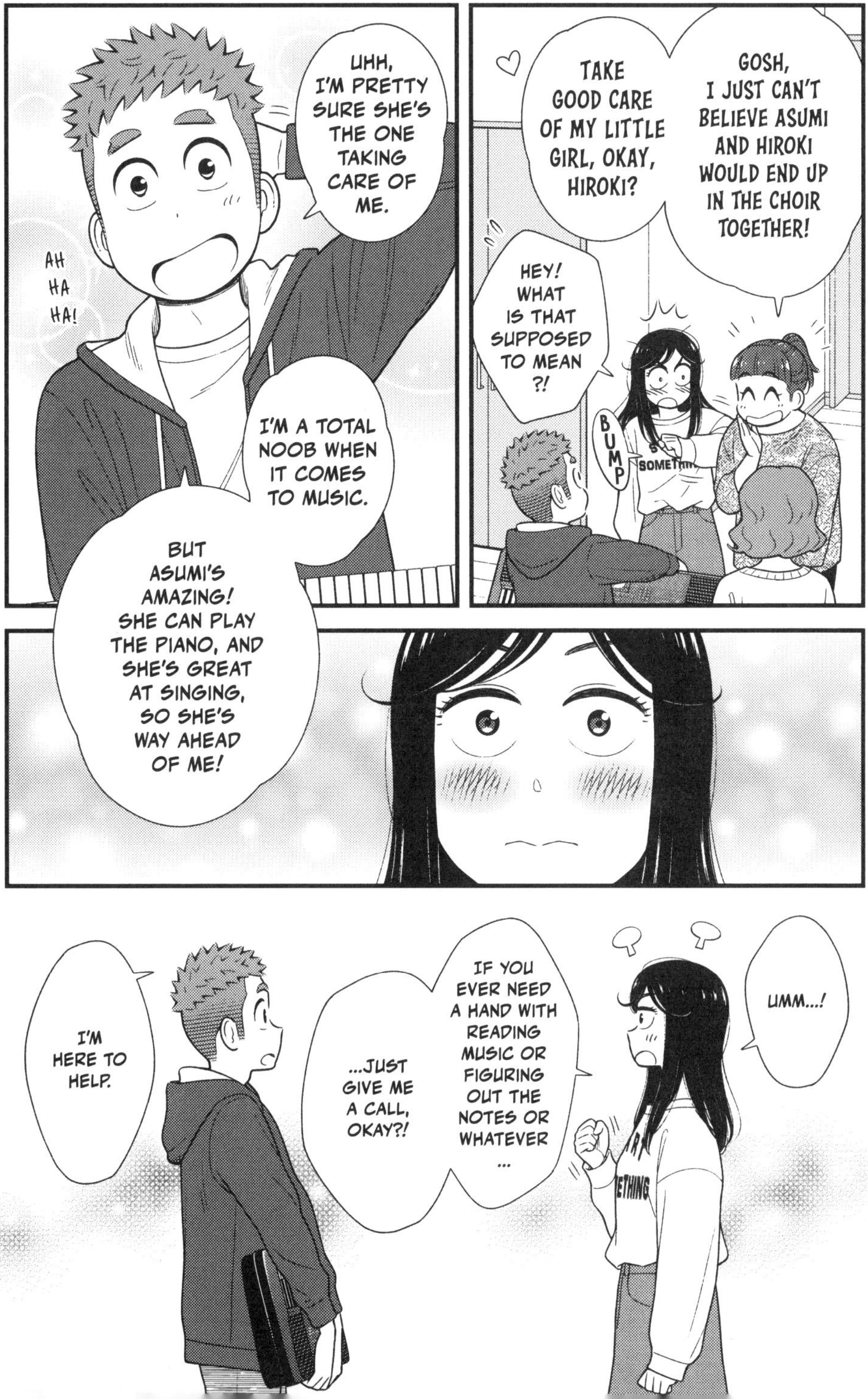
GOSH, I JUST CAN'T BELIEVE ASUMI AND HIROKI WOULD END UP IN THE CHOIR TOGETHER!
TAKE GOOD CARE OF MY LITTLE GIRL, OKAY, HIROKI?
HEY! WHAT IS THAT SUPPOSED TO MEAN?!
BUMP
UHH, I'M PRETTY SURE SHE'S THE ONE TAKING CARE OF ME.
AH HA HA!
I'M A TOTAL NOOB WHEN IT COMES TO MUSIC.
BUT ASUMI'S AMAZING! SHE CAN PLAY THE PIANO, AND SHE'S GREAT AT SINGING, SO SHE'S WAY AHEAD OF ME!
UMM...!
IF YOU EVER NEED A HAND WITH READING MUSIC OR FIGURING OUT THE NOTES OR WHATEVER...
...JUST GIVE ME A CALL, OKAY?!
I'M HERE TO HELP.

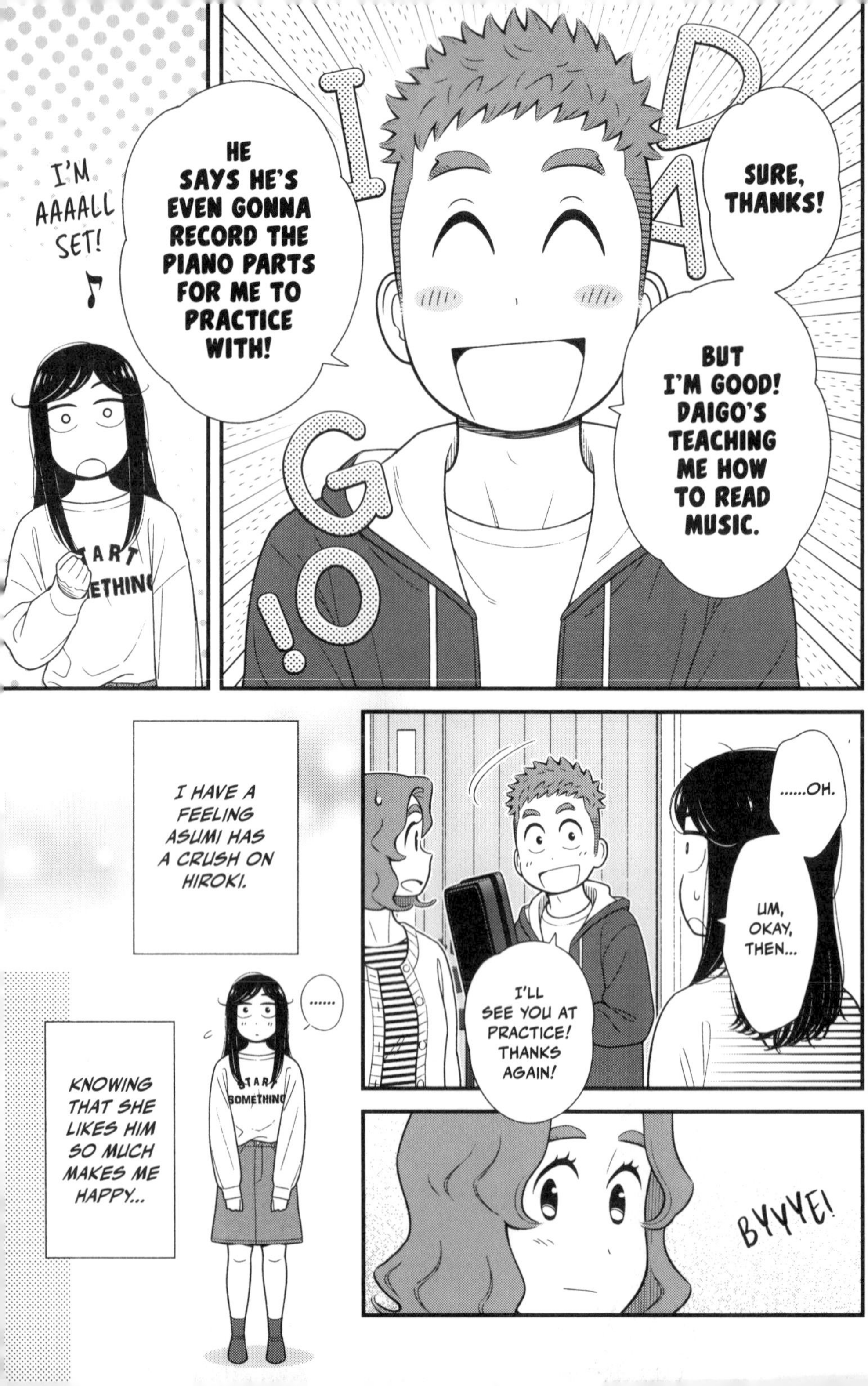
SURE, THANKS!
BUT I'M GOOD! DAIGO'S TEACHING ME HOW TO READ MUSIC.
HE SAYS HE'S EVEN GONNA RECORD THE PIANO PARTS FOR ME TO PRACTICE WITH!
I'M AAAALL SET! ♪
......OH.
UM, OKAY, THEN...
I'LL SEE YOU AT PRACTICE! THANKS AGAIN!
BYYYE!
I HAVE A FEELING ASUMI HAS A CRUSH ON HIROKI.
......
KNOWING THAT SHE LIKES HIM SO MUCH MAKES ME HAPPY...

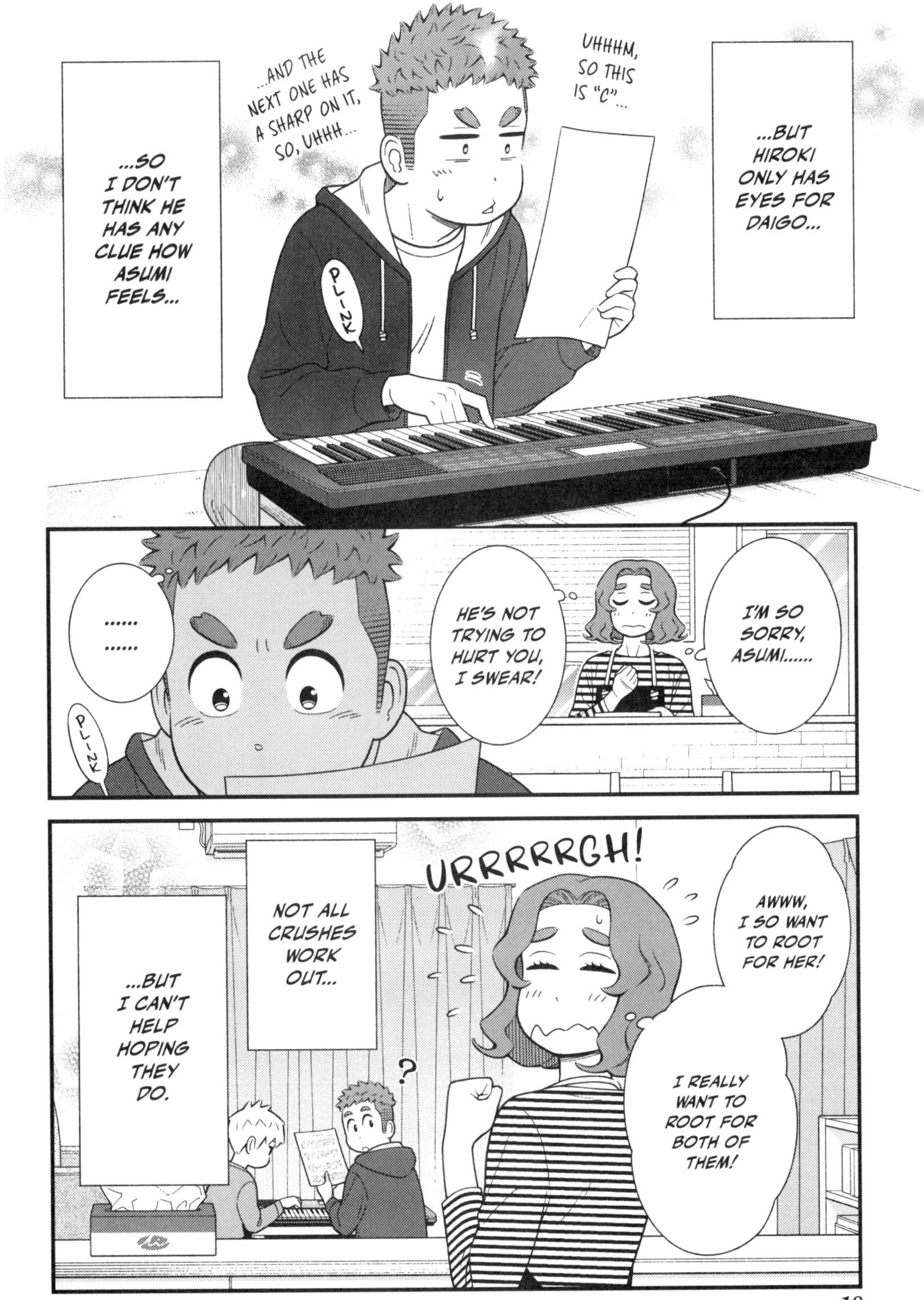
...BUT HIROKI ONLY HAS EYES FOR DAIGO...
UHHHM, SO THIS IS "C"...
...AND THE NEXT ONE HAS A SHARP ON IT, SO, UHHH...
PLINK
...SO I DON'T THINK HE HAS ANY CLUE HOW ASUMI FEELS...
I'M SO SORRY, ASUMI......
HE'S NOT TRYING TO HURT YOU, I SWEAR!
....
PLINK
AWWW, I SO WANT TO ROOT FOR HER!
URRRRRGH!
I REALLY WANT TO ROOT FOR BOTH OF THEM!
NOT ALL CRUSHES WORK OUT...
?
...BUT I CAN'T HELP HOPING THEY DO.

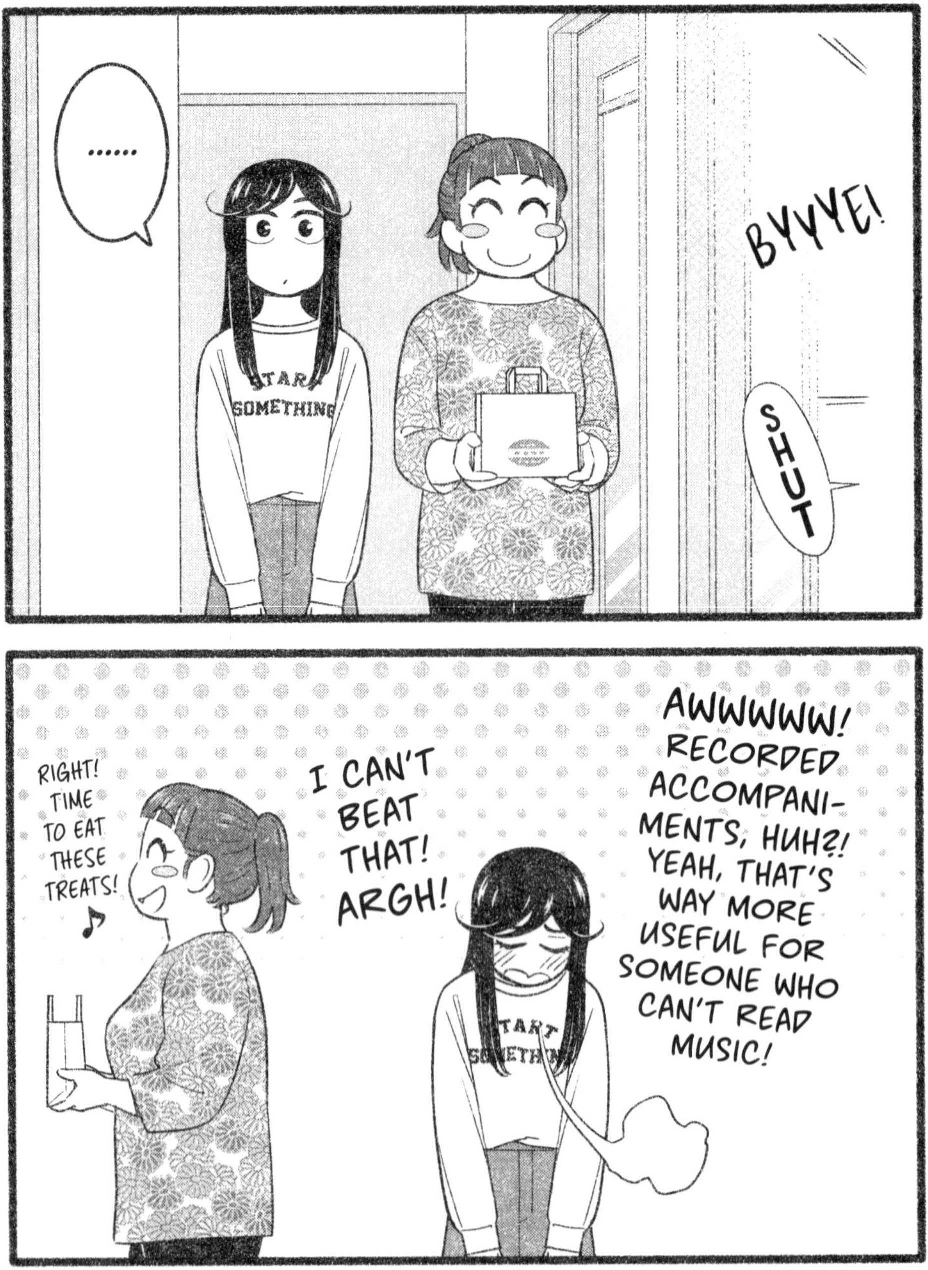
BYYYE!
SHUT
......
AWWWWW! RECORDED ACCOMPANI-MENTS, HUH?! YEAH, THAT'S WAY MORE USEFUL FOR SOMEONE WHO CAN'T READ MUSIC!
I CAN'T BEAT THAT! ARGH!
RIGHT! TIME TO EAT THESE TREATS! ♪

I Think
Our Son
Is Gay

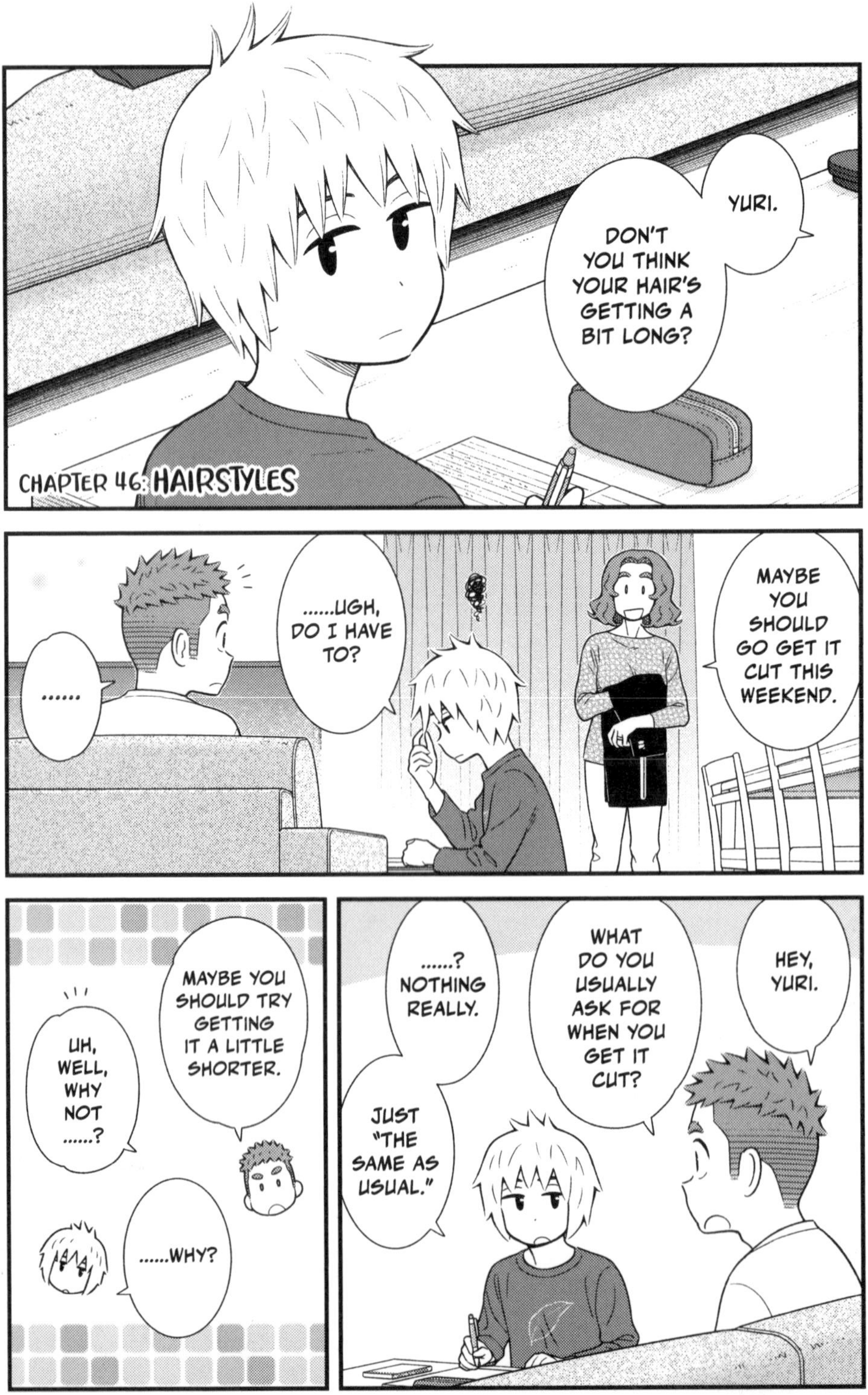
YURI.
DON'T YOU THINK YOUR HAIR'S GETTING A BIT LONG?
CHAPTER 46: HAIRSTYLES
MAYBE YOU SHOULD GO GET IT CUT THIS WEEKEND.
......UGH, DO I HAVE TO?
......
HEY, YURI.
WHAT DO YOU USUALLY ASK FOR WHEN YOU GET IT CUT?
......? NOTHING REALLY.
JUST "THE SAME AS USUAL."
MAYBE YOU SHOULD TRY GETTING IT A LITTLE SHORTER.
UH, WELL, WHY NOT ......?
......WHY?

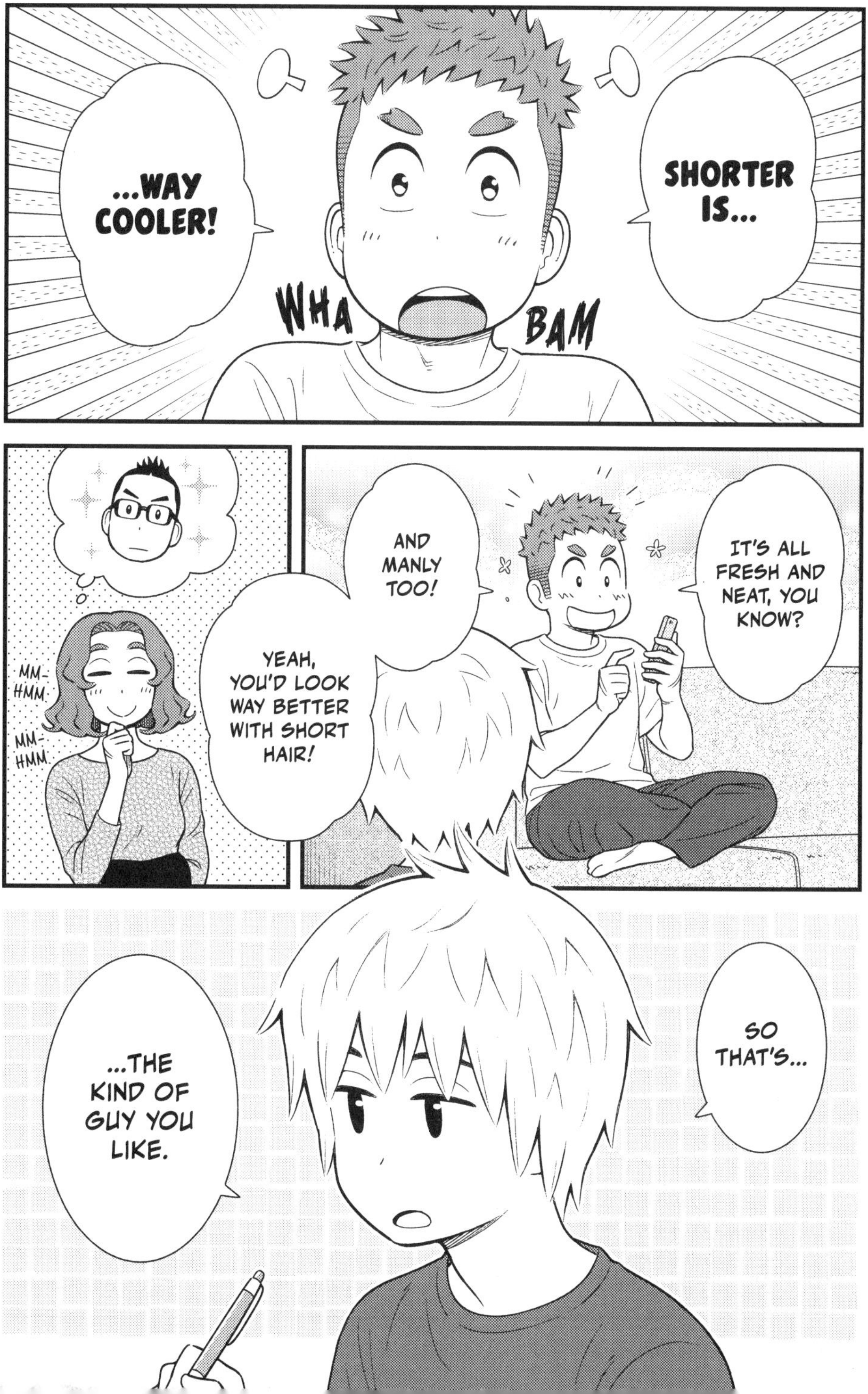
SHORTER IS...
...WAY COOLER!
BAM
WHA
IT'S ALL FRESH AND NEAT, YOU KNOW?
AND MANLY TOO!
YEAH, YOU'D LOOK WAY BETTER WITH SHORT HAIR!
MM-HMM.
MM-HMM.
SO THAT'S...
...THE KIND OF GUY YOU LIKE.

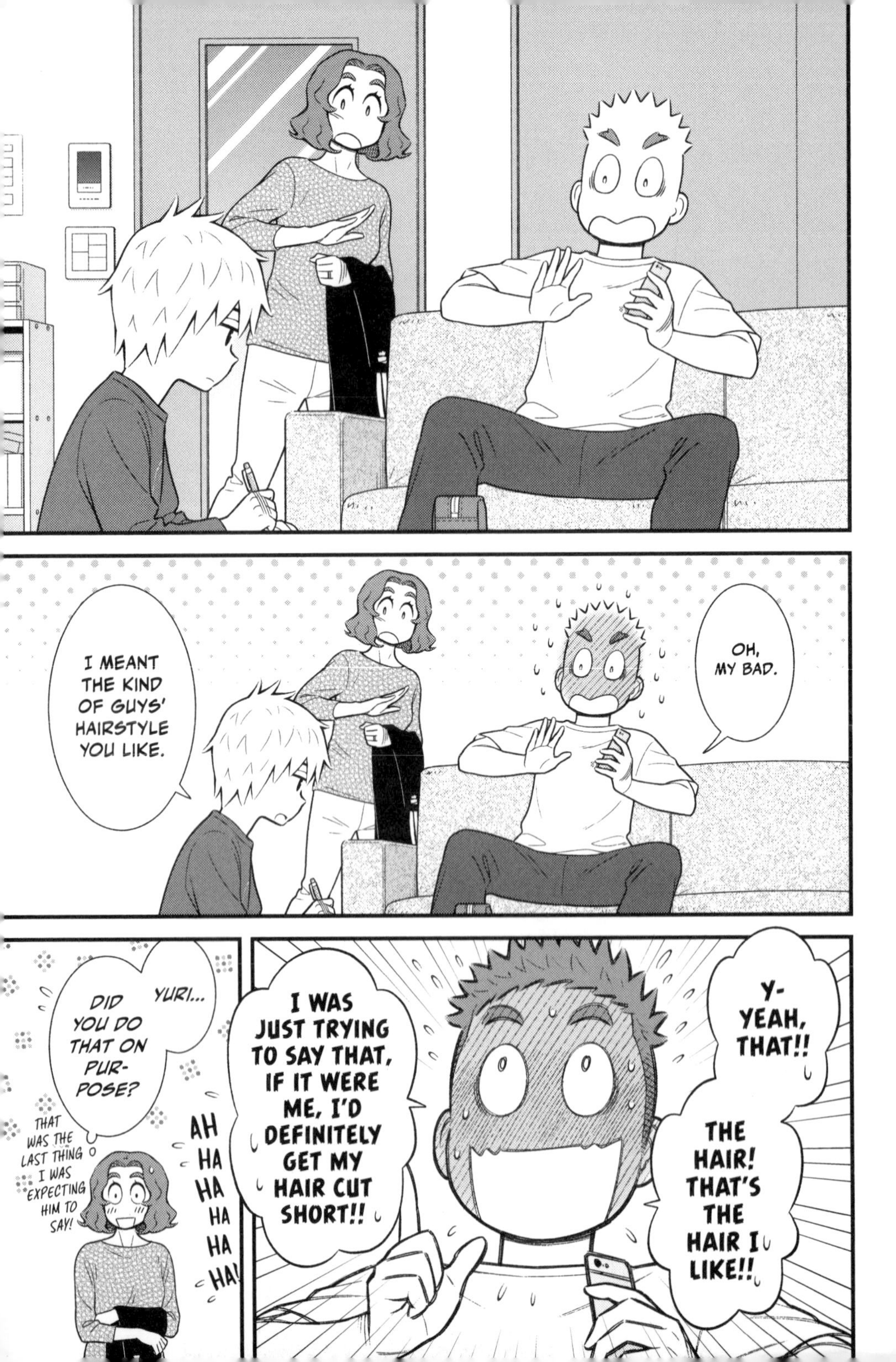
OH, MY BAD.
I MEANT THE KIND OF GUYS' HAIRSTYLE YOU LIKE.
Y-YEAH, THAT!!
THE HAIR! THAT'S THE HAIR I LIKE!!
I WAS JUST TRYING TO SAY THAT, IF IT WERE ME, I'D DEFINITELY GET MY HAIR CUT SHORT!!
YURI...
DID YOU DO THAT ON PURPOSE?
AH HA HA HA HA HA!
THAT WAS THE LAST THING I WAS EXPECTING HIM TO SAY!

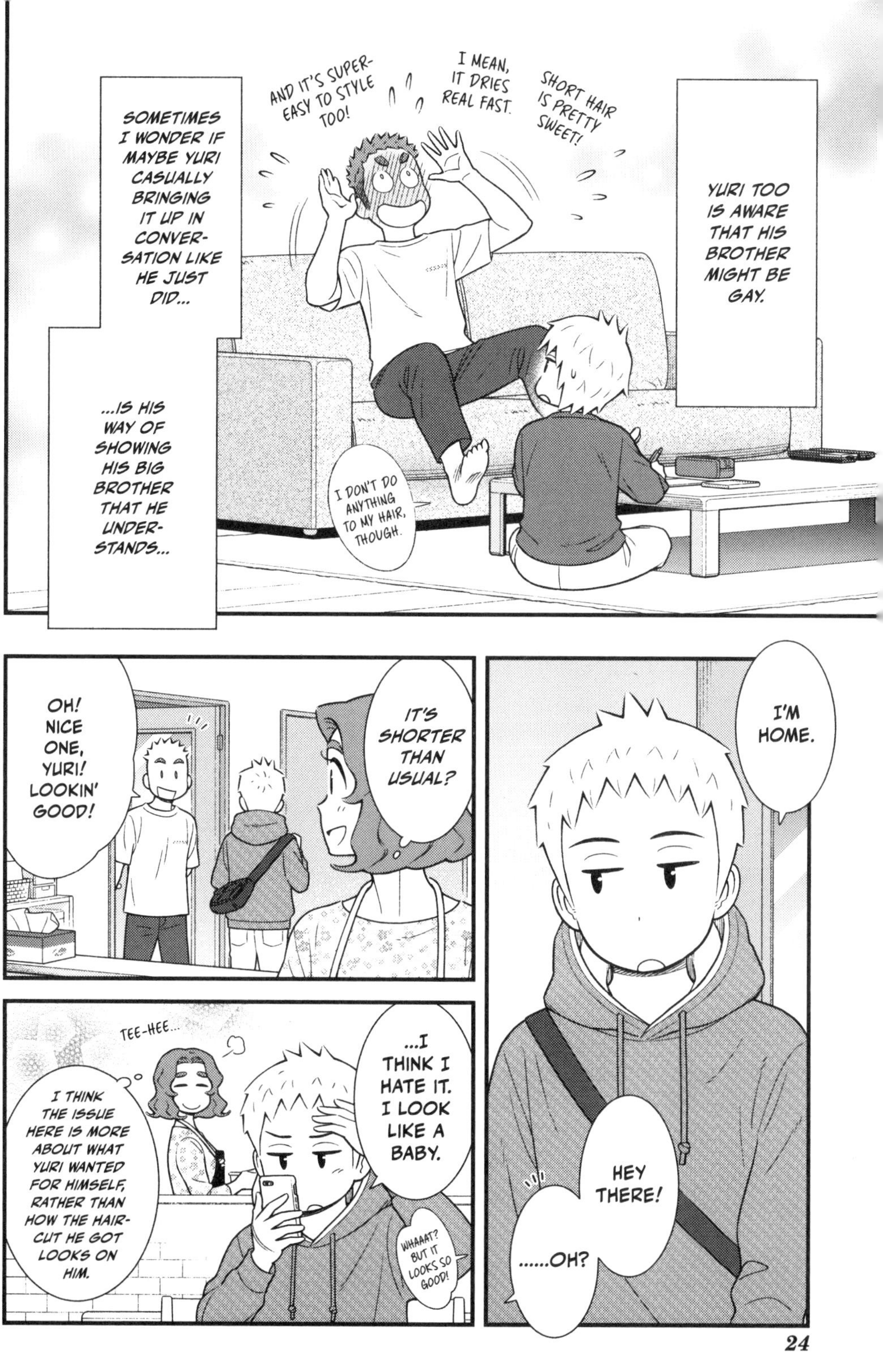

YURI TOO IS AWARE THAT HIS BROTHER MIGHT BE GAY.
SHORT HAIR IS PRETTY SWEET!
I MEAN, IT DRIES REAL FAST.
AND IT'S SUPER-EASY TO STYLE TOO!
SOMETIMES I WONDER IF MAYBE YURI CASUALLY BRINGING IT UP IN CONVER-SATION LIKE HE JUST DID...
I DON'T DO ANYTHING TO MY HAIR, THOUGH.
...IS HIS WAY OF SHOWING HIS BIG BROTHER THAT HE UNDER-STANDS...
I'M HOME.
HEY THERE!
......OH?
IT'S SHORTER THAN USUAL?
OH! NICE ONE, YURI! LOOKIN' GOOD!
...I THINK I HATE IT. I LOOK LIKE A BABY.
WHAAAT? BUT IT LOOKS SO GOOD!
TEE-HEE...
I THINK THE ISSUE HERE IS MORE ABOUT WHAT YURI WANTED FOR HIMSELF, RATHER THAN HOW THE HAIR-CUT HE GOT LOOKS ON HIM.

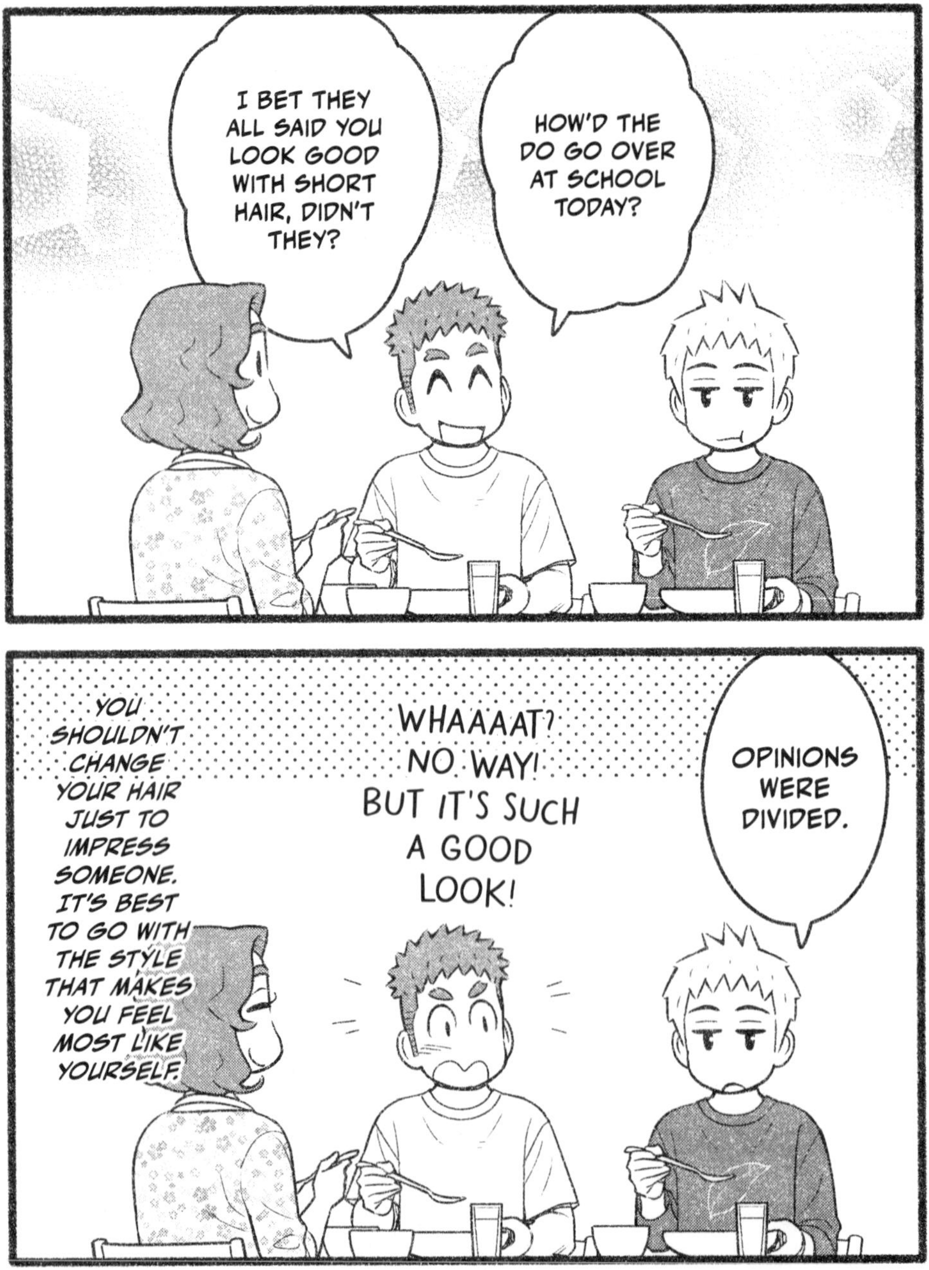
HOW'D THE DO GO OVER AT SCHOOL TODAY?
I BET THEY ALL SAID YOU LOOK GOOD WITH SHORT HAIR, DIDN'T THEY?
OPINIONS WERE DIVIDED.
WHAAAAT? NO WAY! BUT IT'S SUCH A GOOD LOOK!
YOU SHOULDN'T CHANGE YOUR HAIR JUST TO IMPRESS SOMEONE. IT'S BEST TO GO WITH THE STYLE THAT MAKES YOU FEEL MOST LIKE YOURSELF.

I Think
Our Son
Is Gay

Chapter 47: Encouragement

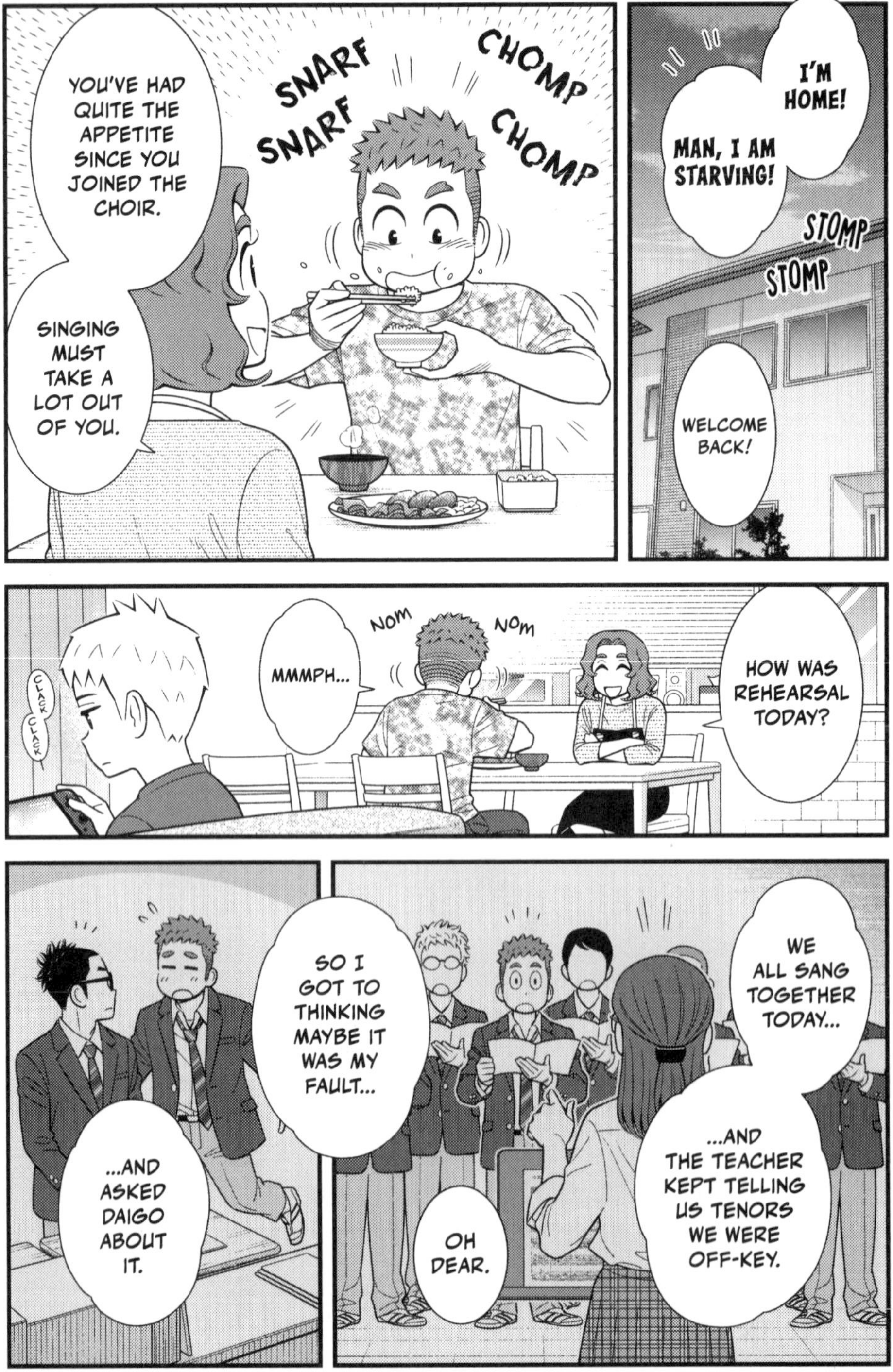
I'M HOME!
MAN, I AM STARVING!
STOMP STOMP
WELCOME BACK!
CHOMP CHOMP
SNARF SNARF
YOU'VE HAD QUITE THE APPETITE SINCE YOU JOINED THE CHOIR.
SINGING MUST TAKE A LOT OUT OF YOU.
HOW WAS REHEARSAL TODAY?
NOM NOM
MMMPH...
CLACK CLACK
WE ALL SANG TOGETHER TODAY...
...AND THE TEACHER KEPT TELLING US TENORS WE WERE OFF-KEY.
OH DEAR.
SO I GOT TO THINKING MAYBE IT WAS MY FAULT...
...AND ASKED DAIGO ABOUT IT.

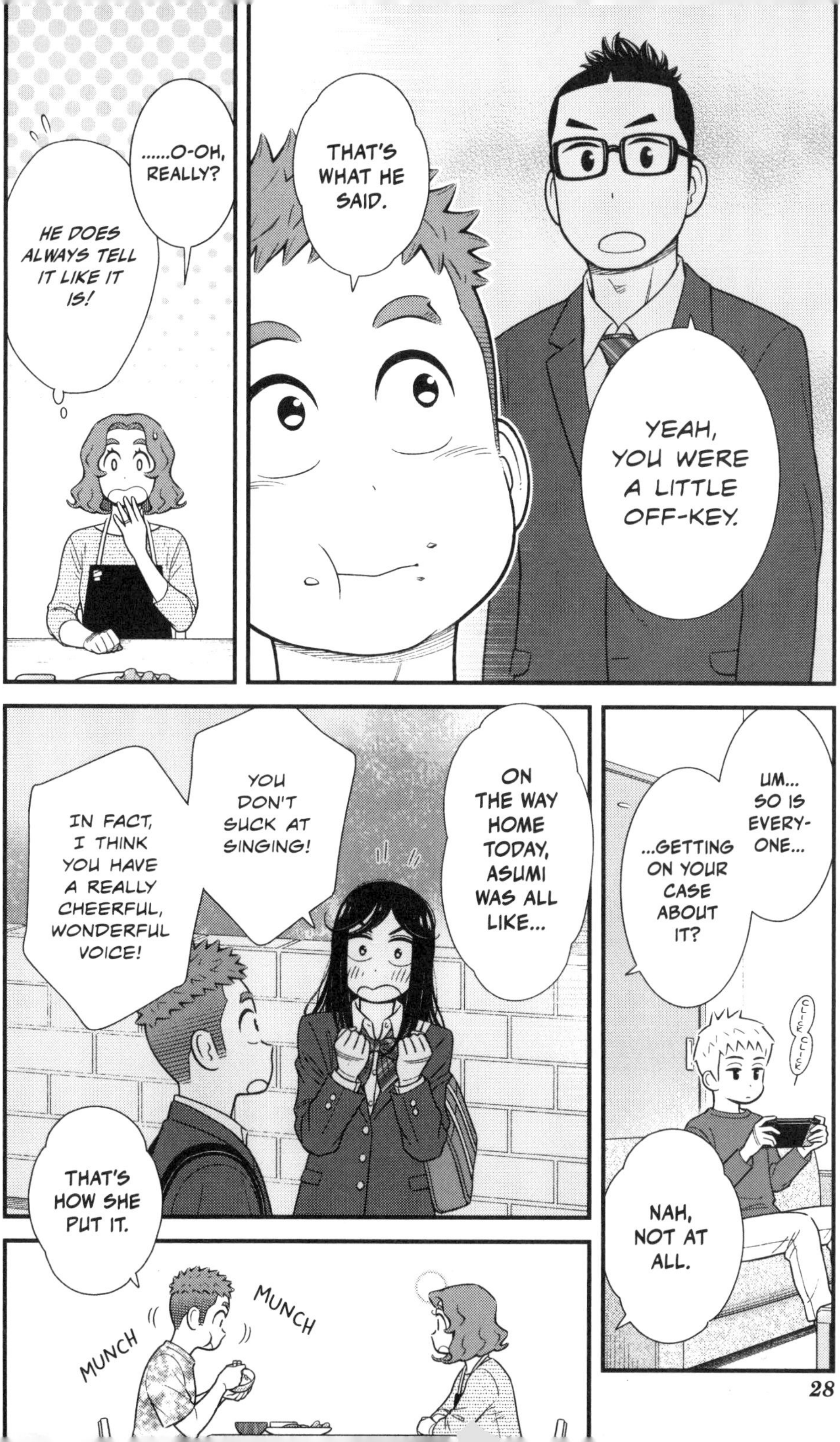
YEAH, YOU WERE A LITTLE OFF-KEY.
THAT'S WHAT HE SAID.
......O-OH, REALLY?
HE DOES ALWAYS TELL IT LIKE IT IS!
UM... SO IS EVERY-ONE...
...GETTING ON YOUR CASE ABOUT IT?
CLICK CLICK
NAH, NOT AT ALL.
ON THE WAY HOME TODAY, ASUMI WAS ALL LIKE...
YOU DON'T SUCK AT SINGING!
IN FACT, I THINK YOU HAVE A REALLY CHEERFUL, WONDERFUL VOICE!
THAT'S HOW SHE PUT IT.
MUNCH
MUNCH

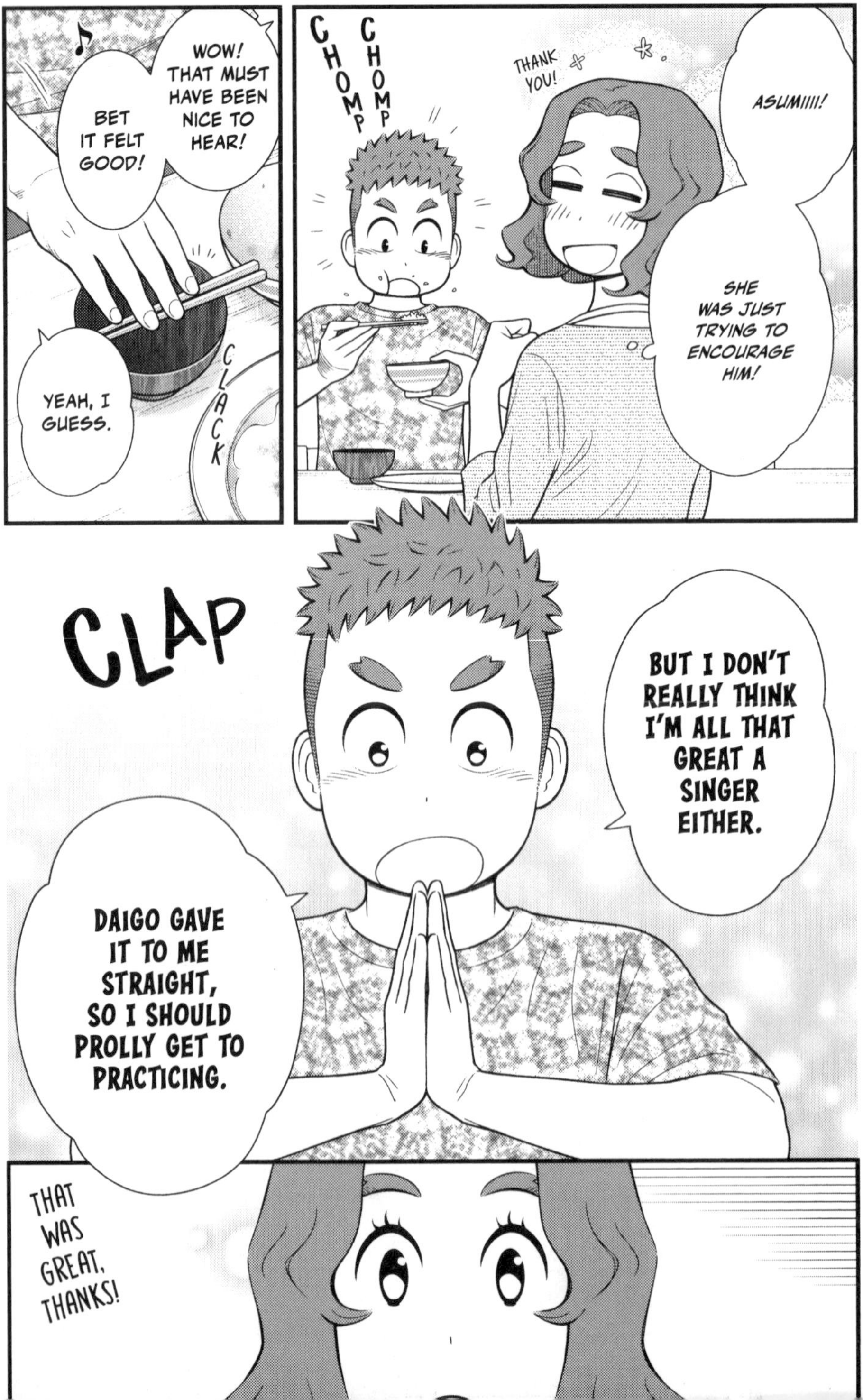
ASUMIIII!
SHE WAS JUST TRYING TO ENCOURAGE HIM!
THANK YOU!
CHOMP CHOMP
WOW! THAT MUST HAVE BEEN NICE TO HEAR!
BET IT FELT GOOD!
CLACK
YEAH, I GUESS.
BUT I DON'T REALLY THINK I'M ALL THAT GREAT A SINGER EITHER.
CLAP
DAIGO GAVE IT TO ME STRAIGHT, SO I SHOULD PROLLY GET TO PRACTICING.
THAT WAS GREAT, THANKS!

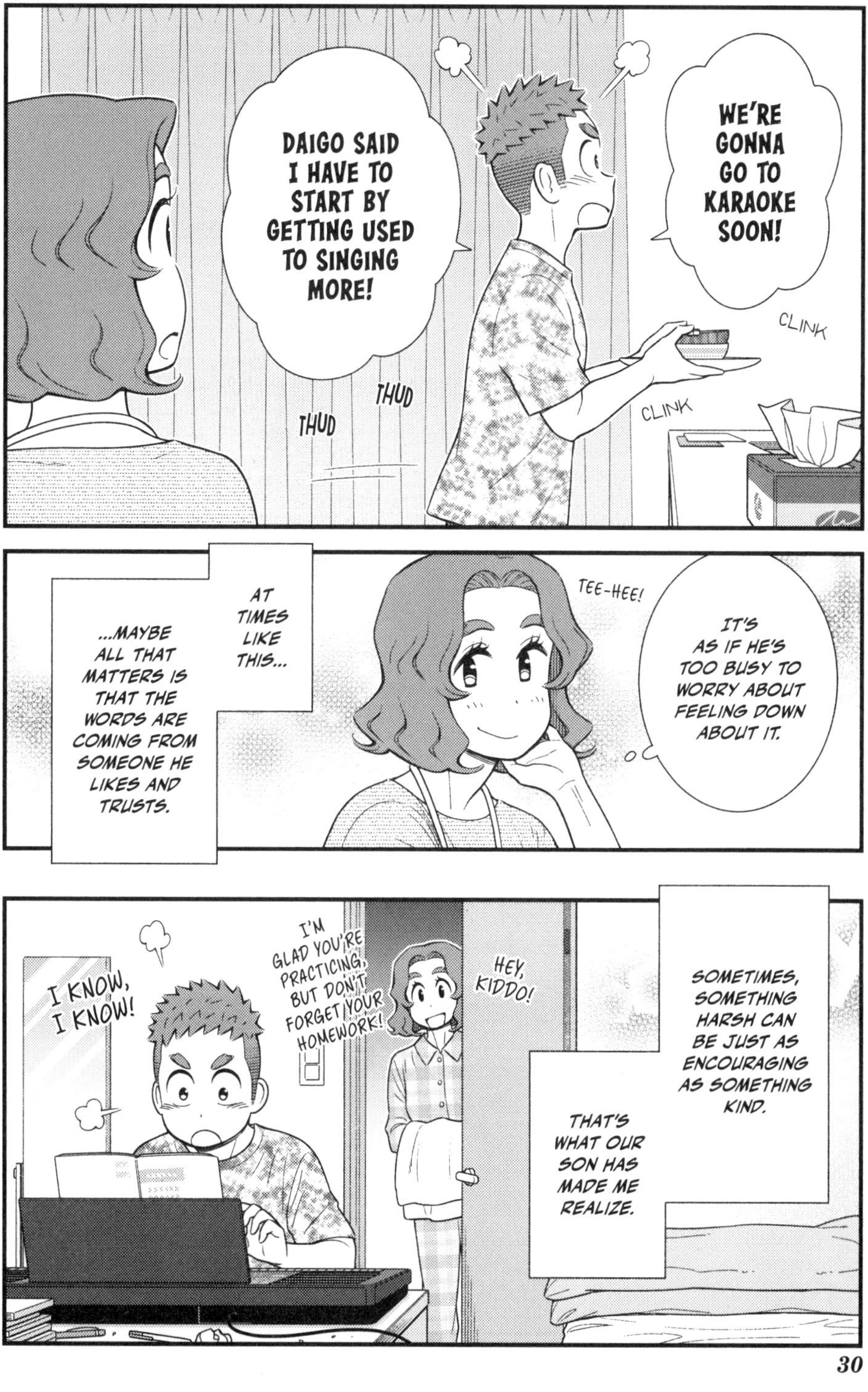
WE'RE GONNA GO TO KARAOKE SOON!
DAIGO SAID I HAVE TO START BY GETTING USED TO SINGING MORE!
CLINK
CLINK
THUD
THUD
TEE-HEE!
IT'S AS IF HE'S TOO BUSY TO WORRY ABOUT FEELING DOWN ABOUT IT.
AT TIMES LIKE THIS...
...MAYBE ALL THAT MATTERS IS THAT THE WORDS ARE COMING FROM SOMEONE HE LIKES AND TRUSTS.
SOMETIMES, SOMETHING HARSH CAN BE JUST AS ENCOURAGING AS SOMETHING KIND.
THAT'S WHAT OUR SON HAS MADE ME REALIZE.
HEY, KIDDO!
I'M GLAD YOU'RE PRACTICING, BUT DON'T FORGET YOUR HOMEWORK!
I KNOW, I KNOW!

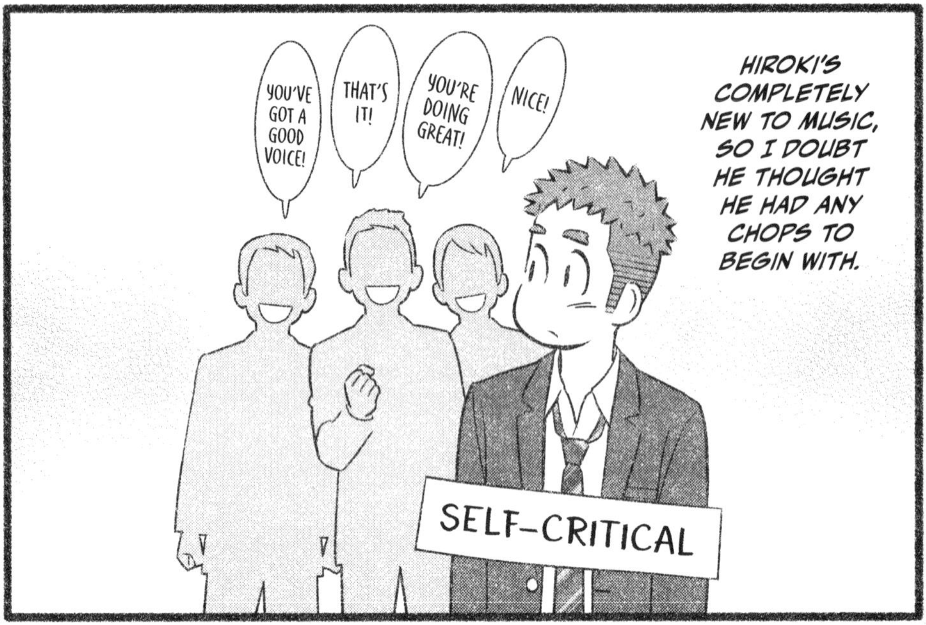
HIROKI'S COMPLETELY NEW TO MUSIC, SO I DOUBT HE THOUGHT HE HAD ANY CHOPS TO BEGIN WITH.
NICE!
YOU'RE DOING GREAT!
THAT'S IT!
YOU'VE GOT A GOOD VOICE!
SELF-CRITICAL

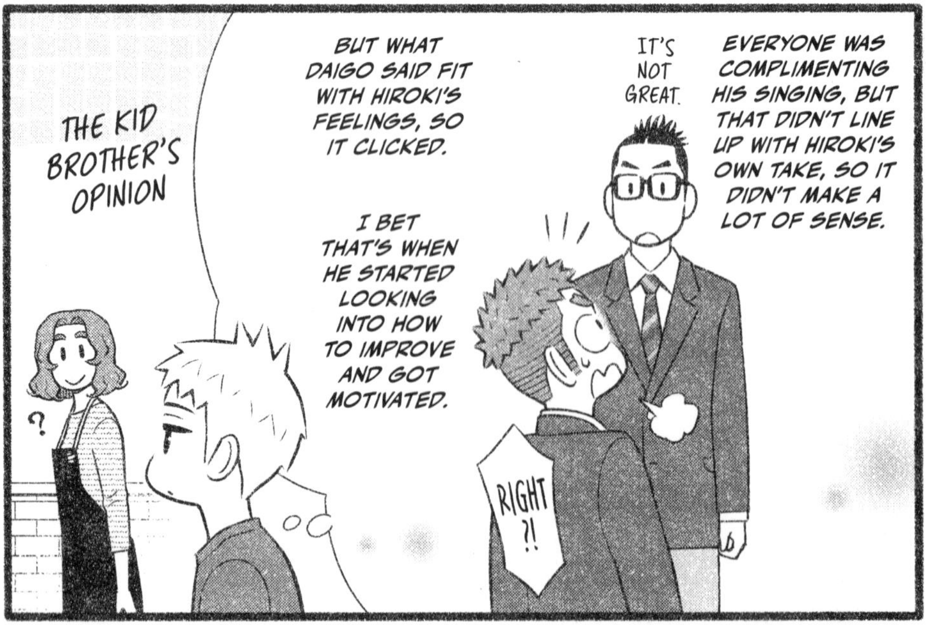
EVERYONE WAS COMPLIMENTING HIS SINGING, BUT THAT DIDN'T LINE UP WITH HIROKI'S OWN TAKE, SO IT DIDN'T MAKE A LOT OF SENSE.
IT'S NOT GREAT.
BUT WHAT DAIGO SAID FIT WITH HIROKI'S FEELINGS, SO IT CLICKED.
THE KID BROTHER'S OPINION
I BET THAT'S WHEN HE STARTED LOOKING INTO HOW TO IMPROVE AND GOT MOTIVATED.
RIGHT ?!
?

I Think
Our Son
Is Gay

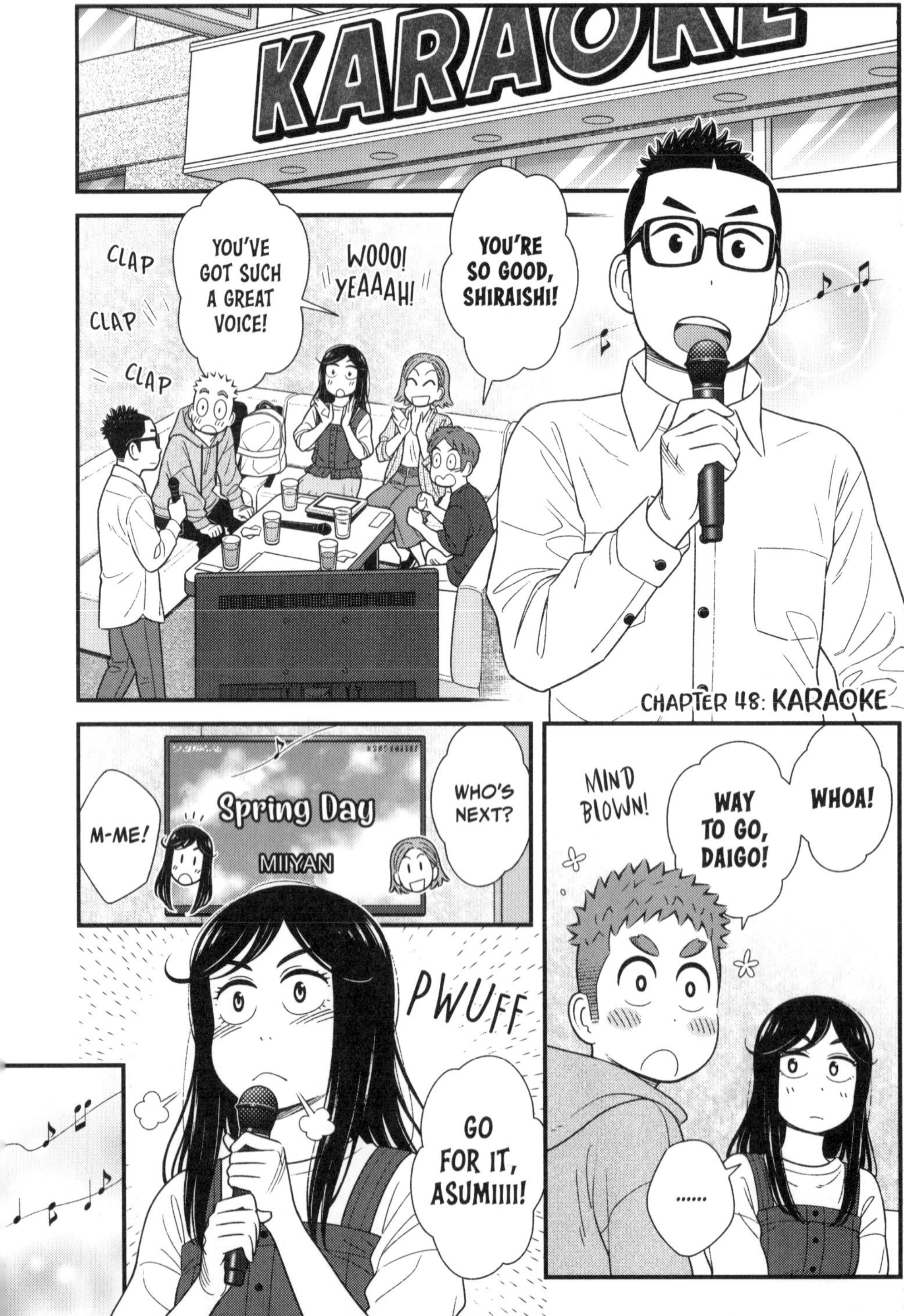
KARAOKE
CHAPTER 48: KARAOKE
YOU'RE SO GOOD, SHIRAISHI!
WOOO! YEAAAH!
YOU'VE GOT SUCH A GREAT VOICE!
CLAP
CLAP
CLAP
WHOA!
WAY TO GO, DAIGO!
MIND BLOWN!
......
WHO'S NEXT?
Spring Day
MIIYAN
M-ME!
PWUFF
GO FOR IT, ASUMIIIII!

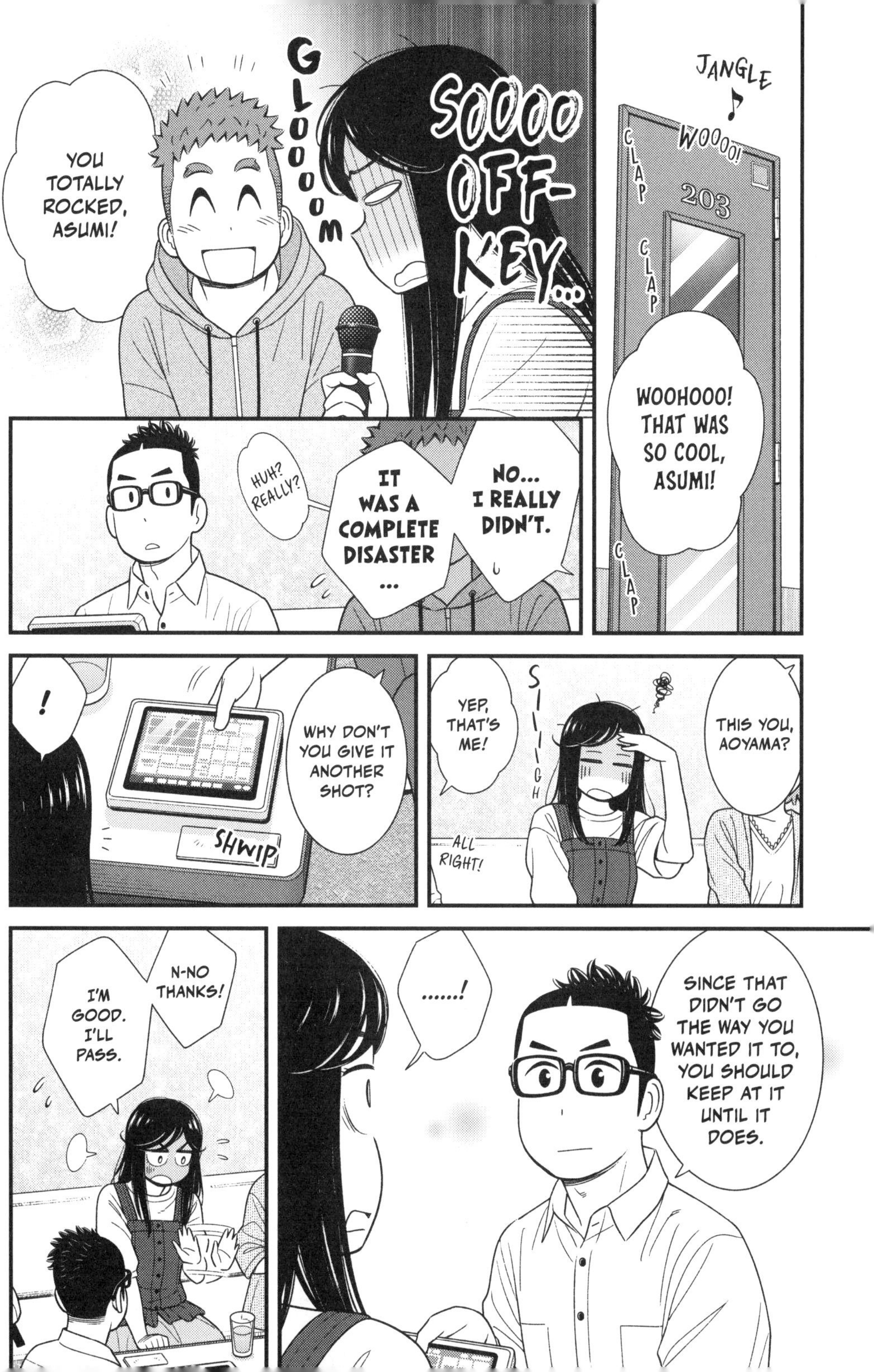
JANGLE
WOOOO!
CLAP
CLAP
203
WOOHOOO! THAT WAS SO COOL, ASUMI!
CLAP
SOOOO OFF-KEY...
GLOOOOOM
YOU TOTALLY ROCKED, ASUMI!
NO... I REALLY DIDN'T.
IT WAS A COMPLETE DISASTER...
HUH? REALLY?
THIS YOU, AOYAMA?
YEP, THAT'S ME!
SIIIIGH
ALL RIGHT!
WHY DON'T YOU GIVE IT ANOTHER SHOT?
SHWIP
!
SINCE THAT DIDN'T GO THE WAY YOU WANTED IT TO, YOU SHOULD KEEP AT IT UNTIL IT DOES.
......!
N-NO THANKS!
I'M GOOD. I'LL PASS.

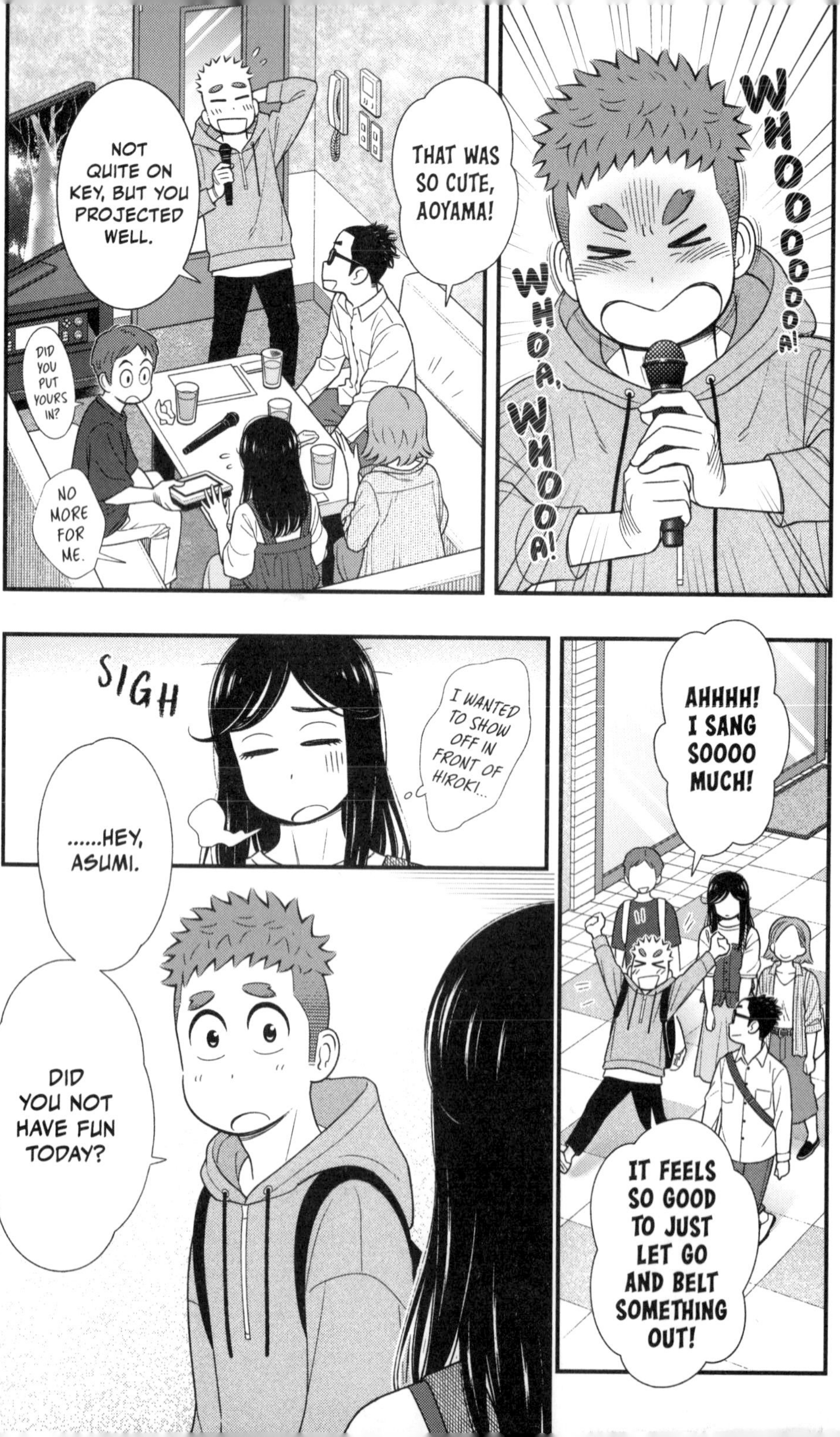
WHOOOOOOOA!
WHOA, WHOOA!
THAT WAS SO CUTE, AOYAMA!
NOT QUITE ON KEY, BUT YOU PROJECTED WELL.
DID YOU PUT YOURS IN?
NO MORE FOR ME.
AHHHH! I SANG SOOOO MUCH!
IT FEELS SO GOOD TO JUST LET GO AND BELT SOMETHING OUT!
I WANTED TO SHOW OFF IN FRONT OF HIROKI...
SIGH
......HEY, ASUMI.
DID YOU NOT HAVE FUN TODAY?

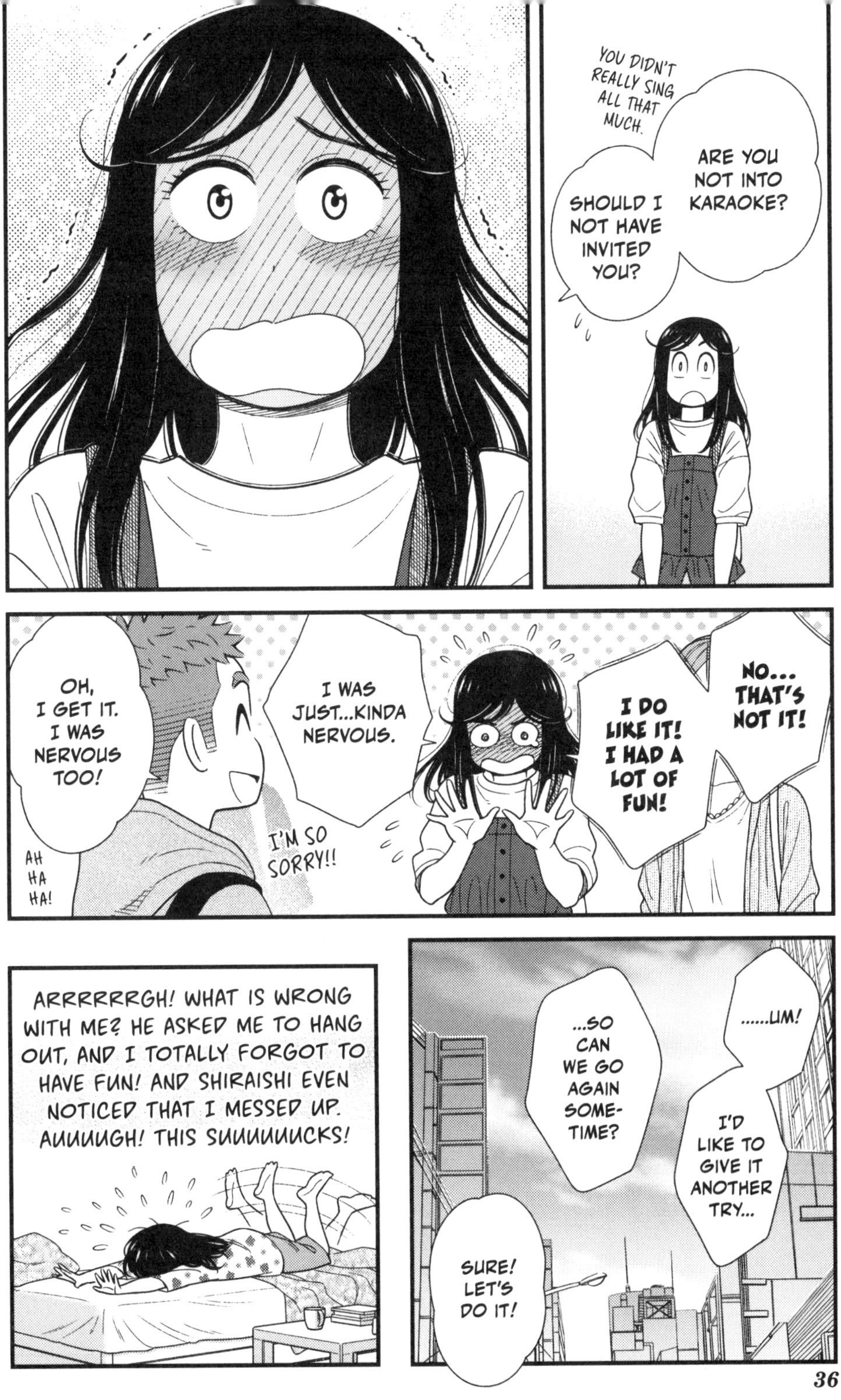
YOU DIDN'T REALLY SING ALL THAT MUCH.
ARE YOU NOT INTO KARAOKE?
SHOULD I NOT HAVE INVITED YOU?
NO... THAT'S NOT IT!
I DO LIKE IT! I HAD A LOT OF FUN!
I WAS JUST...KINDA NERVOUS.
I'M SO SORRY!!
OH, I GET IT. I WAS NERVOUS TOO!
AH HA HA!
......UM!
I'D LIKE TO GIVE IT ANOTHER TRY...
...SO CAN WE GO AGAIN SOME-TIME?
SURE! LET'S DO IT!
ARRRRRRGH! WHAT IS WRONG WITH ME? HE ASKED ME TO HANG OUT, AND I TOTALLY FORGOT TO HAVE FUN! AND SHIRAISHI EVEN NOTICED THAT I MESSED UP. AUUUUGH! THIS SUUUUUUCKS!

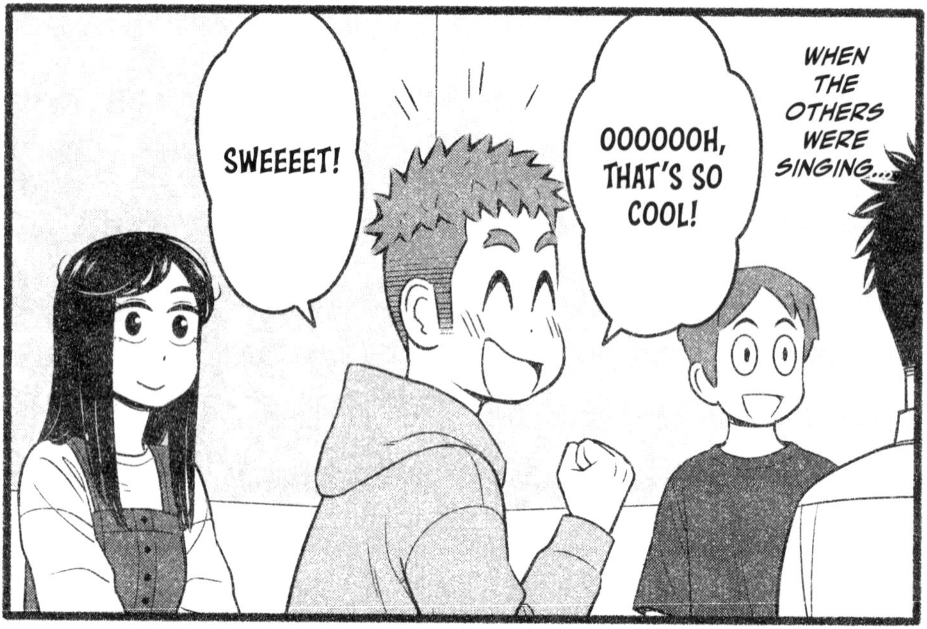
WHEN THE OTHERS WERE SINGING...
OOOOOOH, THAT'S SO COOL!
SWEEEET!

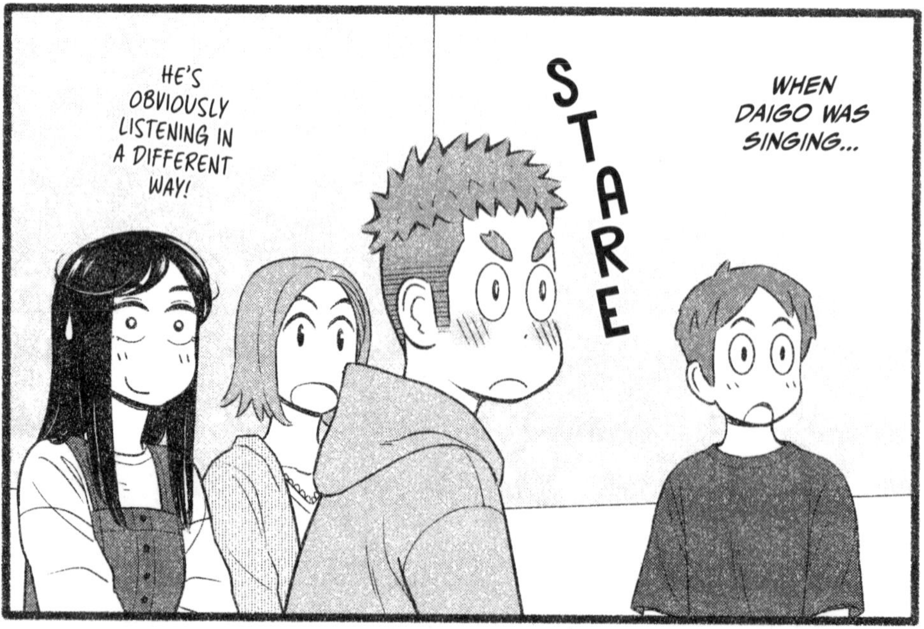
WHEN DAIGO WAS SINGING...
STARE
HE'S OBVIOUSLY LISTENING IN A DIFFERENT WAY!

I Think
Our Son
Is Gay

CHAPTER 49: FOR NOW

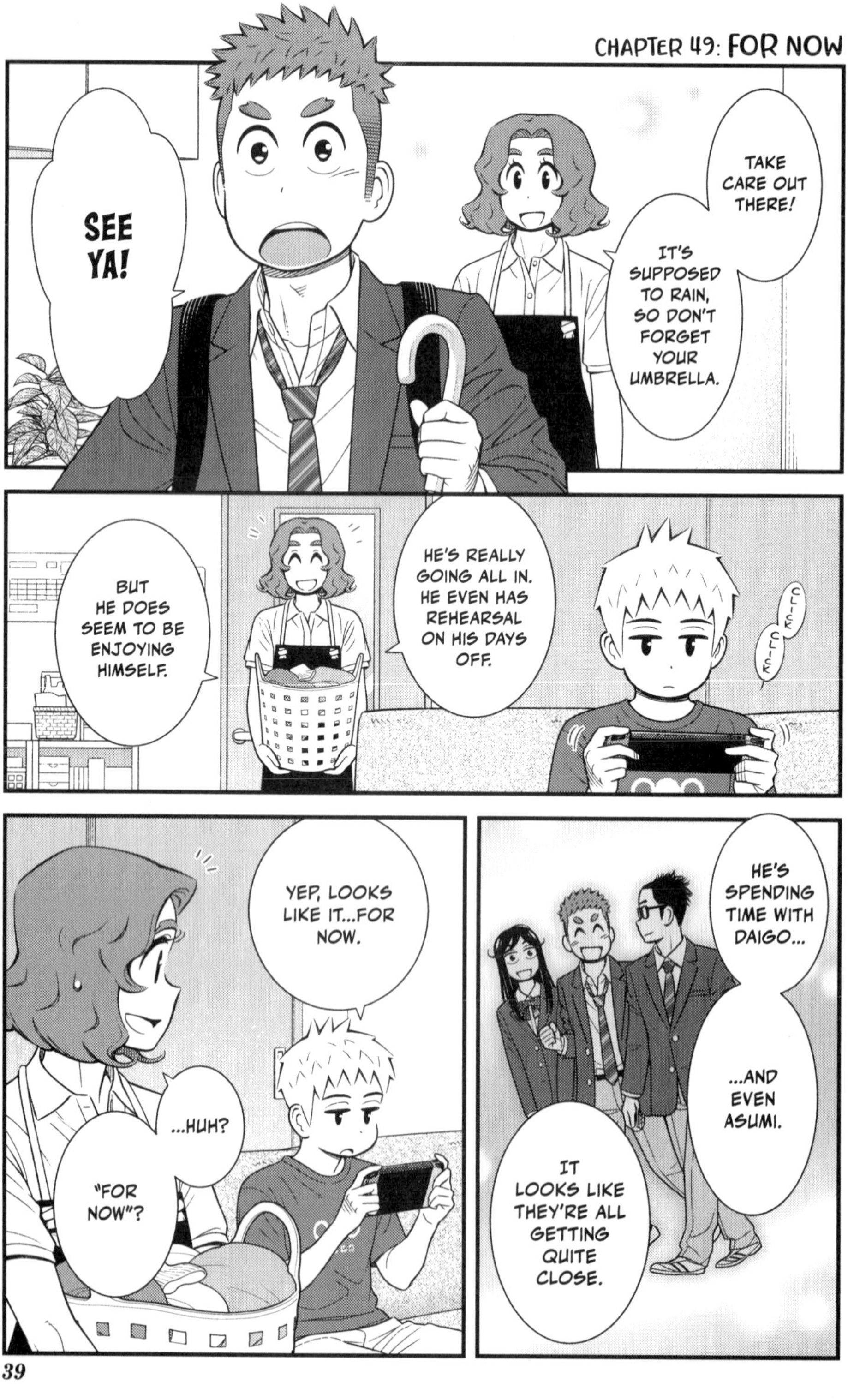
TAKE CARE OUT THERE!
IT'S SUPPOSED TO RAIN, SO DON'T FORGET YOUR UMBRELLA.
SEE YA!
CLICK CLICK
HE'S REALLY GOING ALL IN. HE EVEN HAS REHEARSAL ON HIS DAYS OFF.
BUT HE DOES SEEM TO BE ENJOYING HIMSELF.
HE'S SPENDING TIME WITH DAIGO...
...AND EVEN ASUMI.
IT LOOKS LIKE THEY'RE ALL GETTING QUITE CLOSE.
YEP, LOOKS LIKE IT...FOR NOW.
...HUH?
"FOR NOW"?

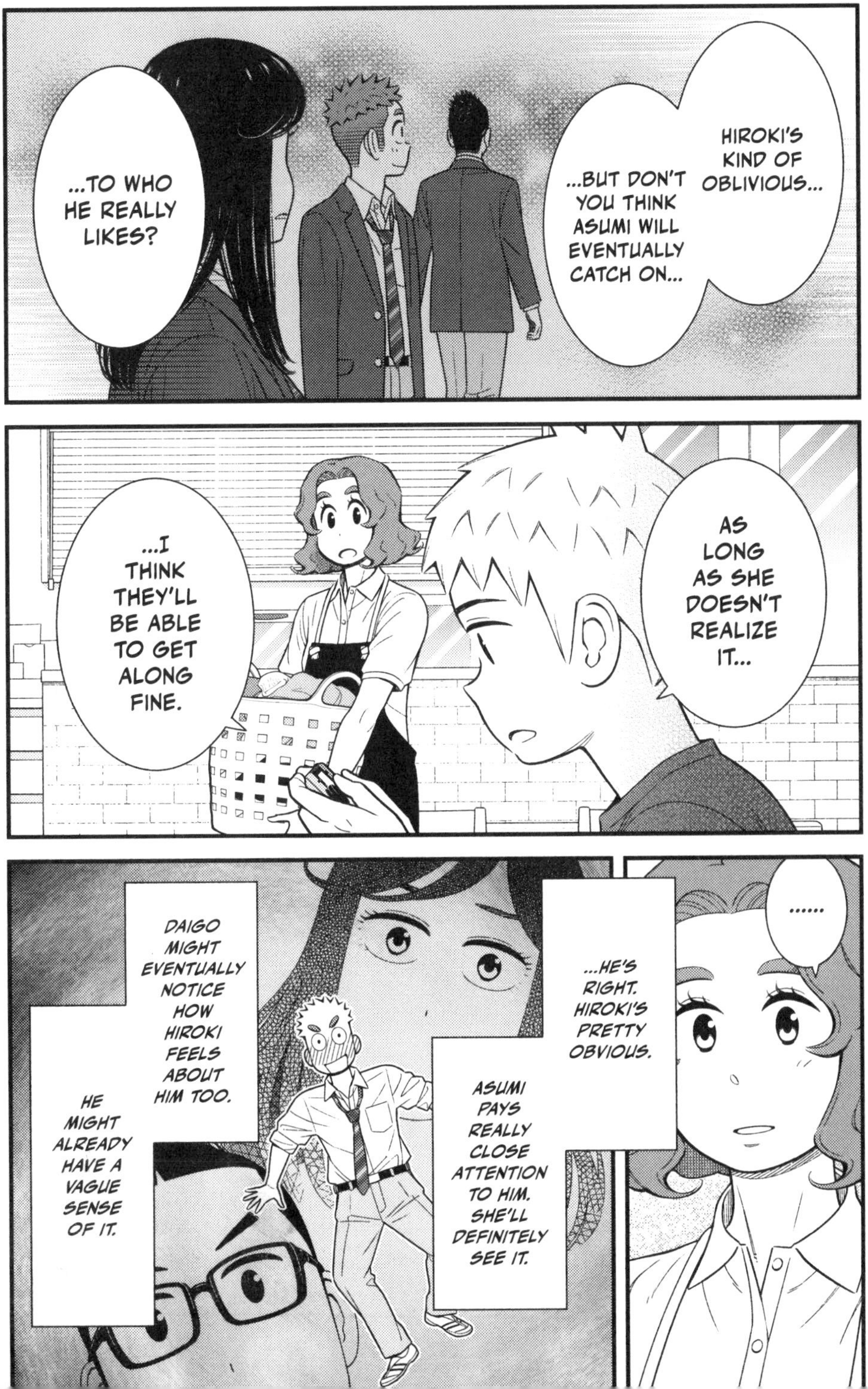
HIROKI'S KIND OF OBLIVIOUS...
...BUT DON'T YOU THINK ASUMI WILL EVENTUALLY CATCH ON...
...TO WHO HE REALLY LIKES?
AS LONG AS SHE DOESN'T REALIZE IT...
...I THINK THEY'LL BE ABLE TO GET ALONG FINE.
......
...HE'S RIGHT. HIROKI'S PRETTY OBVIOUS.
ASUMI PAYS REALLY CLOSE ATTENTION TO HIM. SHE'LL DEFINITELY SEE IT.
DAIGO MIGHT EVENTUALLY NOTICE HOW HIROKI FEELS ABOUT HIM TOO.
HE MIGHT ALREADY HAVE A VAGUE SENSE OF IT.

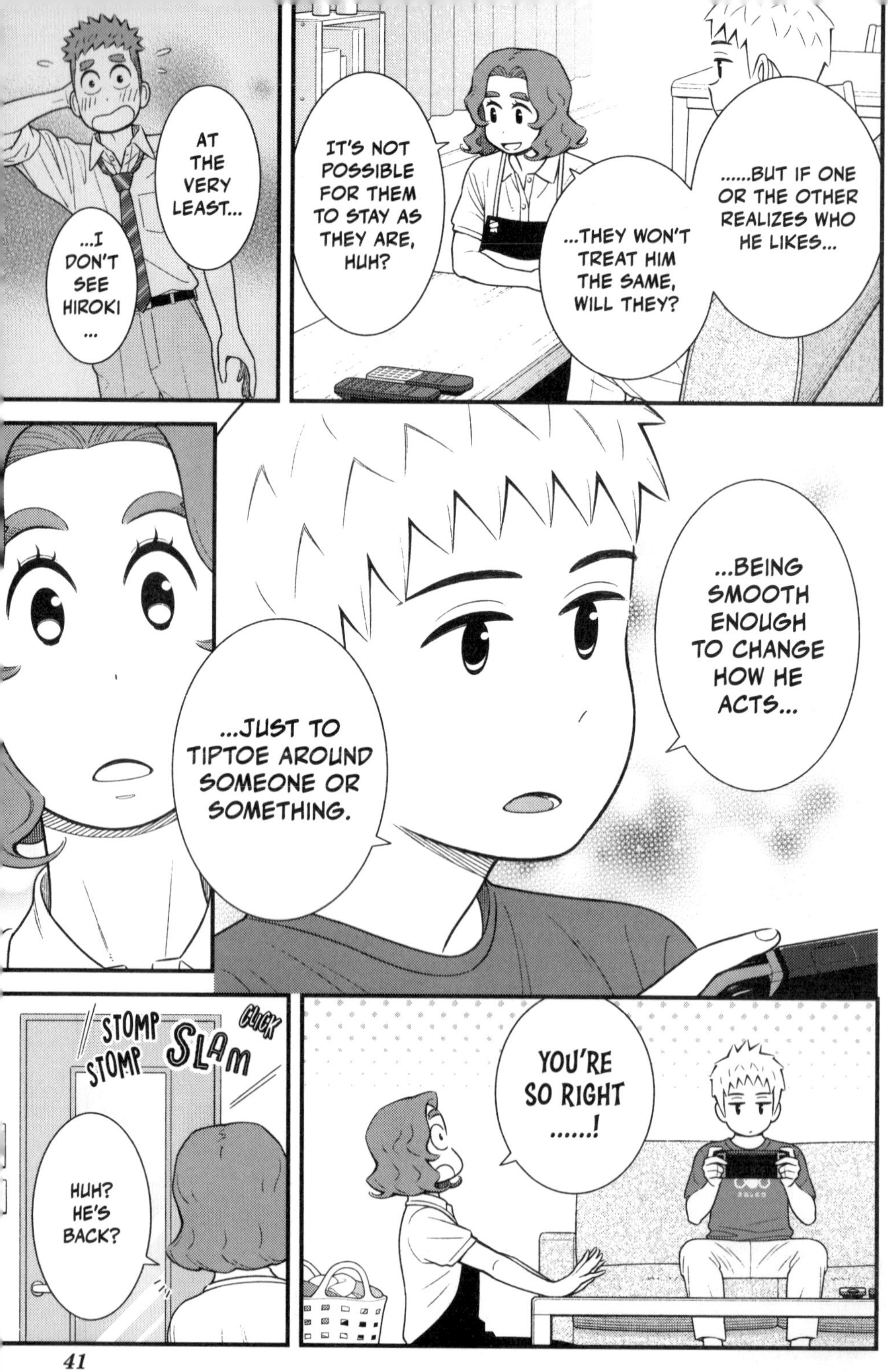
......BUT IF ONE OR THE OTHER REALIZES WHO HE LIKES...
...THEY WON'T TREAT HIM THE SAME, WILL THEY?
IT'S NOT POSSIBLE FOR THEM TO STAY AS THEY ARE, HUH?
AT THE VERY LEAST...
...I DON'T SEE HIROKI ...
...BEING SMOOTH ENOUGH TO CHANGE HOW HE ACTS...
...JUST TO TIPTOE AROUND SOMEONE OR SOMETHING.
YOU'RE SO RIGHT ......!
CLICK
SLAM
STOMP STOMP
HUH? HE'S BACK?

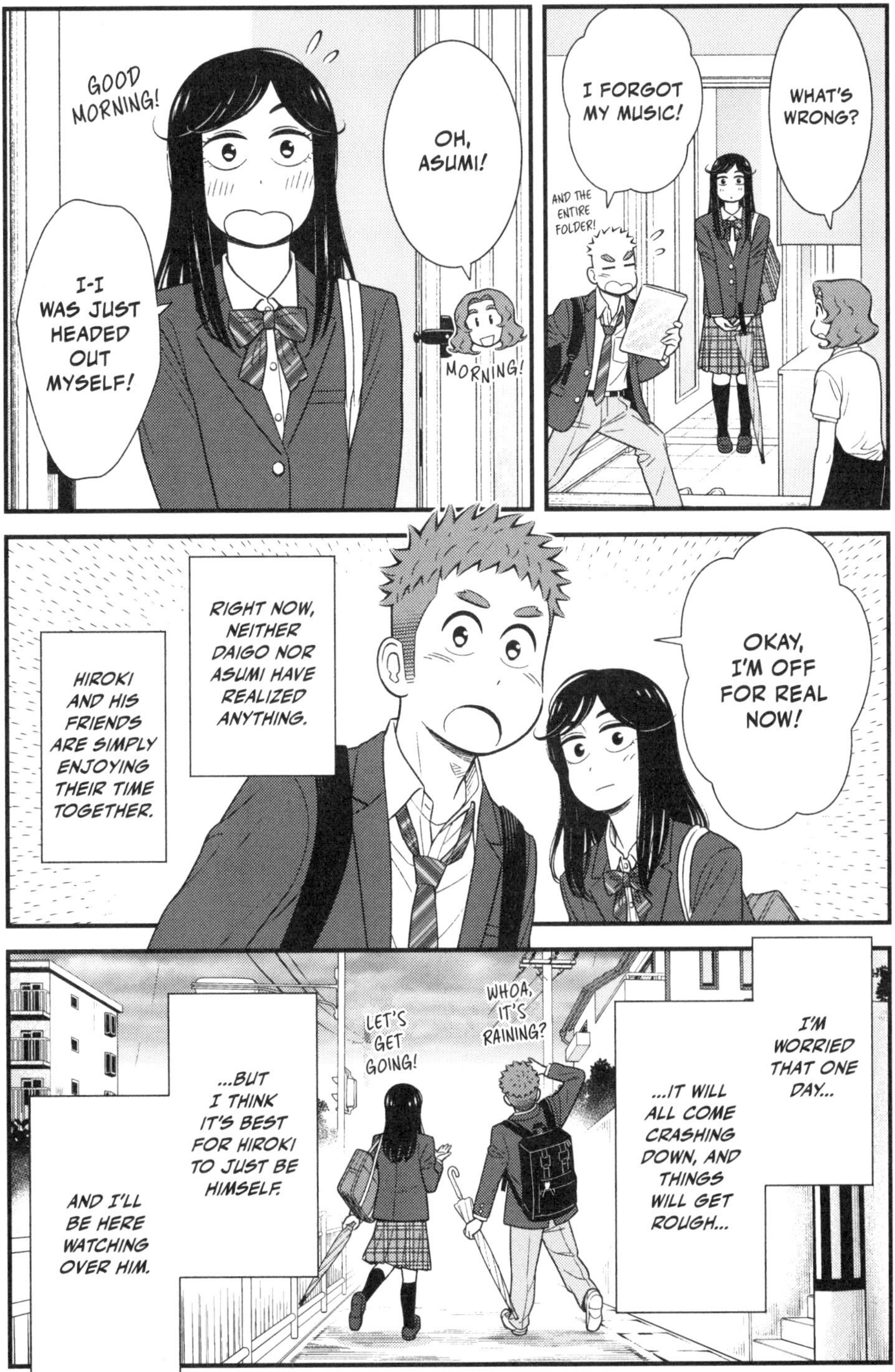
WHAT'S WRONG?
I FORGOT MY MUSIC!
AND THE ENTIRE FOLDER!
OH, ASUMI!
MORNING!
GOOD MORNING!
I-I WAS JUST HEADED OUT MYSELF!
OKAY, I'M OFF FOR REAL NOW!
RIGHT NOW, NEITHER DAIGO NOR ASUMI HAVE REALIZED ANYTHING.
HIROKI AND HIS FRIENDS ARE SIMPLY ENJOYING THEIR TIME TOGETHER.
I'M WORRIED THAT ONE DAY...
...IT WILL ALL COME CRASHING DOWN, AND THINGS WILL GET ROUGH...
WHOA, IT'S RAINING?
LET'S GET GOING!
...BUT I THINK IT'S BEST FOR HIROKI TO JUST BE HIMSELF.
AND I'LL BE HERE WATCHING OVER HIM.

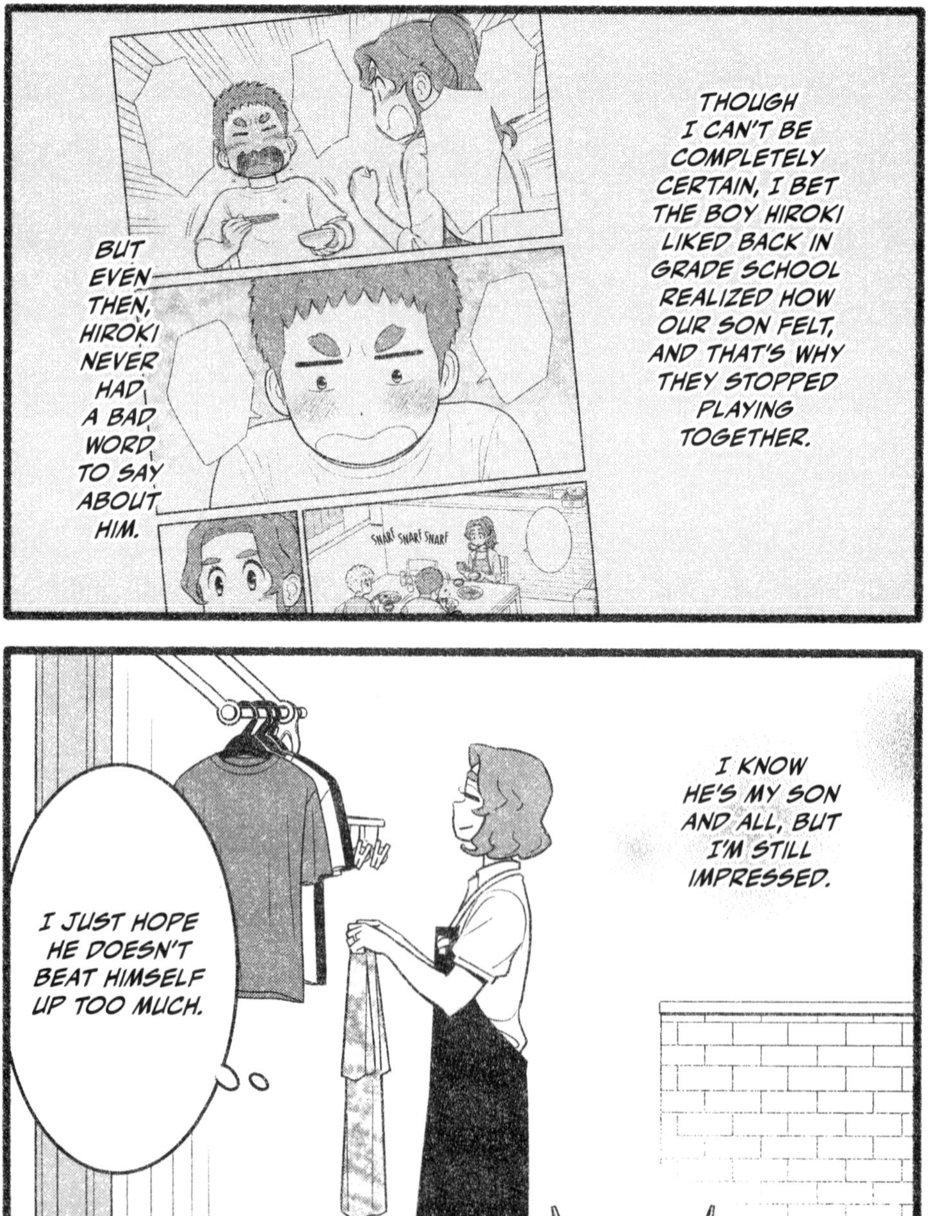
THOUGH I CAN'T BE COMPLETELY CERTAIN, I BET THE BOY HIROKI LIKED BACK IN GRADE SCHOOL REALIZED HOW OUR SON FELT, AND THAT'S WHY THEY STOPPED PLAYING TOGETHER.
BUT EVEN THEN, HIROKI NEVER HAD A BAD WORD TO SAY ABOUT HIM.
SNARF SNARF SNARF
I KNOW HE'S MY SON AND ALL, BUT I'M STILL IMPRESSED.
I JUST HOPE HE DOESN'T BEAT HIMSELF UP TOO MUCH.

I Think
Our Son
Is Gay

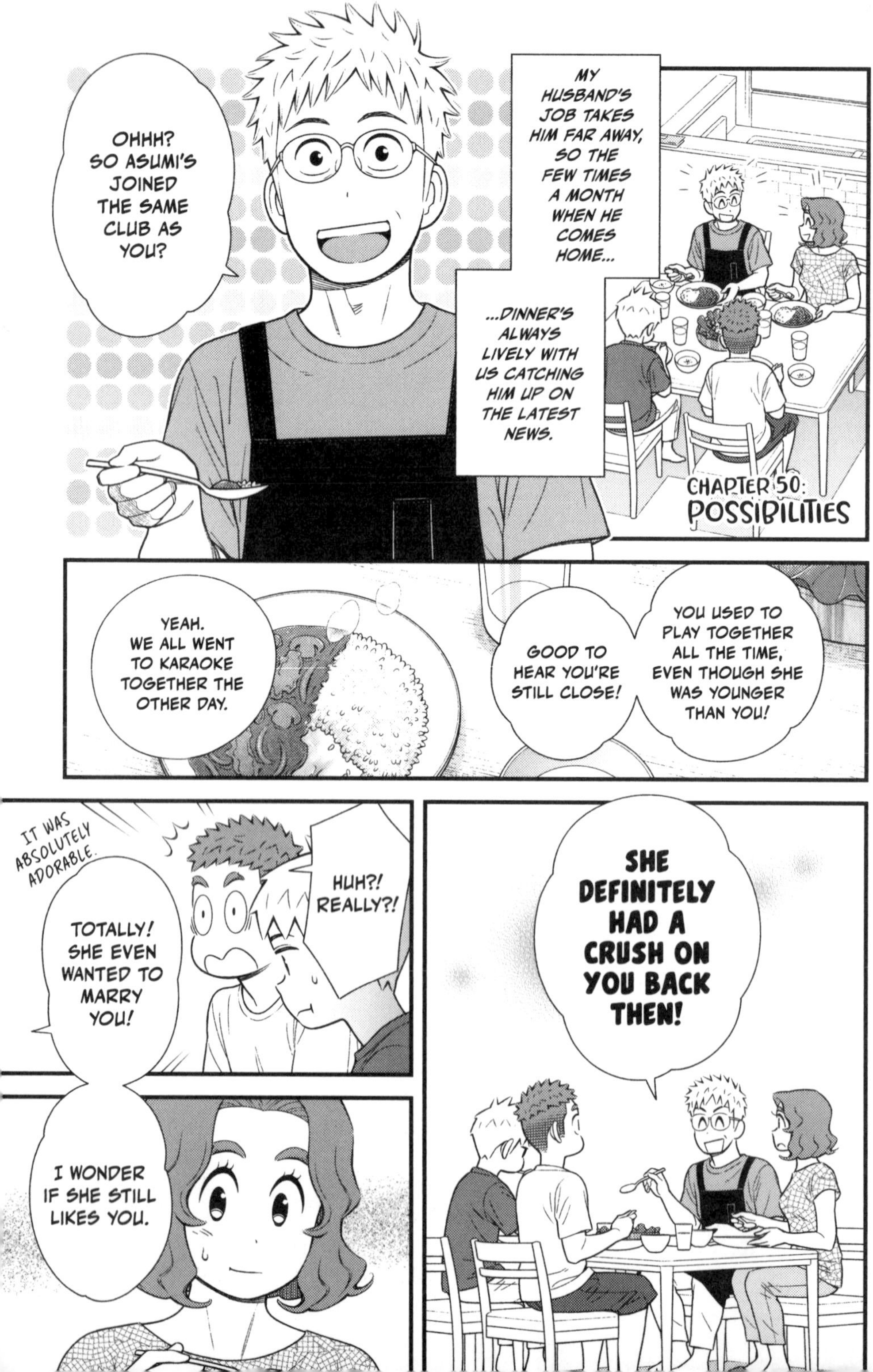
MY HUSBAND'S JOB TAKES HIM FAR AWAY, SO THE FEW TIMES A MONTH WHEN HE COMES HOME...
...DINNER'S ALWAYS LIVELY WITH US CATCHING HIM UP ON THE LATEST NEWS.
CHAPTER 50: POSSIBILITIES
OHHH? SO ASUMI'S JOINED THE SAME CLUB AS YOU?
YOU USED TO PLAY TOGETHER ALL THE TIME, EVEN THOUGH SHE WAS YOUNGER THAN YOU!
GOOD TO HEAR YOU'RE STILL CLOSE!
YEAH. WE ALL WENT TO KARAOKE TOGETHER THE OTHER DAY.
SHE DEFINITELY HAD A CRUSH ON YOU BACK THEN!
HUH?! REALLY?!
TOTALLY! SHE EVEN WANTED TO MARRY YOU!
IT WAS ABSOLUTELY ADORABLE.
I WONDER IF SHE STILL LIKES YOU.

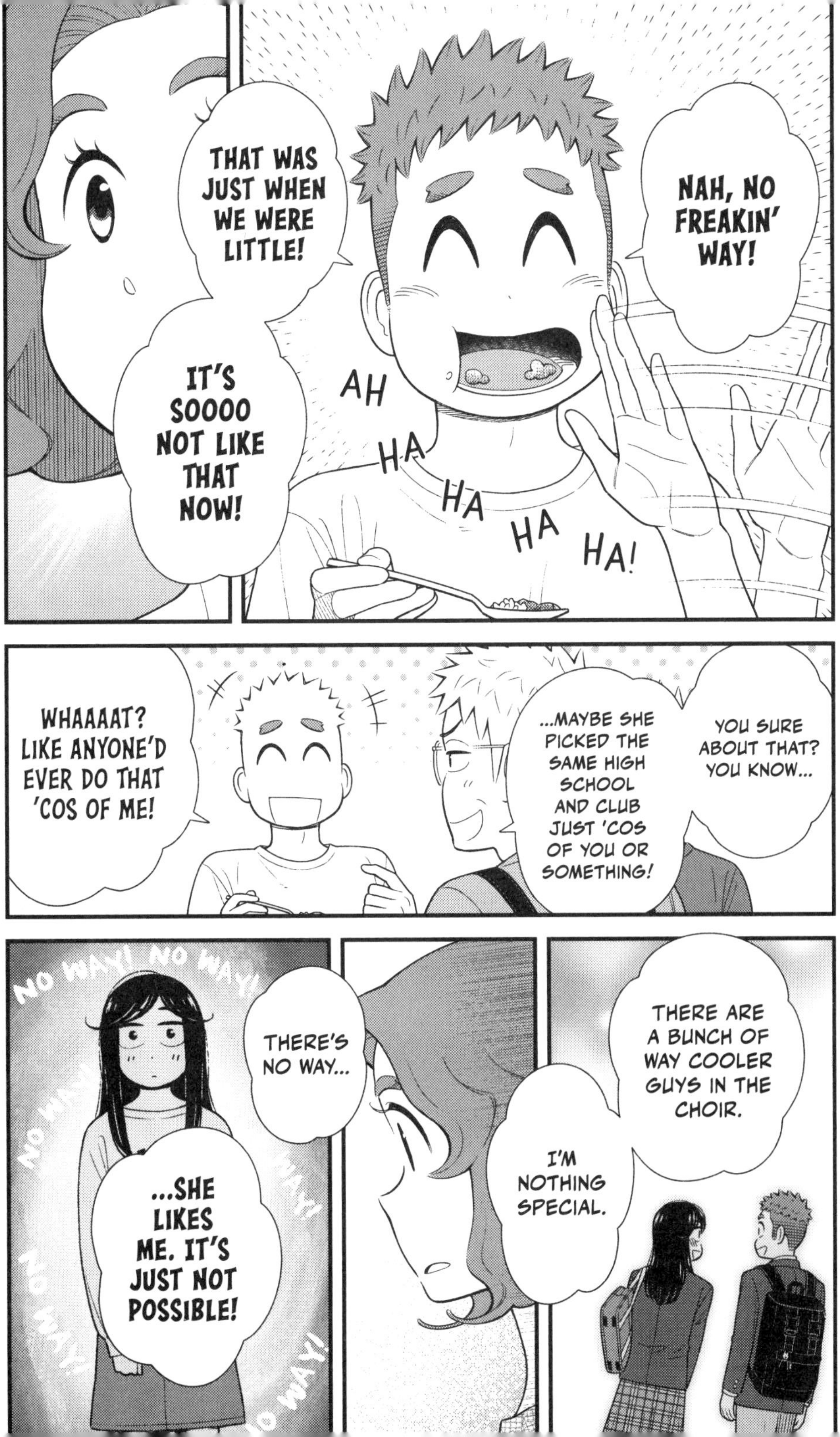
NAH, NO FREAKIN' WAY!
AH HA HA HA HA!
THAT WAS JUST WHEN WE WERE LITTLE!
IT'S SOOOO NOT LIKE THAT NOW!
YOU SURE ABOUT THAT? YOU KNOW...
...MAYBE SHE PICKED THE SAME HIGH SCHOOL AND CLUB JUST 'COS OF YOU OR SOMETHING!
WHAAAAT? LIKE ANYONE'D EVER DO THAT 'COS OF ME!
THERE ARE A BUNCH OF WAY COOLER GUYS IN THE CHOIR.
I'M NOTHING SPECIAL.
THERE'S NO WAY...
...SHE LIKES ME. IT'S JUST NOT POSSIBLE!
NO WAY! NO WAY! NO WAY! WAY! NO WAY! NO WAY!

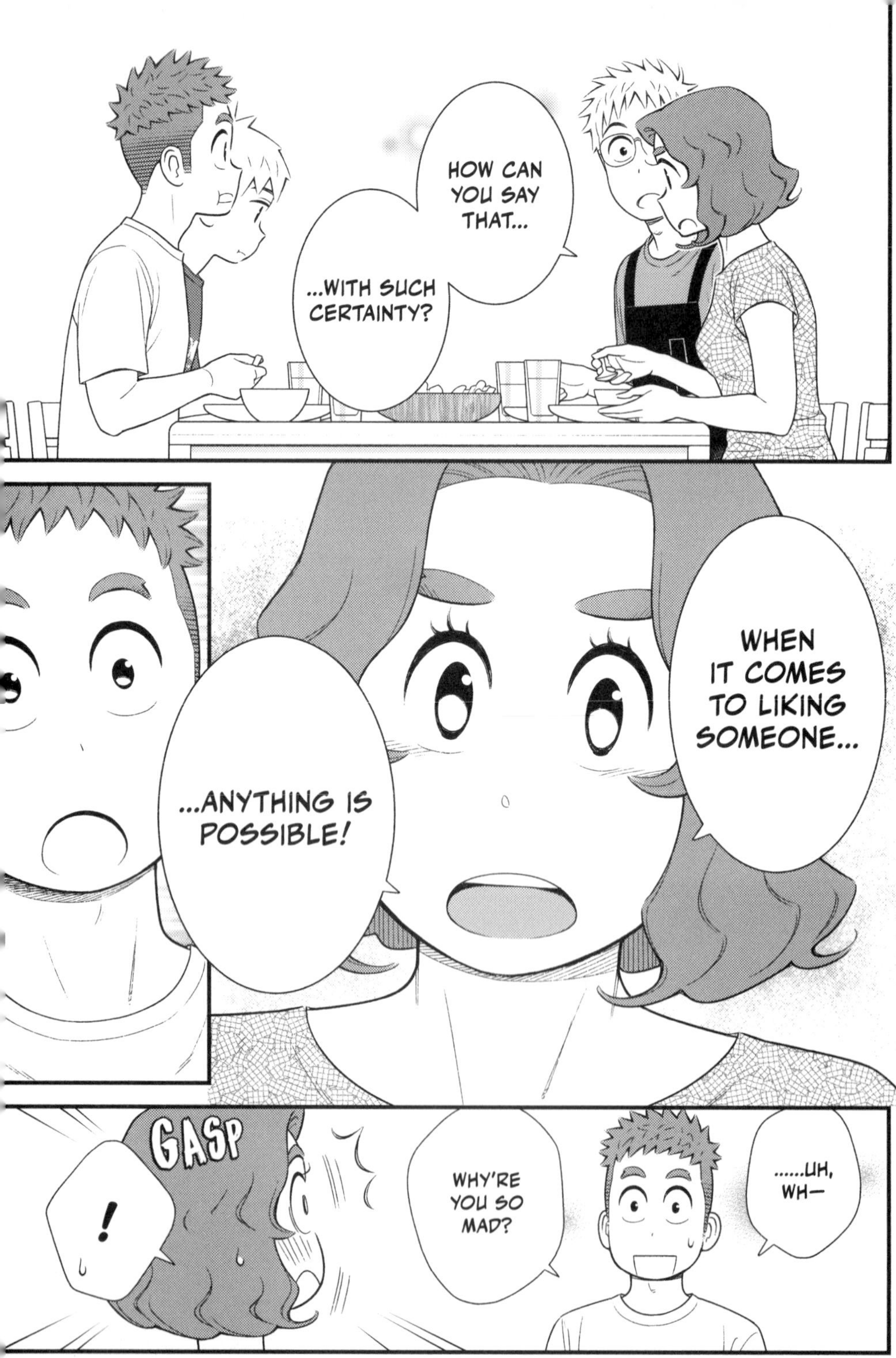
HOW CAN YOU SAY THAT...
...WITH SUCH CERTAINTY?
WHEN IT COMES TO LIKING SOMEONE...
...ANYTHING IS POSSIBLE!
......UH, WH—
WHY'RE YOU SO MAD?
GASP
!

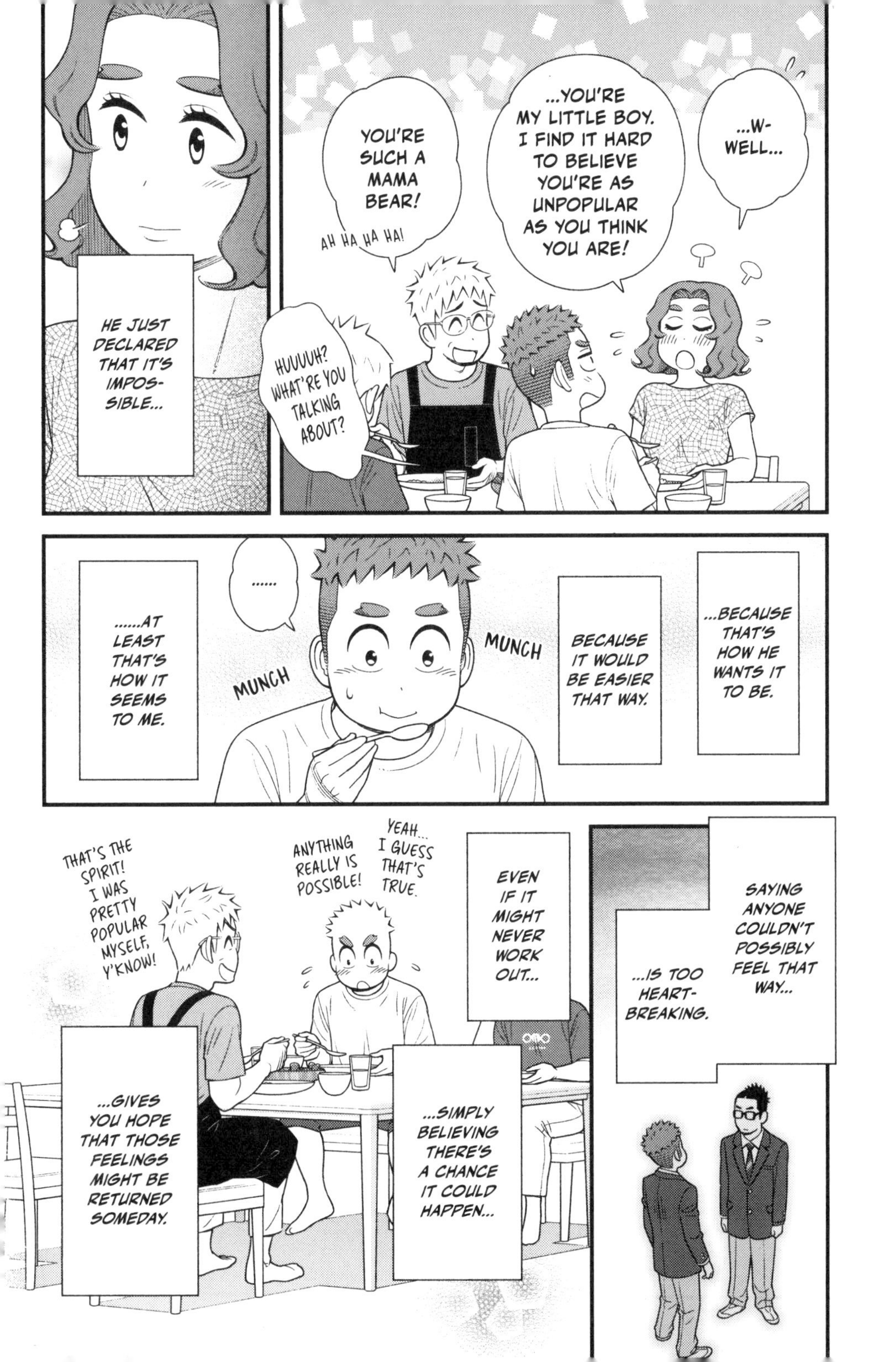
...W-WELL...
...YOU'RE MY LITTLE BOY. I FIND IT HARD TO BELIEVE YOU'RE AS UNPOPULAR AS YOU THINK YOU ARE!
YOU'RE SUCH A MAMA BEAR!
AH HA HA HA!
HUUUUH? WHAT'RE YOU TALKING ABOUT?
HE JUST DECLARED THAT IT'S IMPOSSIBLE...
...BECAUSE THAT'S HOW HE WANTS IT TO BE.
BECAUSE IT WOULD BE EASIER THAT WAY.
MUNCH
MUNCH
......
......AT LEAST THAT'S HOW IT SEEMS TO ME.
SAYING ANYONE COULDN'T POSSIBLY FEEL THAT WAY...
...IS TOO HEART-BREAKING.
EVEN IF IT MIGHT NEVER WORK OUT...
YEAH... I GUESS THAT'S TRUE.
ANYTHING REALLY IS POSSIBLE!
THAT'S THE SPIRIT! I WAS PRETTY POPULAR MYSELF, Y'KNOW!
...SIMPLY BELIEVING THERE'S A CHANCE IT COULD HAPPEN...
...GIVES YOU HOPE THAT THOSE FEELINGS MIGHT BE RETURNED SOMEDAY.

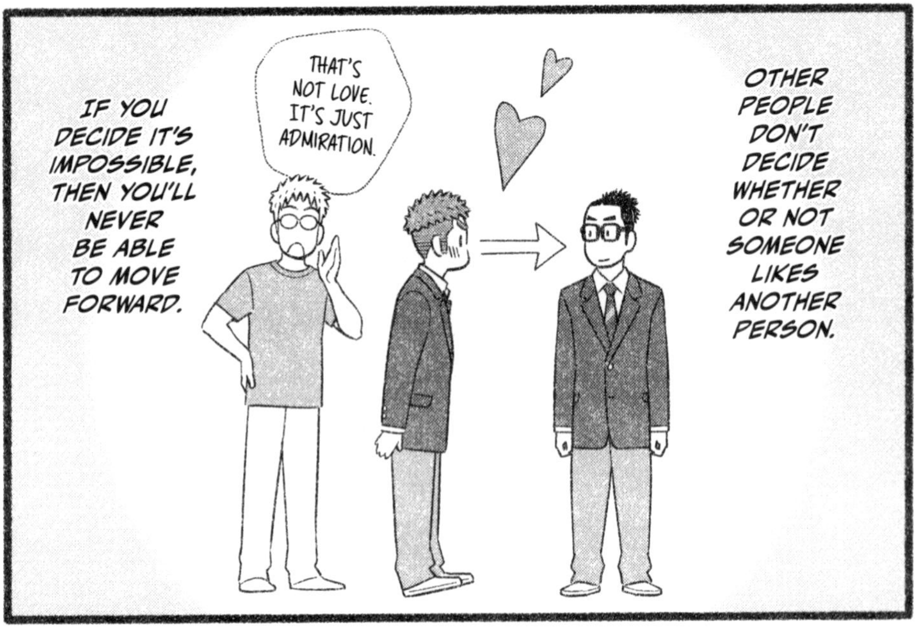
OTHER PEOPLE DON'T DECIDE WHETHER OR NOT SOMEONE LIKES ANOTHER PERSON.
THAT'S NOT LOVE. IT'S JUST ADMIRATION.
IF YOU DECIDE IT'S IMPOSSIBLE, THEN YOU'LL NEVER BE ABLE TO MOVE FORWARD.
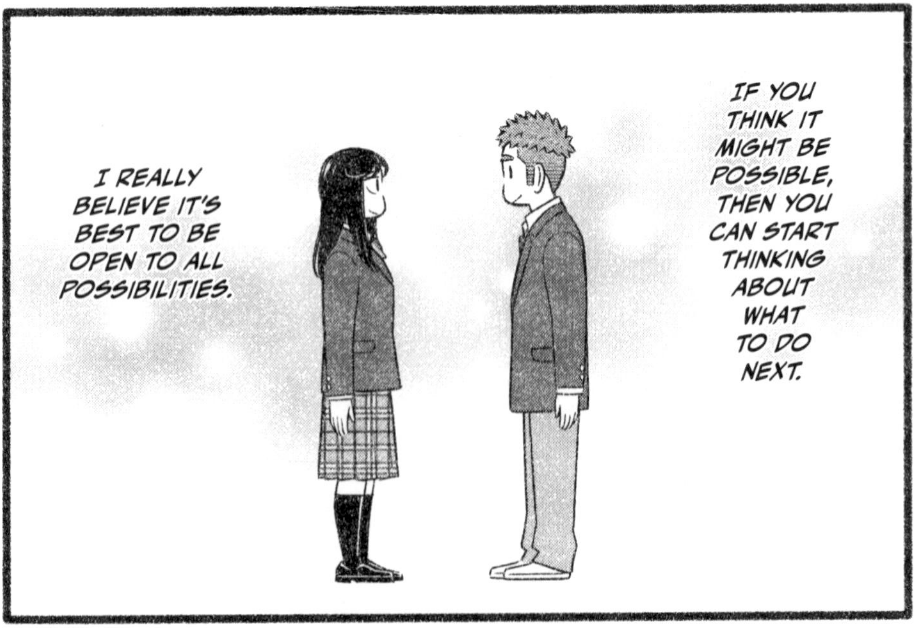
IF YOU THINK IT MIGHT BE POSSIBLE, THEN YOU CAN START THINKING ABOUT WHAT TO DO NEXT.
I REALLY BELIEVE IT'S BEST TO BE OPEN TO ALL POSSIBILITIES.

I Think
Our Son
Is Gay

Chapter 51: The Piano

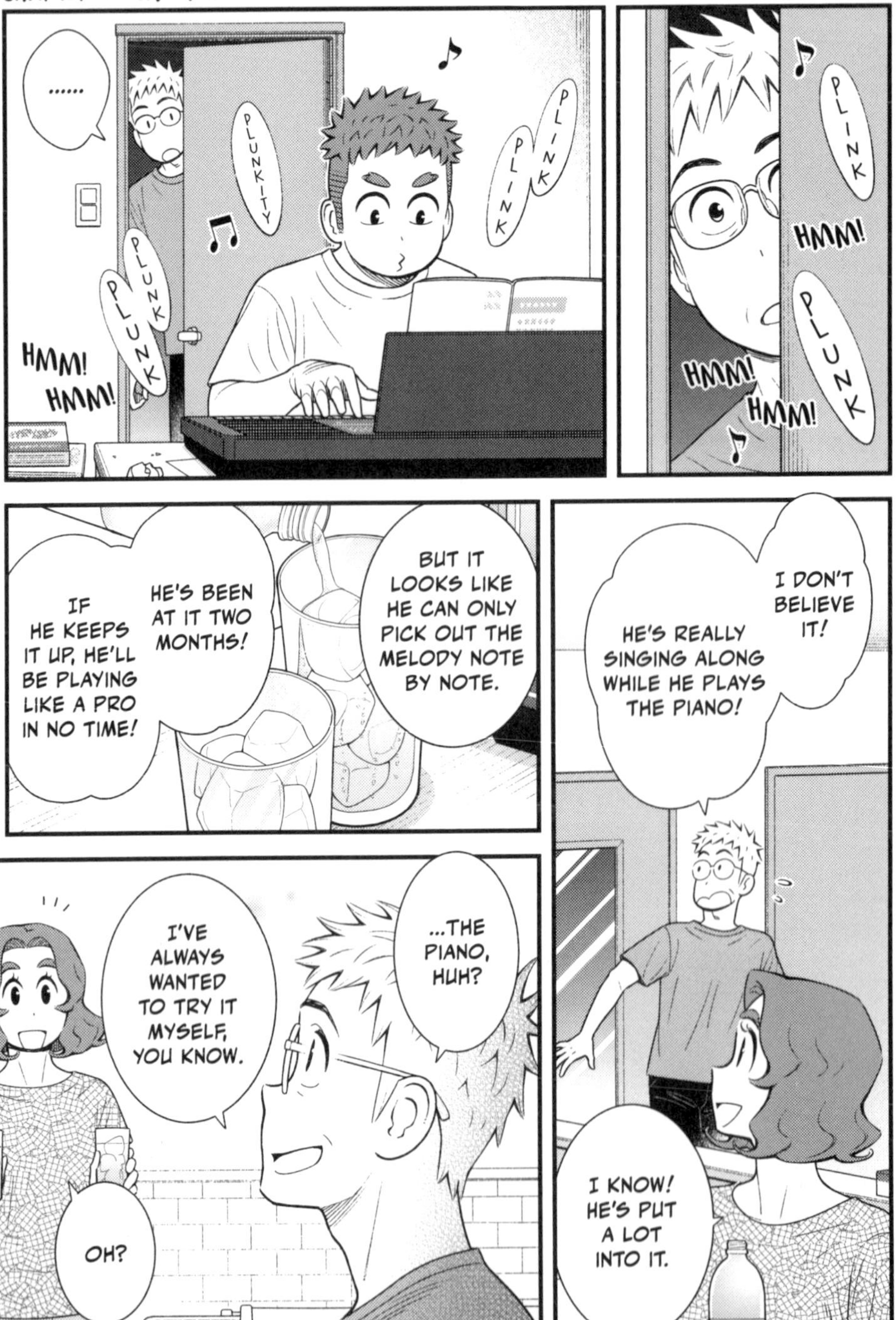
PLINK
HMM!
PLUNK
HMM!
HMM!
......
PLUNKITY
PLINK
PLINK
PLUNK
PLUNK
HMM!
HMM!
I DON'T BELIEVE IT!
HE'S REALLY SINGING ALONG WHILE HE PLAYS THE PIANO!
I KNOW! HE'S PUT A LOT INTO IT.
BUT IT LOOKS LIKE HE CAN ONLY PICK OUT THE MELODY NOTE BY NOTE.
HE'S BEEN AT IT TWO MONTHS!
IF HE KEEPS IT UP, HE'LL BE PLAYING LIKE A PRO IN NO TIME!
...THE PIANO, HUH?
I'VE ALWAYS WANTED TO TRY IT MYSELF, YOU KNOW.
OH?

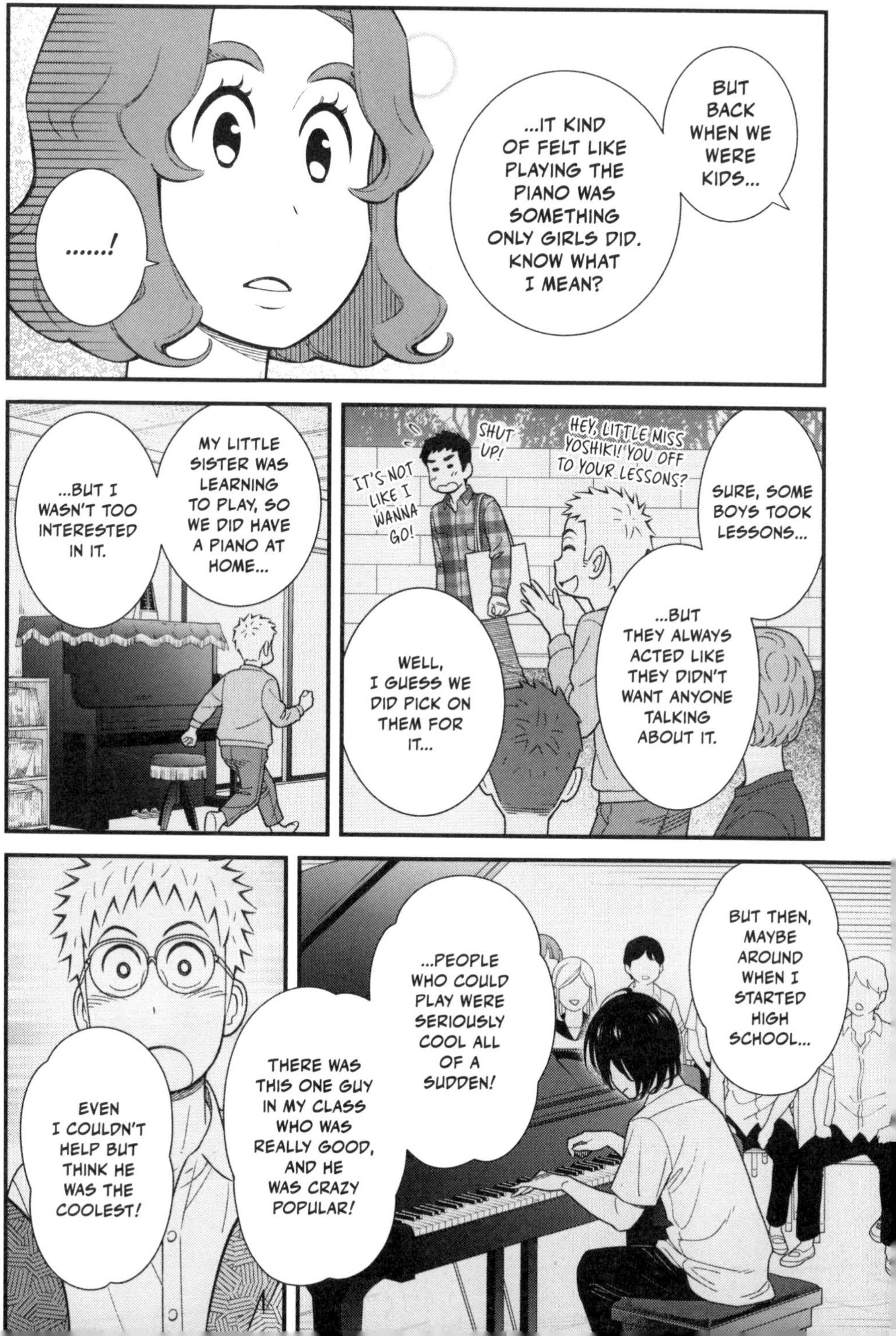
BUT BACK WHEN WE WERE KIDS...
...IT KIND OF FELT LIKE PLAYING THE PIANO WAS SOMETHING ONLY GIRLS DID. KNOW WHAT I MEAN?
......!
SURE, SOME BOYS TOOK LESSONS...
HEY, LITTLE MISS YOSHIKI! YOU OFF TO YOUR LESSONS?
SHUT UP!
IT'S NOT LIKE I WANNA GO!
...BUT THEY ALWAYS ACTED LIKE THEY DIDN'T WANT ANYONE TALKING ABOUT IT.
WELL, I GUESS WE DID PICK ON THEM FOR IT...
MY LITTLE SISTER WAS LEARNING TO PLAY, SO WE DID HAVE A PIANO AT HOME...
...BUT I WASN'T TOO INTERESTED IN IT.
BUT THEN, MAYBE AROUND WHEN I STARTED HIGH SCHOOL...
...PEOPLE WHO COULD PLAY WERE SERIOUSLY COOL ALL OF A SUDDEN!
THERE WAS THIS ONE GUY IN MY CLASS WHO WAS REALLY GOOD, AND HE WAS CRAZY POPULAR!
EVEN I COULDN'T HELP BUT THINK HE WAS THE COOLEST!

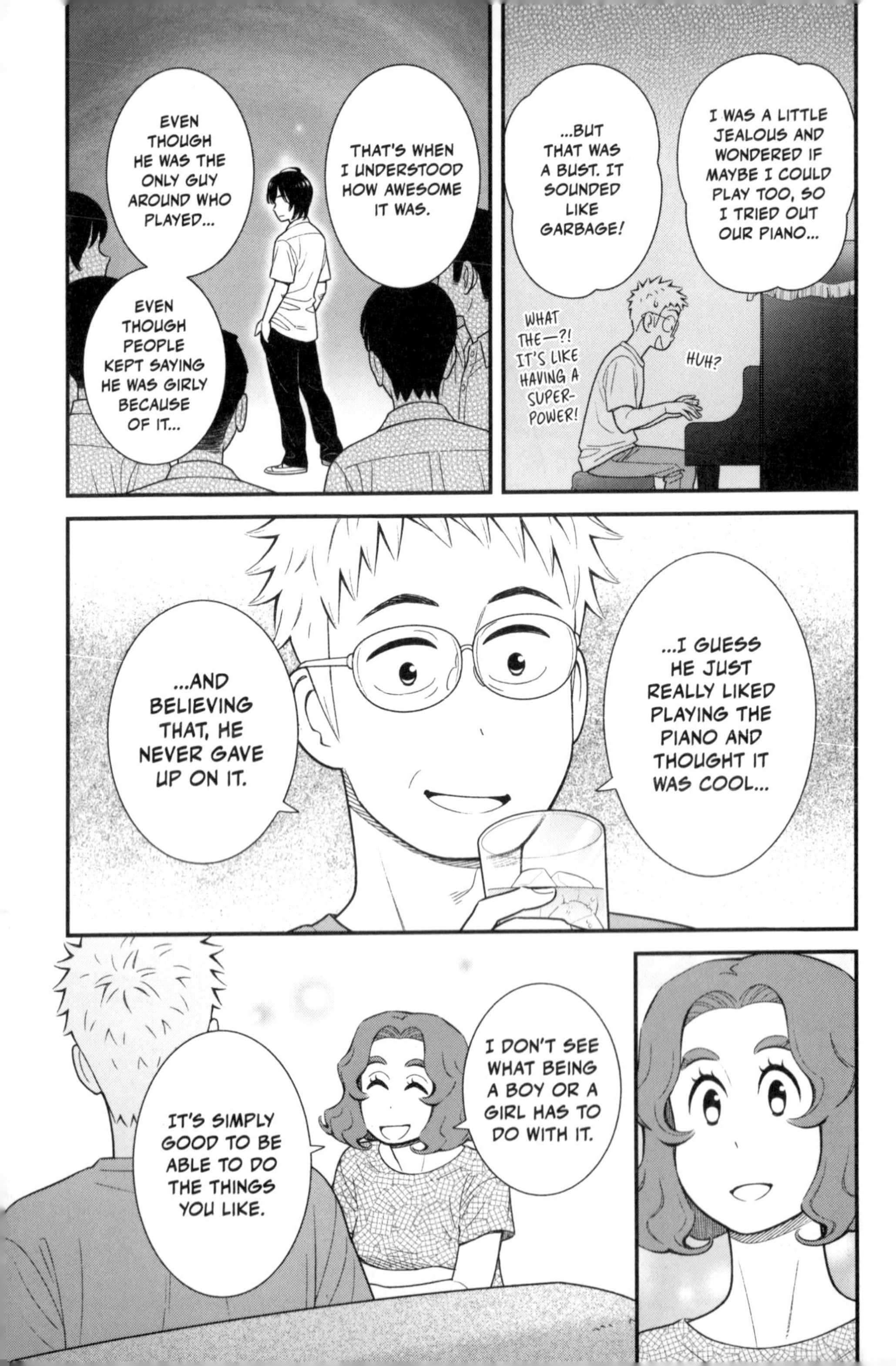
I WAS A LITTLE JEALOUS AND WONDERED IF MAYBE I COULD PLAY TOO, SO I TRIED OUT OUR PIANO...
...BUT THAT WAS A BUST. IT SOUNDED LIKE GARBAGE!
HUH?
WHAT THE—?! IT'S LIKE HAVING A SUPER-POWER!
THAT'S WHEN I UNDERSTOOD HOW AWESOME IT WAS.
EVEN THOUGH HE WAS THE ONLY GUY AROUND WHO PLAYED...
EVEN THOUGH PEOPLE KEPT SAYING HE WAS GIRLY BECAUSE OF IT...
...I GUESS HE JUST REALLY LIKED PLAYING THE PIANO AND THOUGHT IT WAS COOL...
...AND BELIEVING THAT, HE NEVER GAVE UP ON IT.
I DON'T SEE WHAT BEING A BOY OR A GIRL HAS TO DO WITH IT.
IT'S SIMPLY GOOD TO BE ABLE TO DO THE THINGS YOU LIKE.

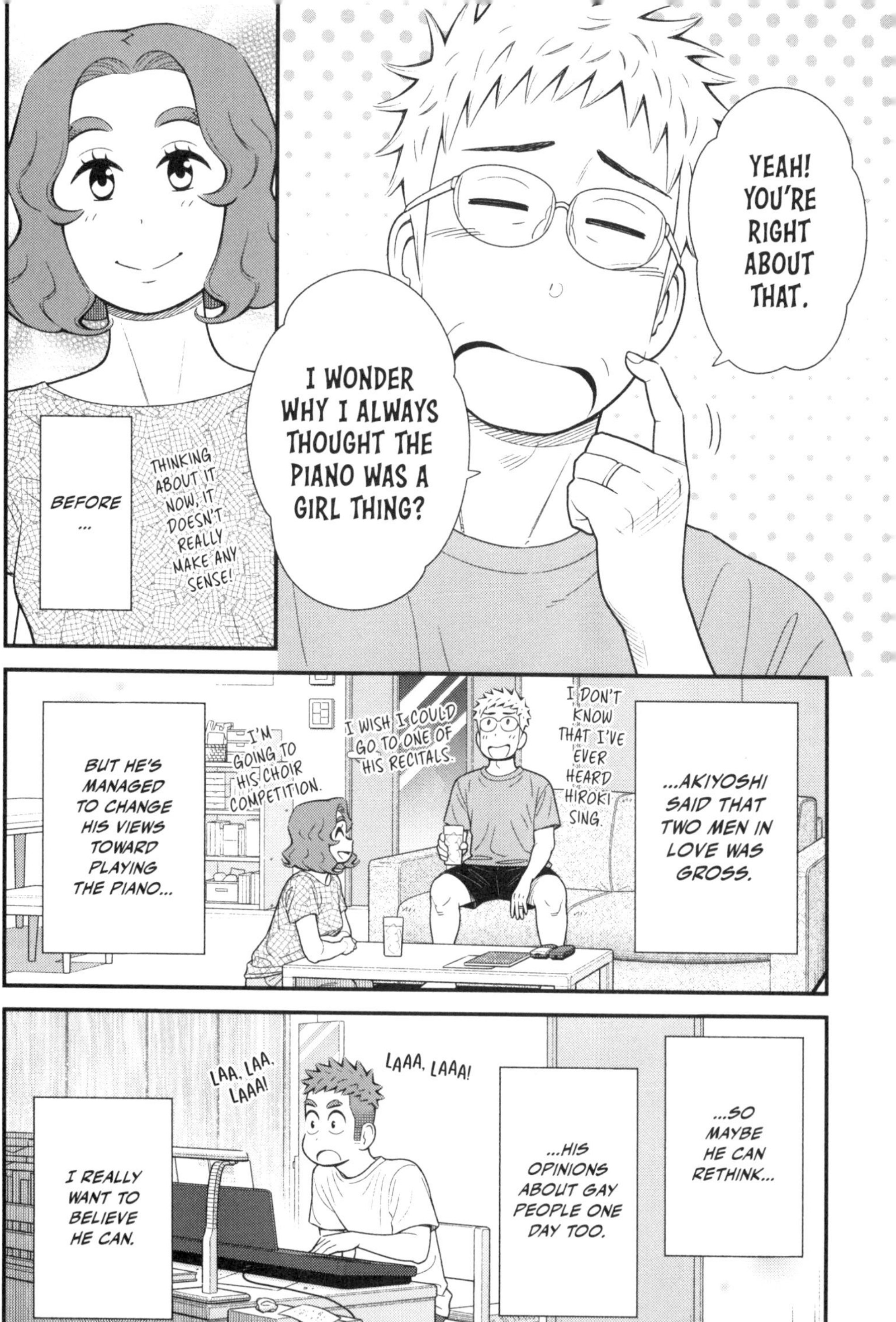
YEAH! YOU'RE RIGHT ABOUT THAT.
I WONDER WHY I ALWAYS THOUGHT THE PIANO WAS A GIRL THING?
THINKING ABOUT IT NOW, IT DOESN'T REALLY MAKE ANY SENSE!
BEFORE ...
...AKIYOSHI SAID THAT TWO MEN IN LOVE WAS GROSS.
I DON'T KNOW THAT I'VE EVER HEARD HIROKI SING.
I WISH I COULD GO TO ONE OF HIS RECITALS.
I'M GOING TO HIS CHOIR COMPETITION.
BUT HE'S MANAGED TO CHANGE HIS VIEWS TOWARD PLAYING THE PIANO...
...SO MAYBE HE CAN RETHINK...
...HIS OPINIONS ABOUT GAY PEOPLE ONE DAY TOO.
LAAA, LAAA!
LAA, LAA, LAAA!
I REALLY WANT TO BELIEVE HE CAN.

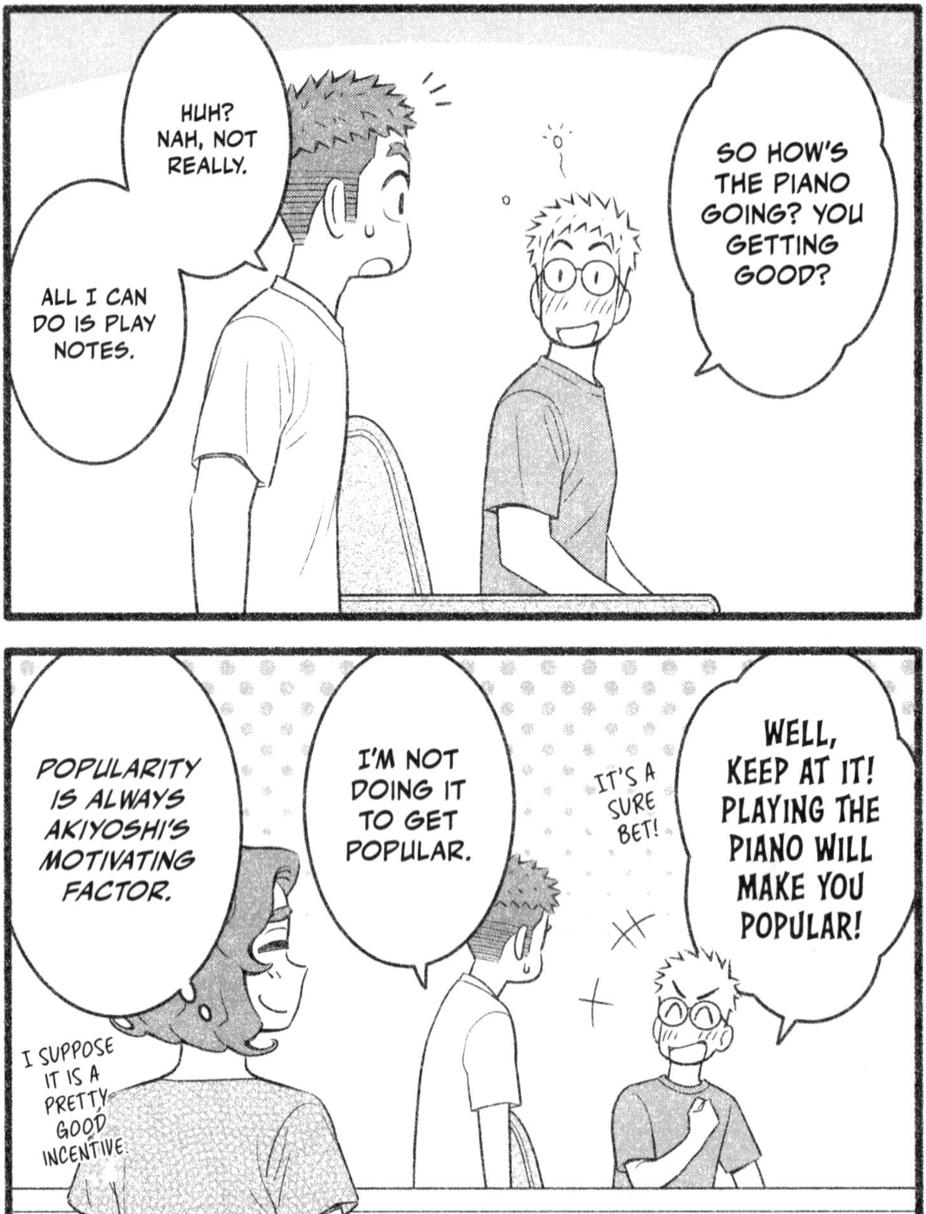
SO HOW'S THE PIANO GOING? YOU GETTING GOOD?
HUH? NAH, NOT REALLY.
ALL I CAN DO IS PLAY NOTES.
WELL, KEEP AT IT! PLAYING THE PIANO WILL MAKE YOU POPULAR!
IT'S A SURE BET!
I'M NOT DOING IT TO GET POPULAR.
POPULARITY IS ALWAYS AKIYOSHI'S MOTIVATING FACTOR.
I SUPPOSE IT IS A PRETTY GOOD INCENTIVE.

I Think
Our Son
Is Gay

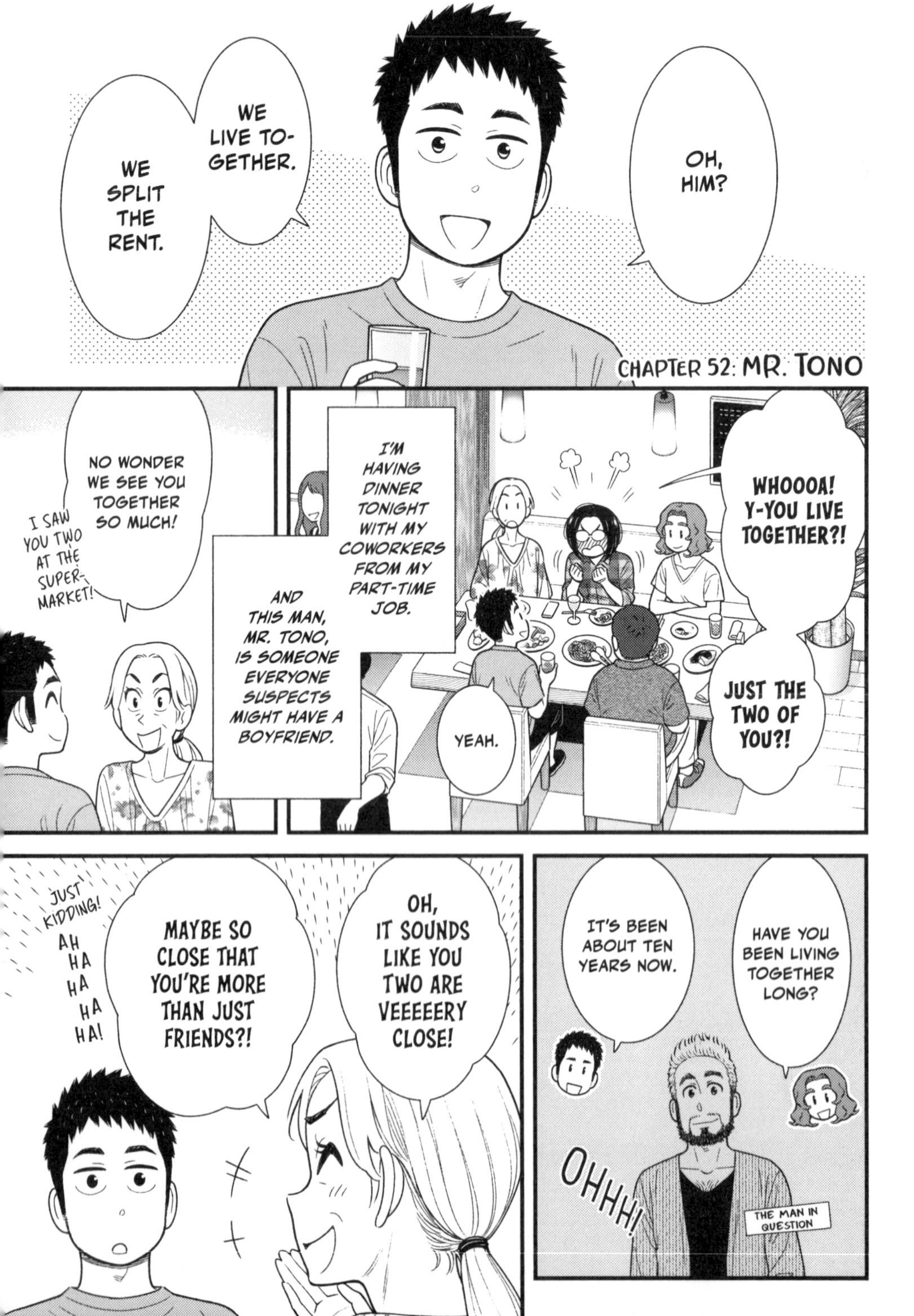
OH, HIM?
WE LIVE TOGETHER.
WE SPLIT THE RENT.
CHAPTER 52: MR. TONO
WHOOOA! Y-YOU LIVE TOGETHER?!
I'M HAVING DINNER TONIGHT WITH MY COWORKERS FROM MY PART-TIME JOB.
JUST THE TWO OF YOU?!
AND THIS MAN, MR. TONO, IS SOMEONE EVERYONE SUSPECTS MIGHT HAVE A BOYFRIEND.
YEAH.
NO WONDER WE SEE YOU TOGETHER SO MUCH!
I SAW YOU TWO AT THE SUPERMARKET!
HAVE YOU BEEN LIVING TOGETHER LONG?
IT'S BEEN ABOUT TEN YEARS NOW.
OHHH!
THE MAN IN QUESTION
OH, IT SOUNDS LIKE YOU TWO ARE VEEEEERY CLOSE!
MAYBE SO CLOSE THAT YOU'RE MORE THAN JUST FRIENDS?!
JUST KIDDING!
AH HA HA HA HA!

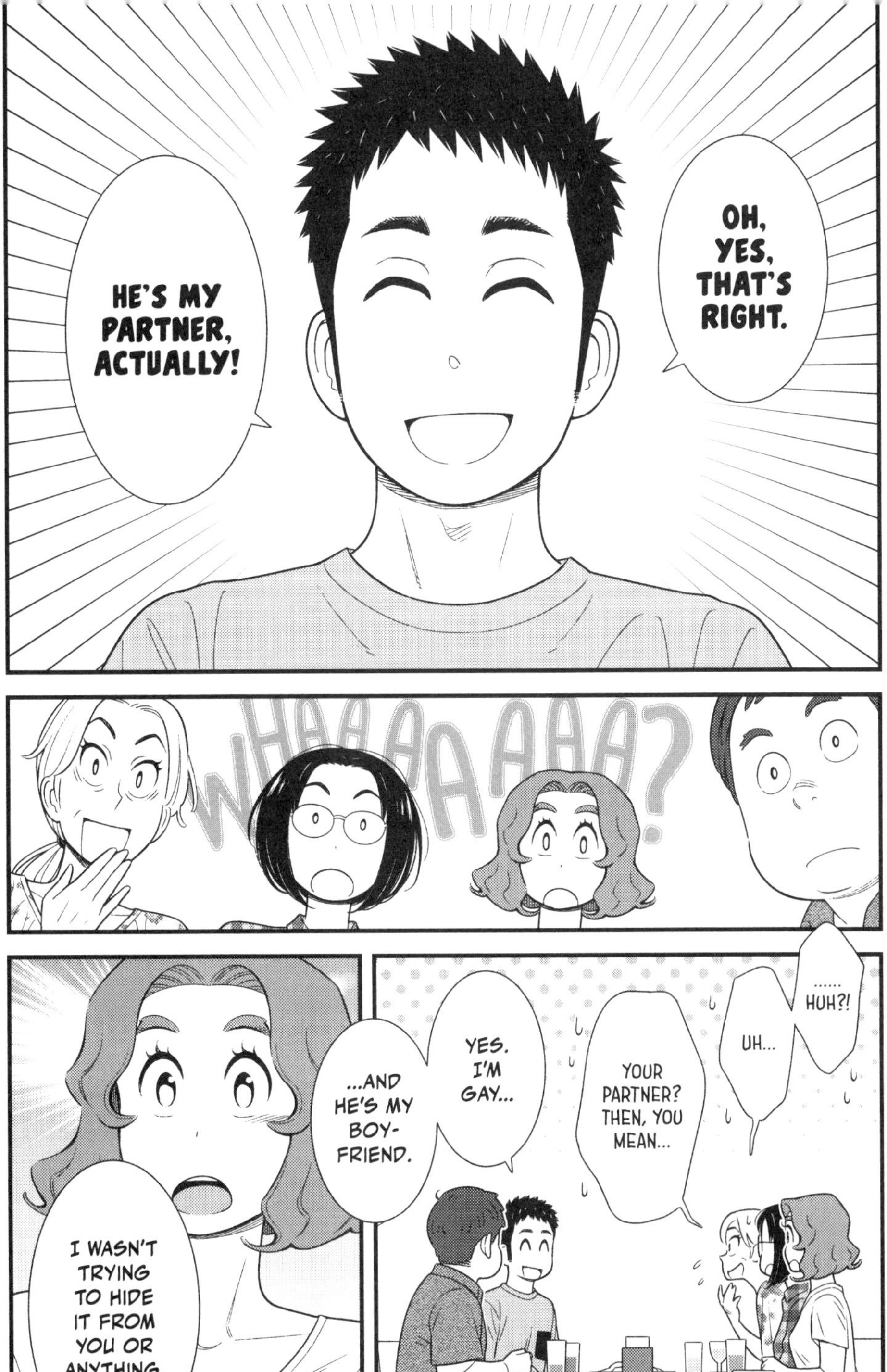
OH, YES, THAT'S RIGHT.
HE'S MY PARTNER, ACTUALLY!
WHAAAAAAA?
......HUH?!
UH...
YOUR PARTNER? THEN, YOU MEAN...
YES. I'M GAY...
...AND HE'S MY BOY-FRIEND.
I WASN'T TRYING TO HIDE IT FROM YOU OR ANYTHING.

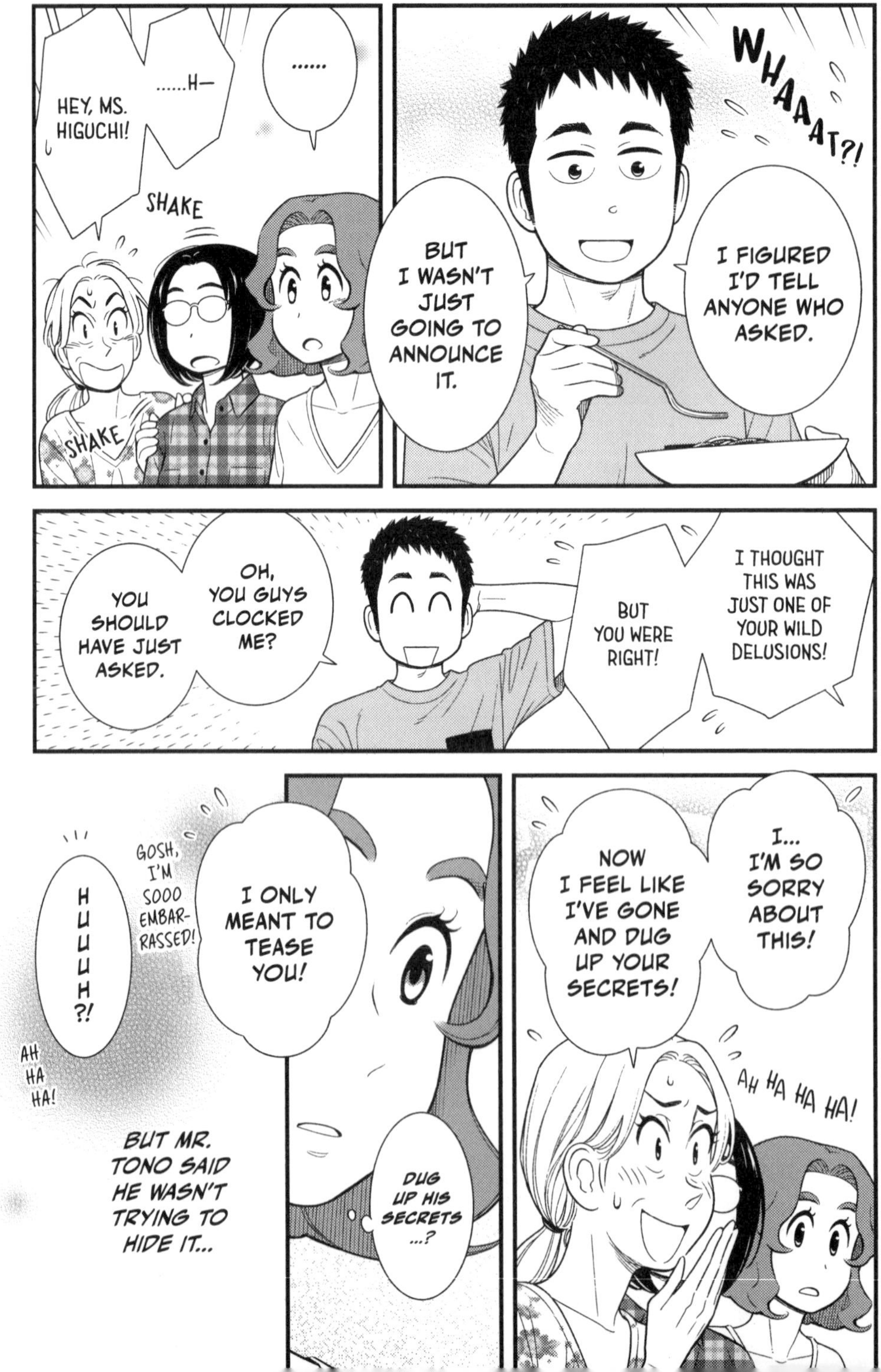
WHAAAT?!
I FIGURED I'D TELL ANYONE WHO ASKED.
BUT I WASN'T JUST GOING TO ANNOUNCE IT.
......
......H—
HEY, MS. HIGUCHI!
SHAKE
SHAKE
I THOUGHT THIS WAS JUST ONE OF YOUR WILD DELUSIONS!
BUT YOU WERE RIGHT!
OH, YOU GUYS CLOCKED ME?
YOU SHOULD HAVE JUST ASKED.
I... I'M SO SORRY ABOUT THIS!
NOW I FEEL LIKE I'VE GONE AND DUG UP YOUR SECRETS!
AH HA HA HA!
I ONLY MEANT TO TEASE YOU!
GOSH, I'M SOOO EMBARRASSED!
HUUUH?!
DUG UP HIS SECRETS...?
AH HA HA!
BUT MR. TONO SAID HE WASN'T TRYING TO HIDE IT...

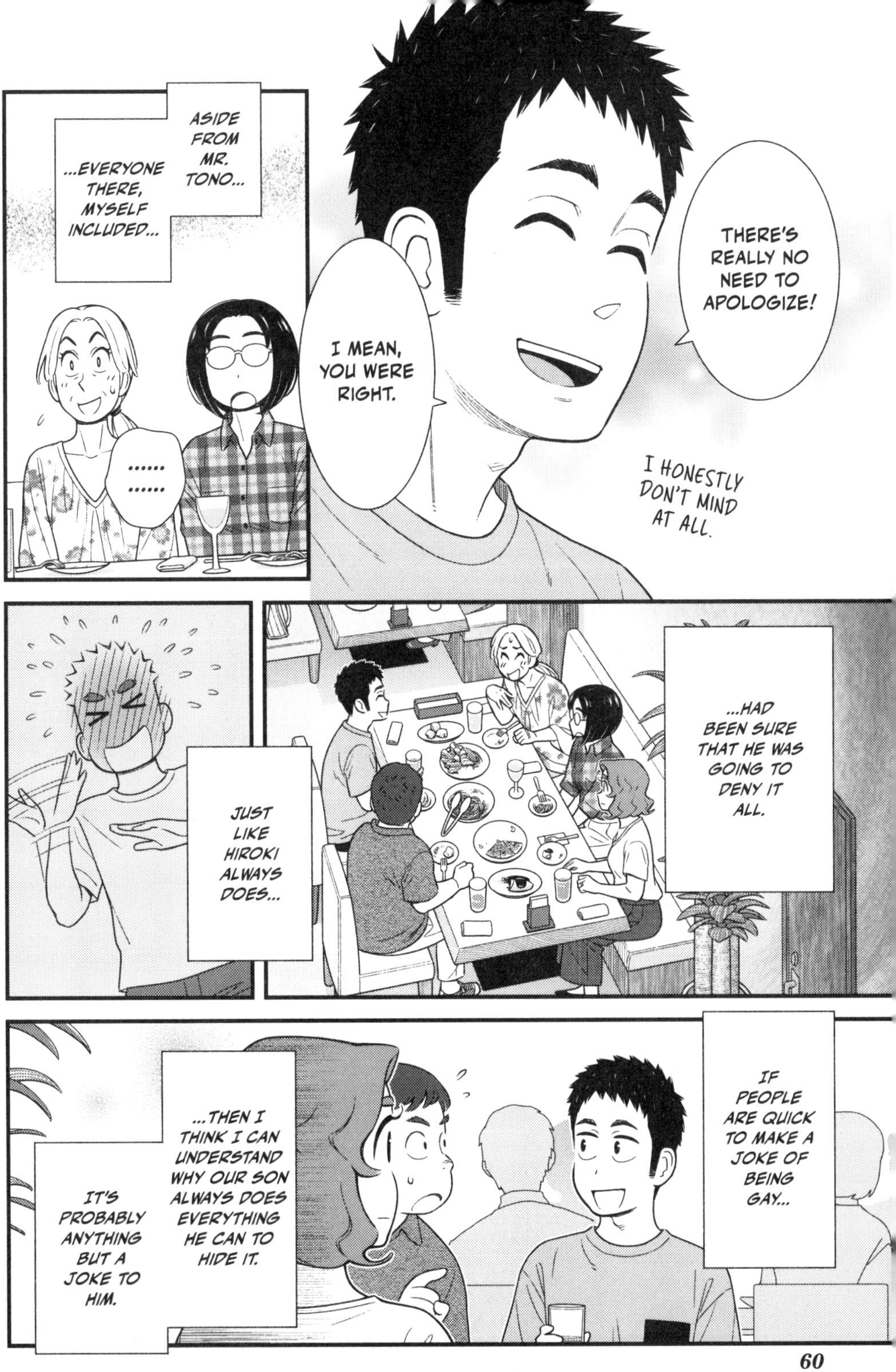
THERE'S REALLY NO NEED TO APOLOGIZE!
I MEAN, YOU WERE RIGHT.
I HONESTLY DON'T MIND AT ALL.
ASIDE FROM MR. TONO...
...EVERYONE THERE, MYSELF INCLUDED...
......
......
...HAD BEEN SURE THAT HE WAS GOING TO DENY IT ALL.
JUST LIKE HIROKI ALWAYS DOES...
IF PEOPLE ARE QUICK TO MAKE A JOKE OF BEING GAY...
...THEN I THINK I CAN UNDERSTAND WHY OUR SON ALWAYS DOES EVERYTHING HE CAN TO HIDE IT.
IT'S PROBABLY ANYTHING BUT A JOKE TO HIM.

Chapter 53: You're Just Fine

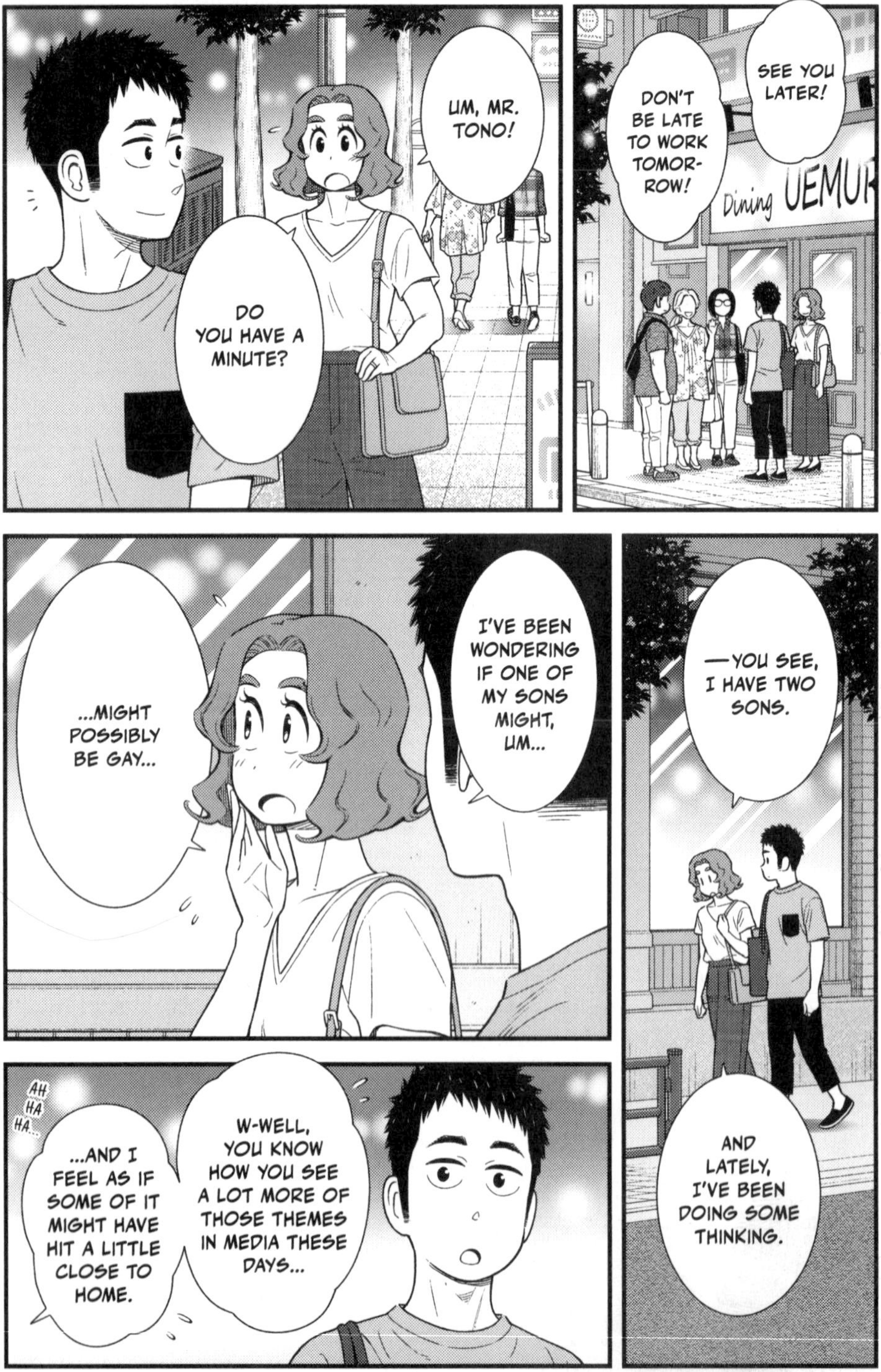
SEE YOU LATER!
DON'T BE LATE TO WORK TOMORROW!
UM, MR. TONO!
DO YOU HAVE A MINUTE?
—YOU SEE, I HAVE TWO SONS.
AND LATELY, I'VE BEEN DOING SOME THINKING.
I'VE BEEN WONDERING IF ONE OF MY SONS MIGHT, UM...
...MIGHT POSSIBLY BE GAY...
W-WELL, YOU KNOW HOW YOU SEE A LOT MORE OF THOSE THEMES IN MEDIA THESE DAYS...
...AND I FEEL AS IF SOME OF IT MIGHT HAVE HIT A LITTLE CLOSE TO HOME.
AH HA HA...

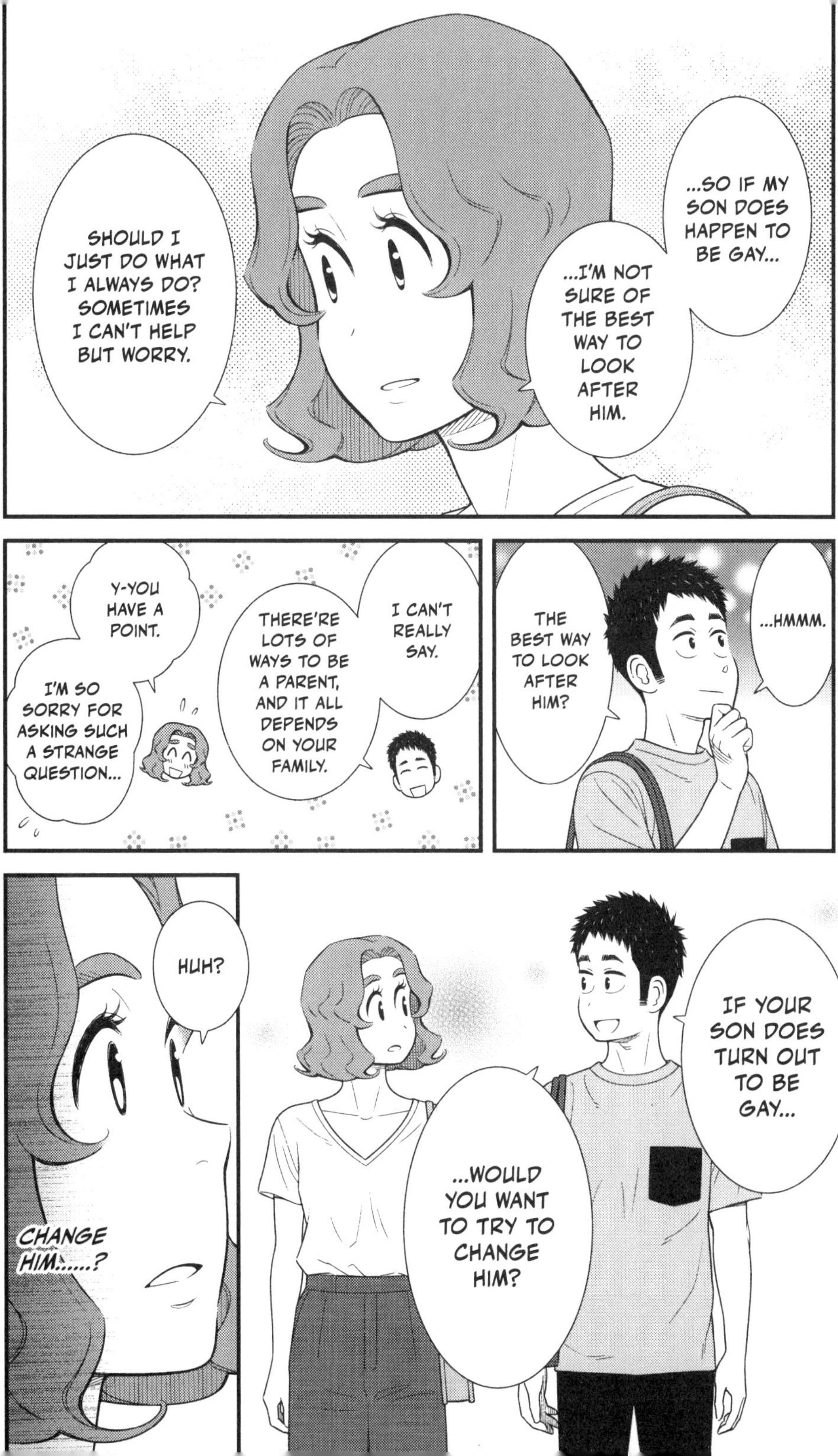
...SO IF MY SON DOES HAPPEN TO BE GAY...
...I'M NOT SURE OF THE BEST WAY TO LOOK AFTER HIM.
SHOULD I JUST DO WHAT I ALWAYS DO? SOMETIMES I CAN'T HELP BUT WORRY.
...HMMM.
THE BEST WAY TO LOOK AFTER HIM?
I CAN'T REALLY SAY.
THERE'RE LOTS OF WAYS TO BE A PARENT, AND IT ALL DEPENDS ON YOUR FAMILY.
Y-YOU HAVE A POINT.
I'M SO SORRY FOR ASKING SUCH A STRANGE QUESTION...
IF YOUR SON DOES TURN OUT TO BE GAY...
...WOULD YOU WANT TO TRY TO CHANGE HIM?
HUH?
CHANGE HIM......?

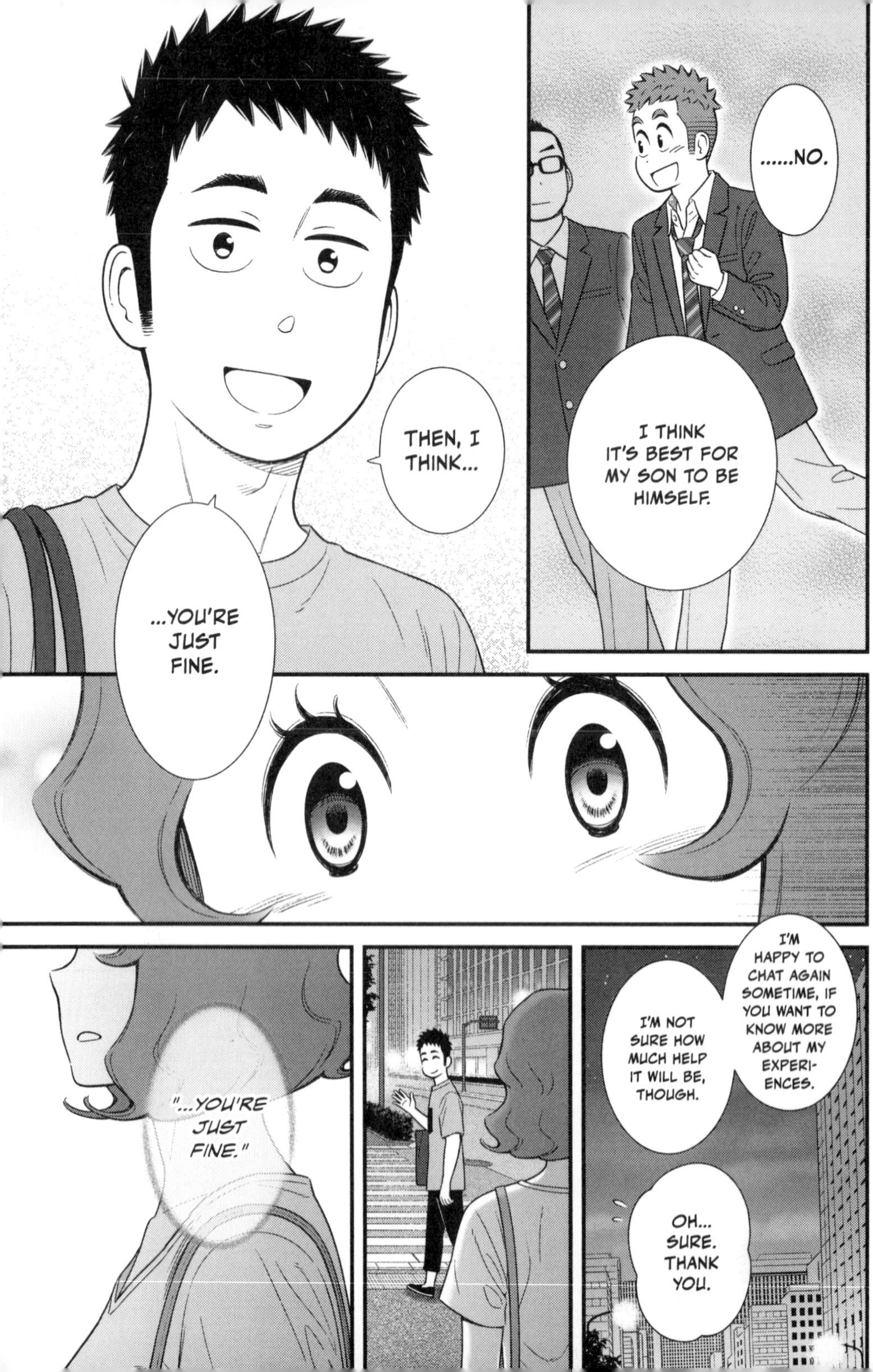
......NO.
I THINK IT'S BEST FOR MY SON TO BE HIMSELF.
THEN, I THINK...
...YOU'RE JUST FINE.
I'M HAPPY TO CHAT AGAIN SOMETIME, IF YOU WANT TO KNOW MORE ABOUT MY EXPERI-ENCES.
I'M NOT SURE HOW MUCH HELP IT WILL BE, THOUGH.
OH... SURE. THANK YOU.
"...YOU'RE JUST FINE."

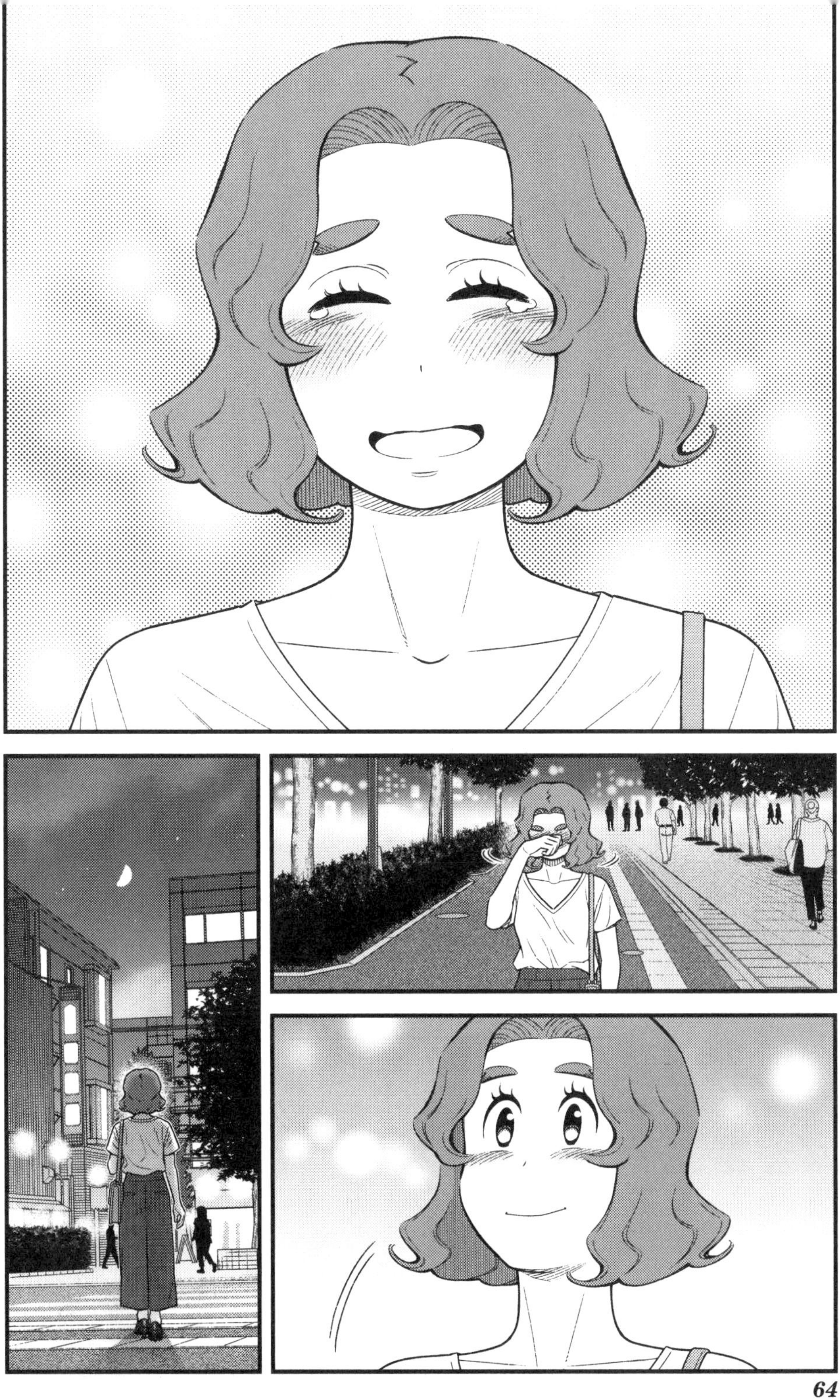

Chapter 54: Not Quite Right

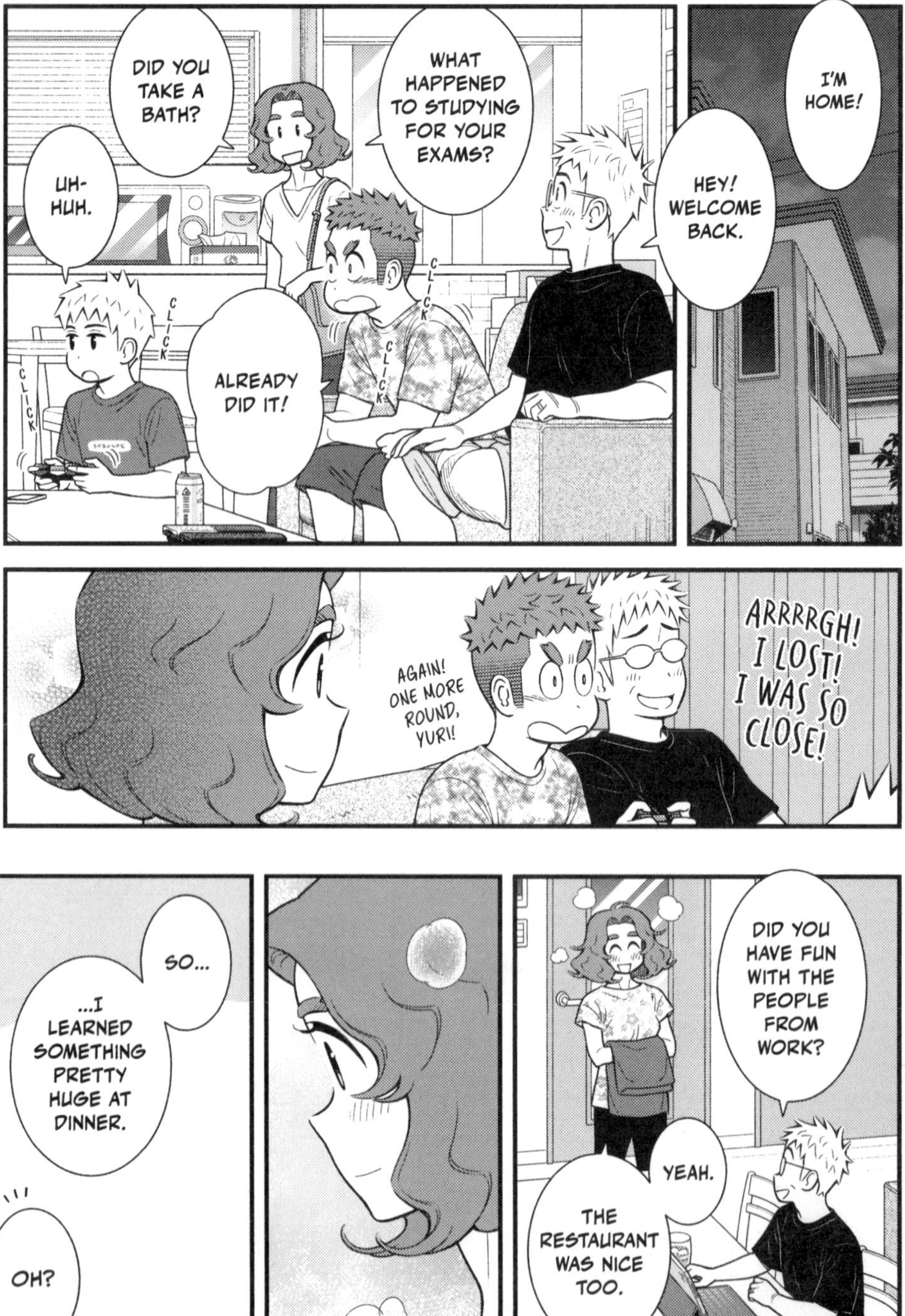

I'M HOME!
HEY! WELCOME BACK.
WHAT HAPPENED TO STUDYING FOR YOUR EXAMS?
DID YOU TAKE A BATH?
CLICK
CLICK
ALREADY DID IT!
UH-HUH.
CLICK
CLICK
ARRRRGH! I LOST! I WAS SO CLOSE!
AGAIN! ONE MORE ROUND, YURI!
DID YOU HAVE FUN WITH THE PEOPLE FROM WORK?
YEAH.
THE RESTAURANT WAS NICE TOO.
SO...
...I LEARNED SOMETHING PRETTY HUGE AT DINNER.
OH?

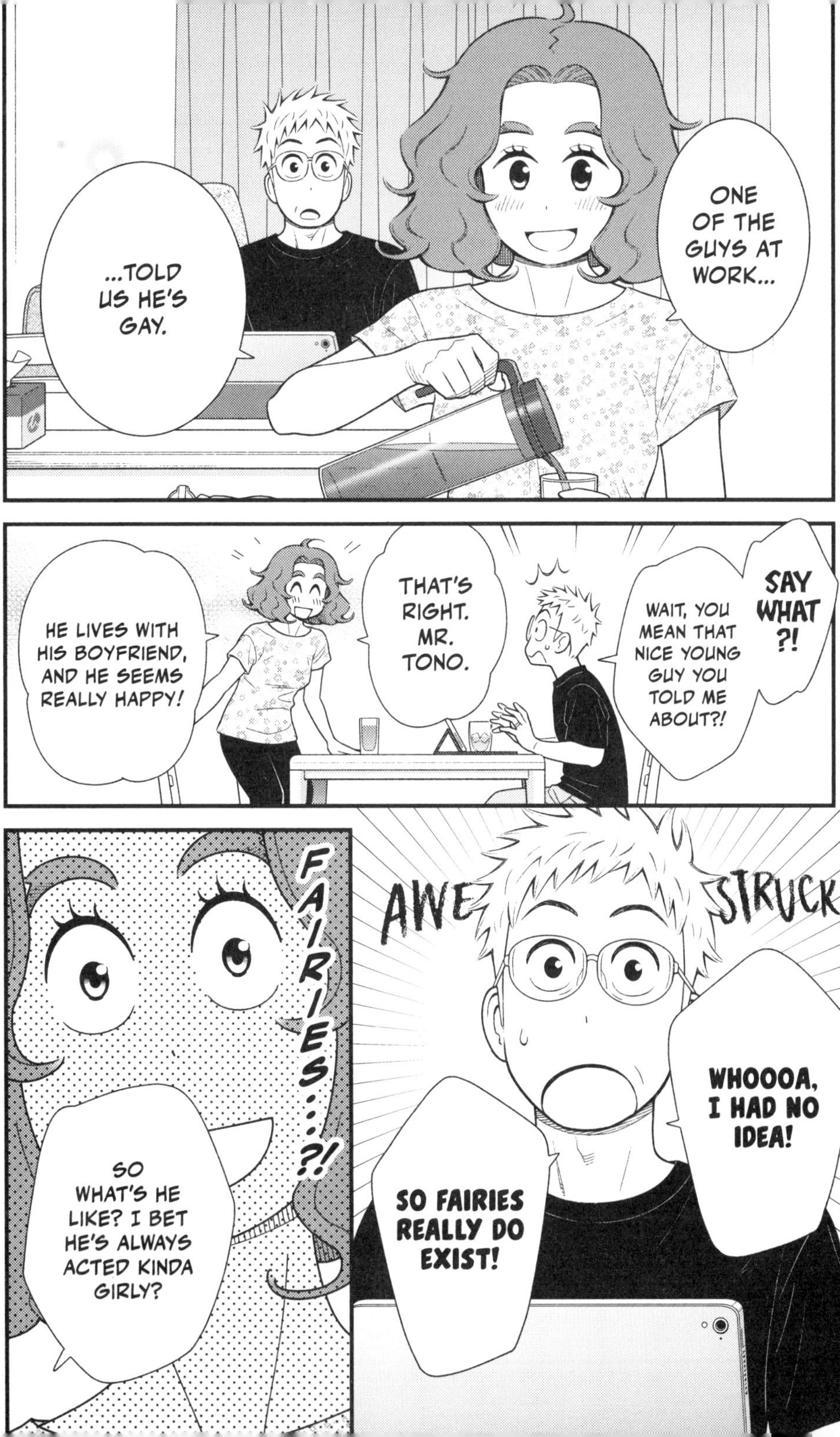
ONE OF THE GUYS AT WORK...
...TOLD US HE'S GAY.
SAY WHAT?!
WAIT, YOU MEAN THAT NICE YOUNG GUY YOU TOLD ME ABOUT?!
THAT'S RIGHT. MR. TONO.
HE LIVES WITH HIS BOYFRIEND, AND HE SEEMS REALLY HAPPY!
AWE STRUCK
WHOOOA, I HAD NO IDEA!
SO FAIRIES REALLY DO EXIST!
FAIRIES...?!
SO WHAT'S HE LIKE? I BET HE'S ALWAYS ACTED KINDA GIRLY?

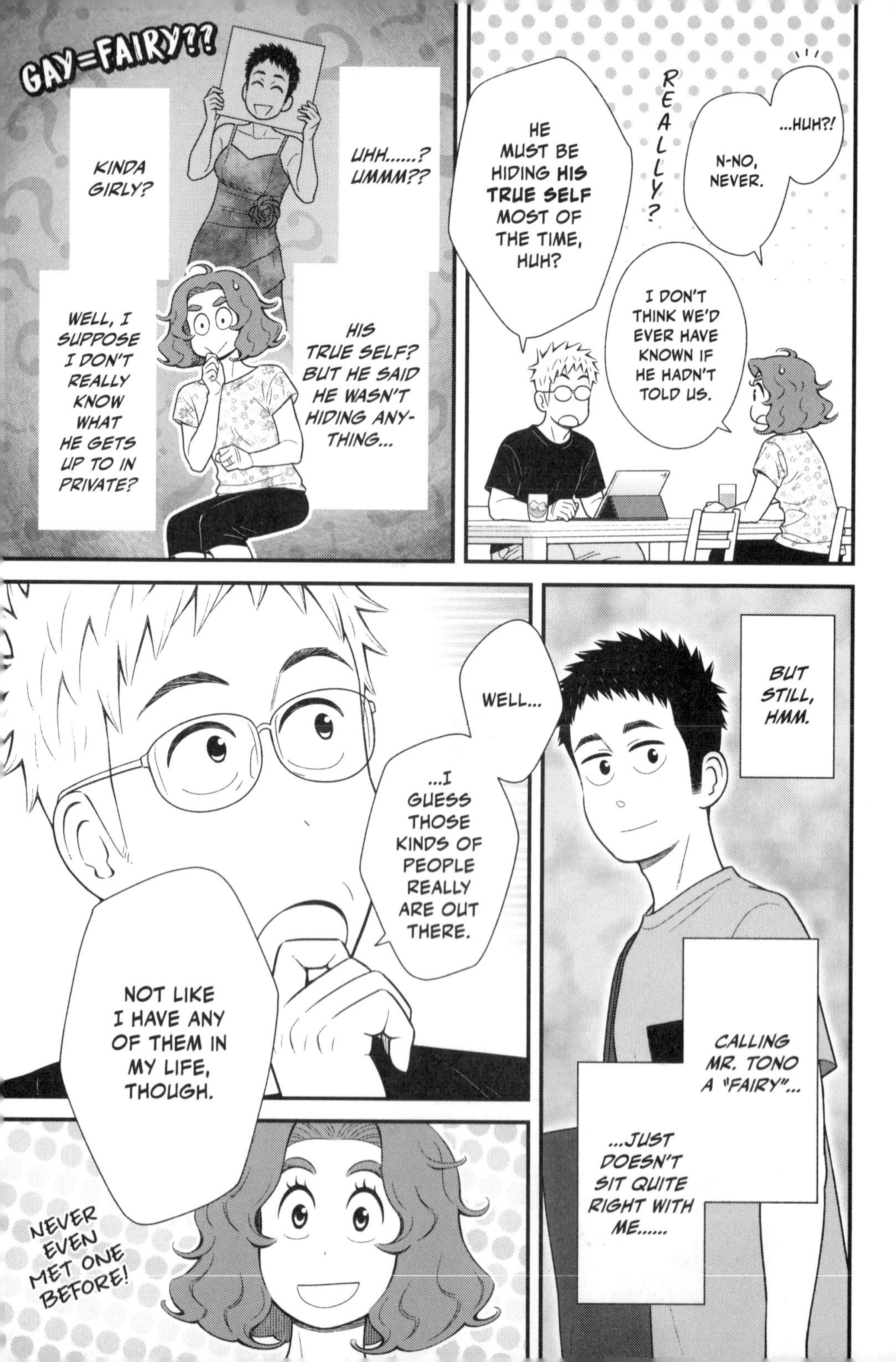

...HUH?!
N-NO, NEVER.
REALLY?
HE MUST BE HIDING **HIS TRUE SELF** MOST OF THE TIME, HUH?
I DON'T THINK WE'D EVER HAVE KNOWN IF HE HADN'T TOLD US.
GAY=FAIRY??
UHH......? UMMM??
KINDA GIRLY?
HIS TRUE SELF? BUT HE SAID HE WASN'T HIDING ANY-THING...
WELL, I SUPPOSE I DON'T REALLY KNOW WHAT HE GETS UP TO IN PRIVATE?
BUT STILL, HMM.
CALLING MR. TONO A "FAIRY"...
...JUST DOESN'T SIT QUITE RIGHT WITH ME......
WELL...
...I GUESS THOSE KINDS OF PEOPLE REALLY ARE OUT THERE.
NOT LIKE I HAVE ANY OF THEM IN MY LIFE, THOUGH.
NEVER EVEN MET ONE BEFORE!

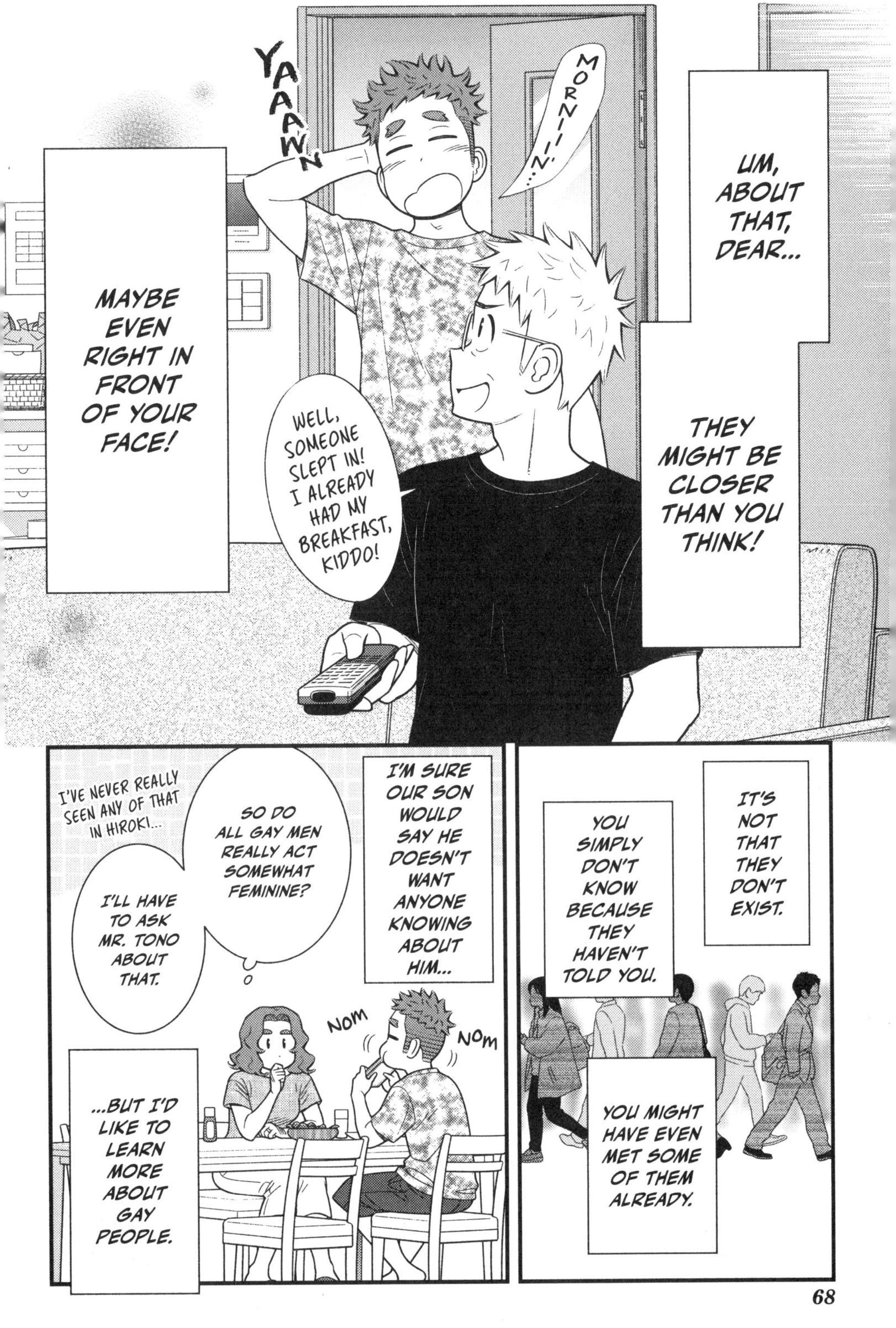
UM, ABOUT THAT, DEAR...
THEY MIGHT BE CLOSER THAN YOU THINK!
MORNIIIN'...
YAAAWN
WELL, SOMEONE SLEPT IN! I ALREADY HAD MY BREAKFAST, KIDDO!
MAYBE EVEN RIGHT IN FRONT OF YOUR FACE!
IT'S NOT THAT THEY DON'T EXIST.
YOU SIMPLY DON'T KNOW BECAUSE THEY HAVEN'T TOLD YOU.
YOU MIGHT HAVE EVEN MET SOME OF THEM ALREADY.
I'M SURE OUR SON WOULD SAY HE DOESN'T WANT ANYONE KNOWING ABOUT HIM...
SO DO ALL GAY MEN REALLY ACT SOMEWHAT FEMININE?
I'VE NEVER REALLY SEEN ANY OF THAT IN HIROKI...
I'LL HAVE TO ASK MR. TONO ABOUT THAT.
NOM
NOM
...BUT I'D LIKE TO LEARN MORE ABOUT GAY PEOPLE.

CHAPTER 55: IDEALS VS REALITY

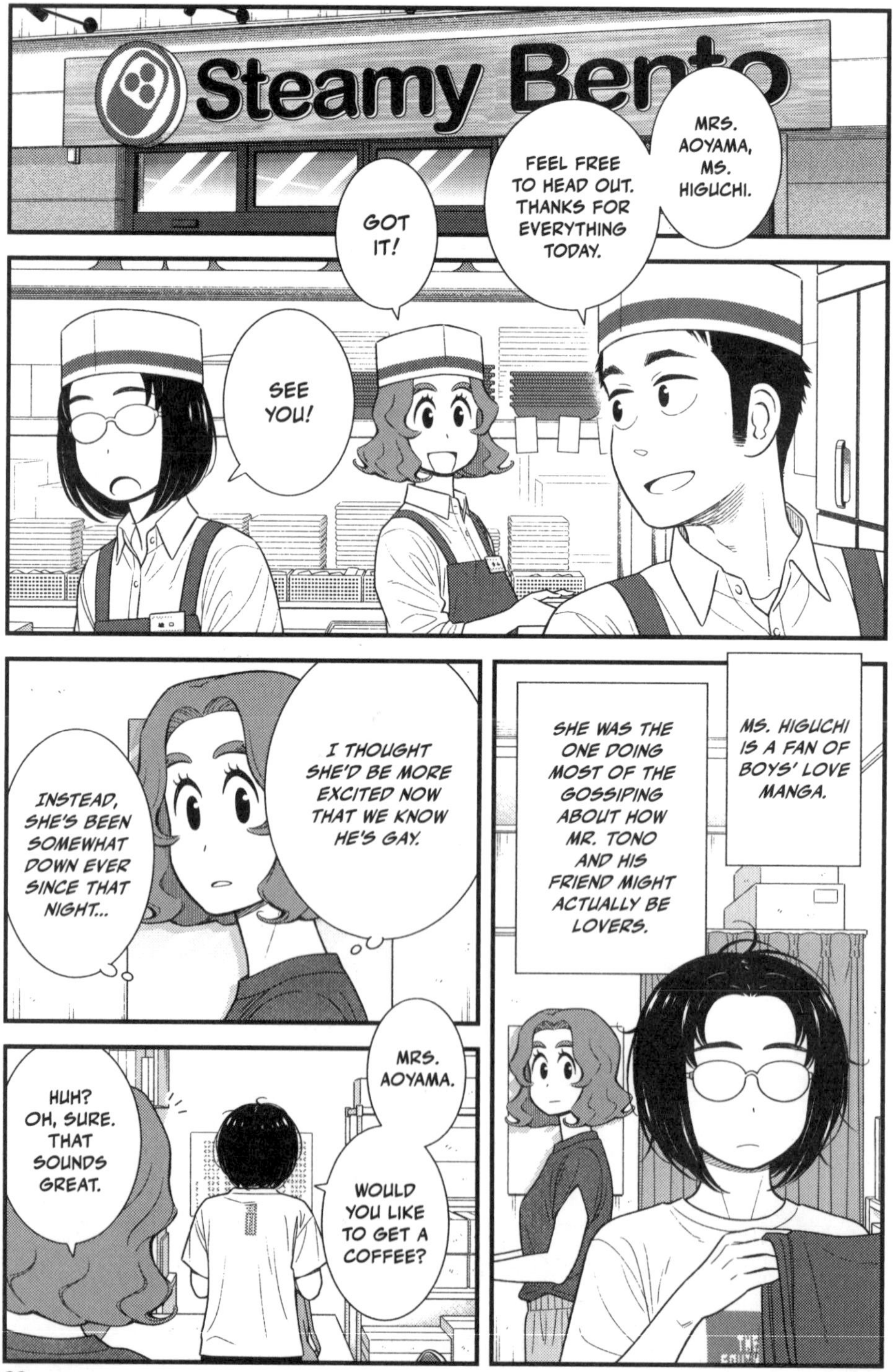

Steamy Bento
MRS. AOYAMA, MS. HIGUCHI.
FEEL FREE TO HEAD OUT. THANKS FOR EVERYTHING TODAY.
GOT IT!
SEE YOU!
MS. HIGUCHI IS A FAN OF BOYS' LOVE MANGA.
SHE WAS THE ONE DOING MOST OF THE GOSSIPING ABOUT HOW MR. TONO AND HIS FRIEND MIGHT ACTUALLY BE LOVERS.
I THOUGHT SHE'D BE MORE EXCITED NOW THAT WE KNOW HE'S GAY.
INSTEAD, SHE'S BEEN SOMEWHAT DOWN EVER SINCE THAT NIGHT...
MRS. AOYAMA.
WOULD YOU LIKE TO GET A COFFEE?
HUH? OH, SURE. THAT SOUNDS GREAT.

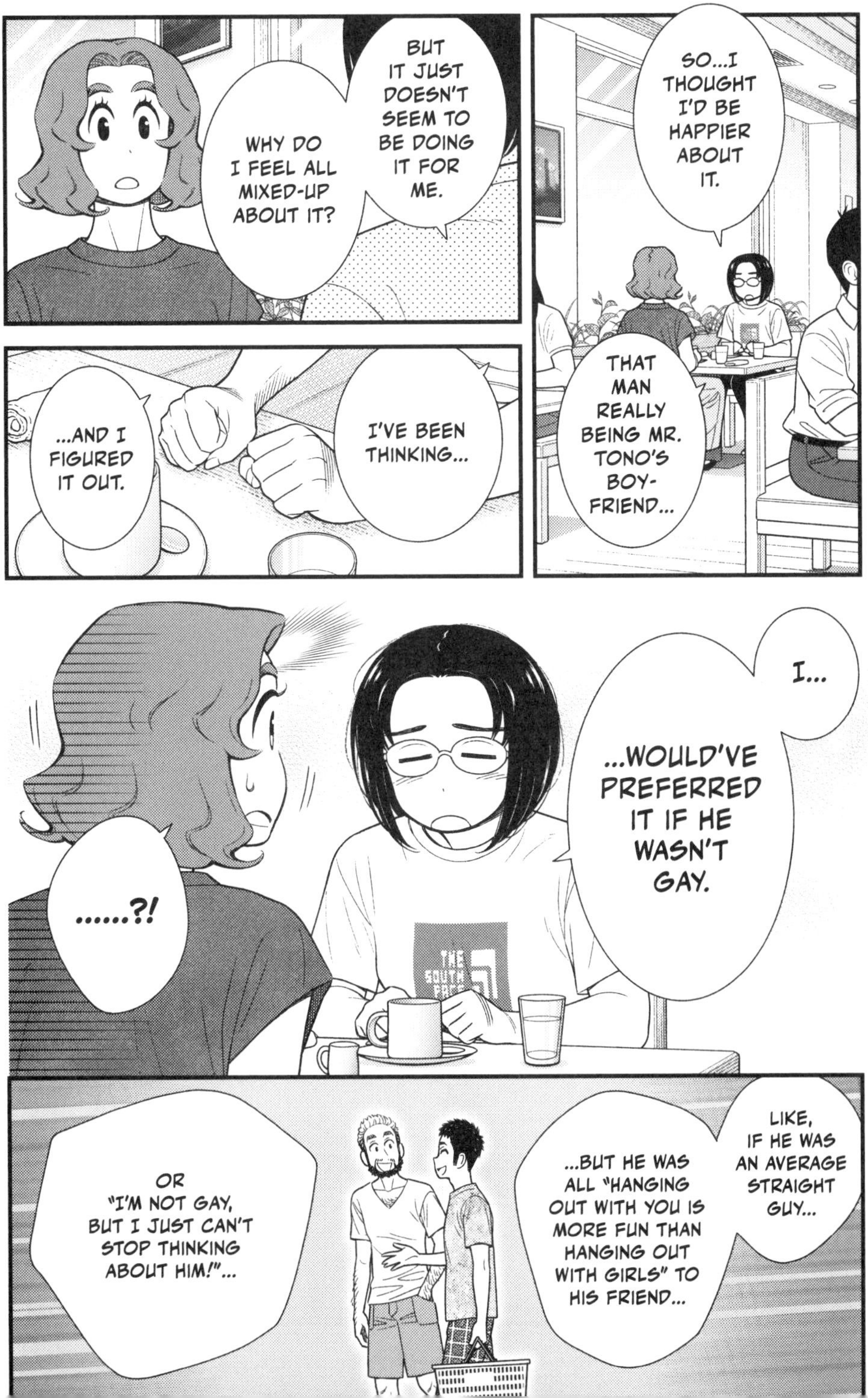
SO...I THOUGHT I'D BE HAPPIER ABOUT IT.
THAT MAN REALLY BEING MR. TONO'S BOY-FRIEND...
BUT IT JUST DOESN'T SEEM TO BE DOING IT FOR ME.
WHY DO I FEEL ALL MIXED-UP ABOUT IT?
I'VE BEEN THINKING...
...AND I FIGURED IT OUT.
I...
...WOULD'VE PREFERRED IT IF HE WASN'T GAY.
......?!
LIKE, IF HE WAS AN AVERAGE STRAIGHT GUY...
...BUT HE WAS ALL "HANGING OUT WITH YOU IS MORE FUN THAN HANGING OUT WITH GIRLS" TO HIS FRIEND...
OR "I'M NOT GAY, BUT I JUST CAN'T STOP THINKING ABOUT HIM!"...

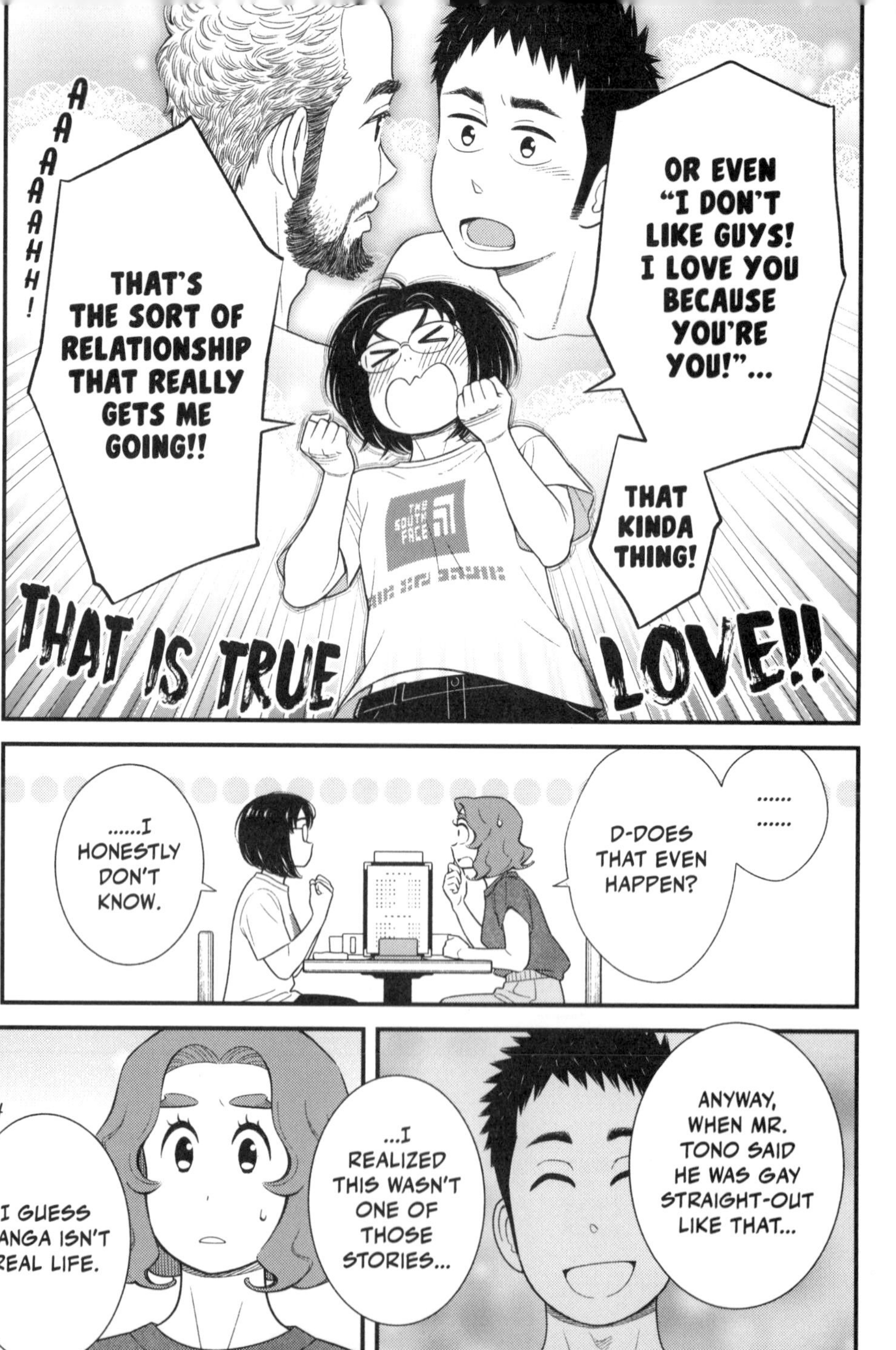
OR EVEN "I DON'T LIKE GUYS! I LOVE YOU BECAUSE YOU'RE YOU!"...
THAT KINDA THING!
AAAAAAAHHH!
THAT'S THE SORT OF RELATIONSHIP THAT REALLY GETS ME GOING!!
THE SOUTH FACE
THAT IS TRUE LOVE!!
......
......
D-DOES THAT EVEN HAPPEN?
......I HONESTLY DON'T KNOW.
ANYWAY, WHEN MR. TONO SAID HE WAS GAY STRAIGHT-OUT LIKE THAT...
...I REALIZED THIS WASN'T ONE OF THOSE STORIES...
SIGH
I GUESS MANGA ISN'T REAL LIFE.

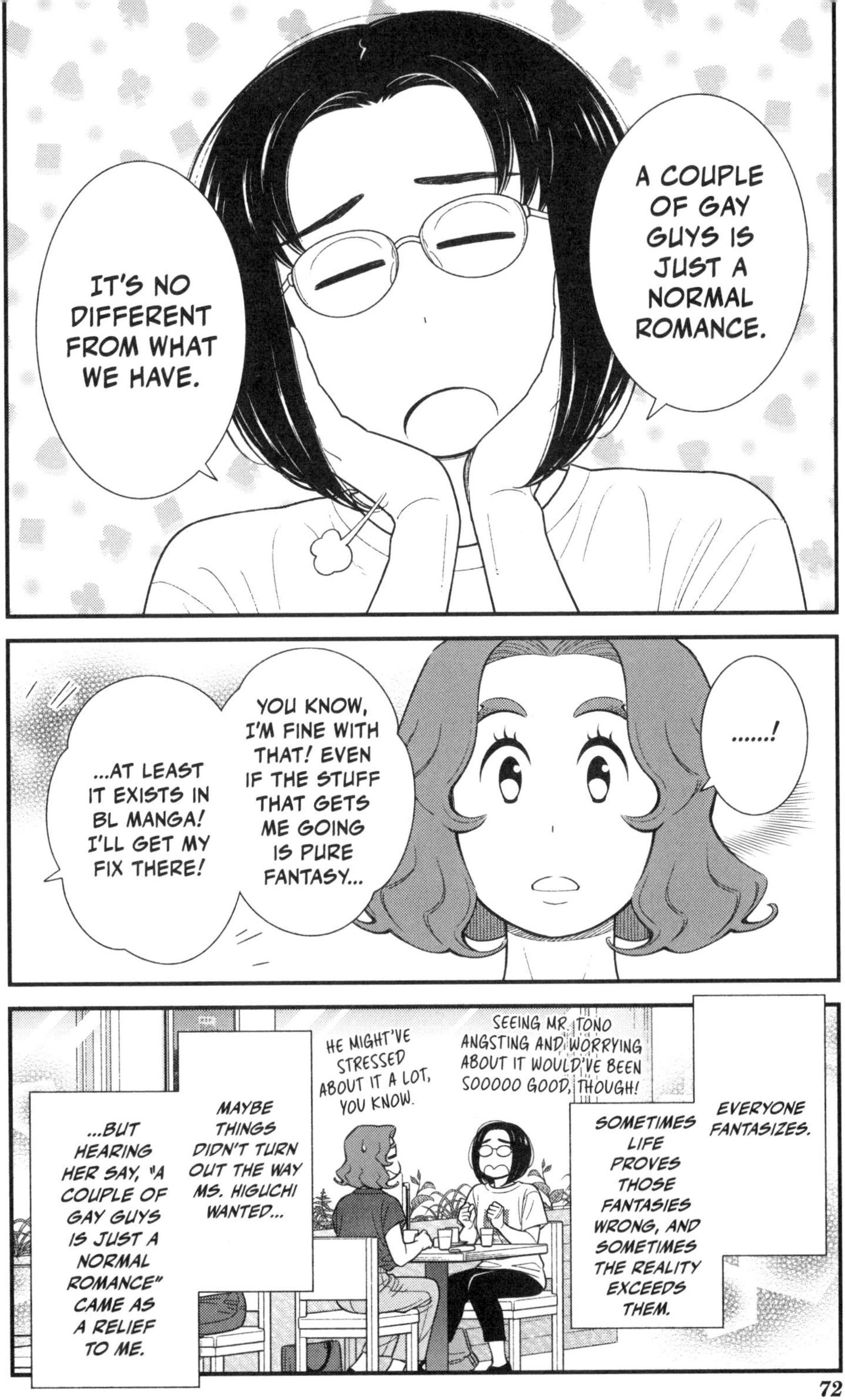
A COUPLE OF GAY GUYS IS JUST A NORMAL ROMANCE.
IT'S NO DIFFERENT FROM WHAT WE HAVE.
......!
YOU KNOW, I'M FINE WITH THAT! EVEN IF THE STUFF THAT GETS ME GOING IS PURE FANTASY...
...AT LEAST IT EXISTS IN BL MANGA! I'LL GET MY FIX THERE!
EVERYONE FANTASIZES.
SOMETIMES LIFE PROVES THOSE FANTASIES WRONG, AND SOMETIMES THE REALITY EXCEEDS THEM.
SEEING MR. TONO ANGSTING AND WORRYING ABOUT IT WOULD'VE BEEN SOOOOO GOOD, THOUGH!
HE MIGHT'VE STRESSED ABOUT IT A LOT, YOU KNOW.
MAYBE THINGS DIDN'T TURN OUT THE WAY MS. HIGUCHI WANTED...
...BUT HEARING HER SAY, "A COUPLE OF GAY GUYS IS JUST A NORMAL ROMANCE" CAME AS A RELIEF TO ME.

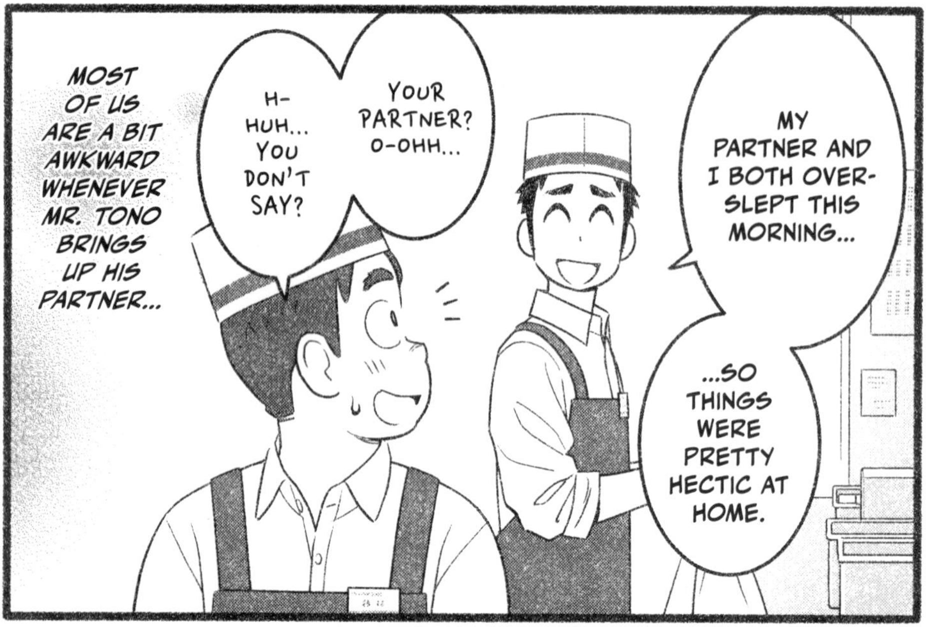
MY PARTNER AND I BOTH OVER-SLEPT THIS MORNING...
...SO THINGS WERE PRETTY HECTIC AT HOME.
YOUR PARTNER? O-OHH...
H-HUH... YOU DON'T SAY?
MOST OF US ARE A BIT AWKWARD WHENEVER MR. TONO BRINGS UP HIS PARTNER...
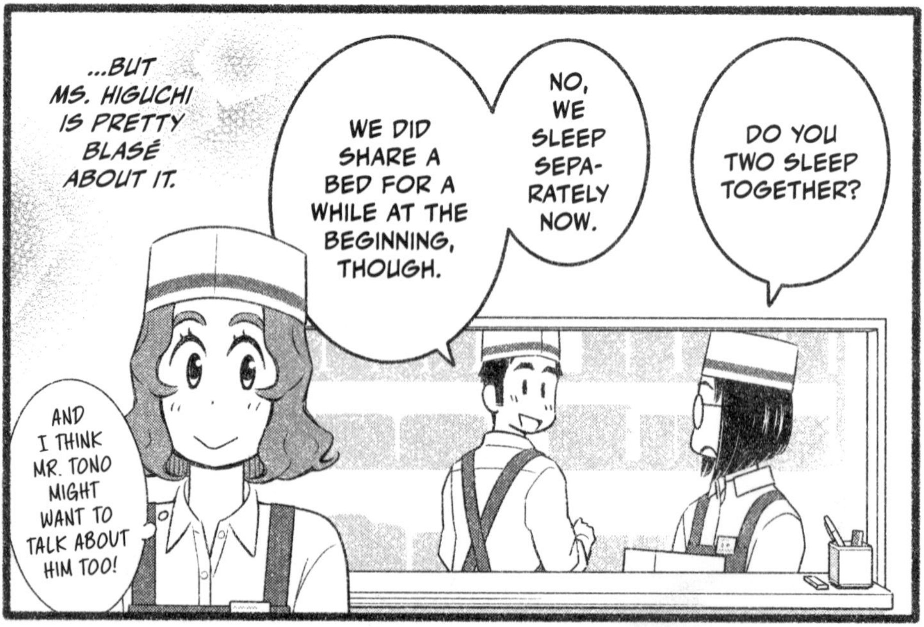
DO YOU TWO SLEEP TOGETHER?
NO, WE SLEEP SEPA-RATELY NOW.
WE DID SHARE A BED FOR A WHILE AT THE BEGINNING, THOUGH.
...BUT MS. HIGUCHI IS PRETTY BLASÉ ABOUT IT.
AND I THINK MR. TONO MIGHT WANT TO TALK ABOUT HIM TOO!

I Think
Our Son
Is Gay

CHAPTER 56: YUKATA

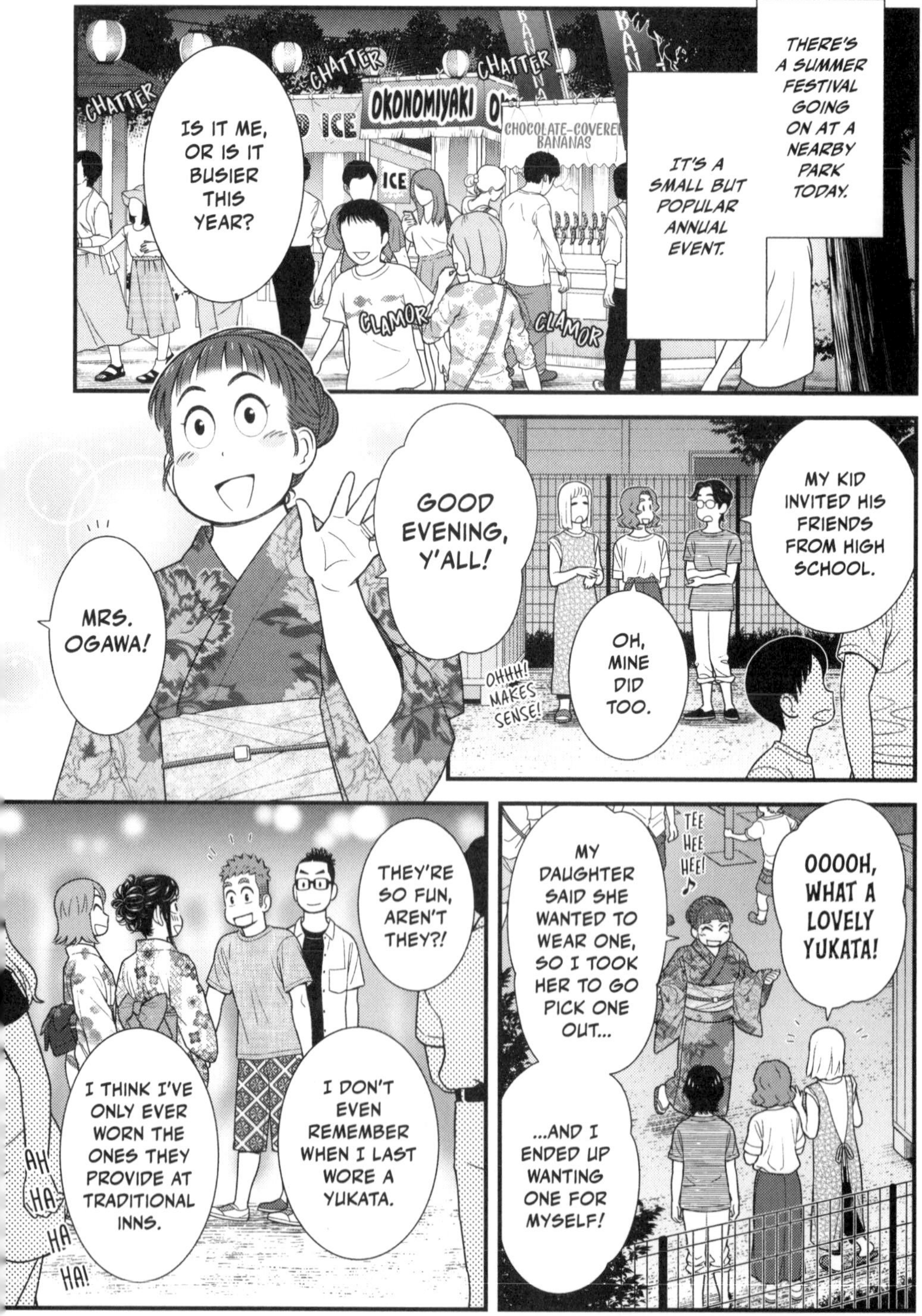

THERE'S A SUMMER FESTIVAL GOING ON AT A NEARBY PARK TODAY.
IT'S A SMALL BUT POPULAR ANNUAL EVENT.
BANANA
CHOCOLATE-COVERED BANANAS
CHATTER
OKONOMIYAKI
CHATTER
ICE
IS IT ME, OR IS IT BUSIER THIS YEAR?
CHATTER
CLAMOR
CLAMOR
MY KID INVITED HIS FRIENDS FROM HIGH SCHOOL.
OH, MINE DID TOO.
OHHH! MAKES SENSE!
GOOD EVENING, Y'ALL!
MRS. OGAWA!
OOOOH, WHAT A LOVELY YUKATA!
TEE HEE HEE!
MY DAUGHTER SAID SHE WANTED TO WEAR ONE, SO I TOOK HER TO GO PICK ONE OUT...
...AND I ENDED UP WANTING ONE FOR MYSELF!
THEY'RE SO FUN, AREN'T THEY?!
I DON'T EVEN REMEMBER WHEN I LAST WORE A YUKATA.
I THINK I'VE ONLY EVER WORN THE ONES THEY PROVIDE AT TRADITIONAL INNS.
AH HA HA HA!

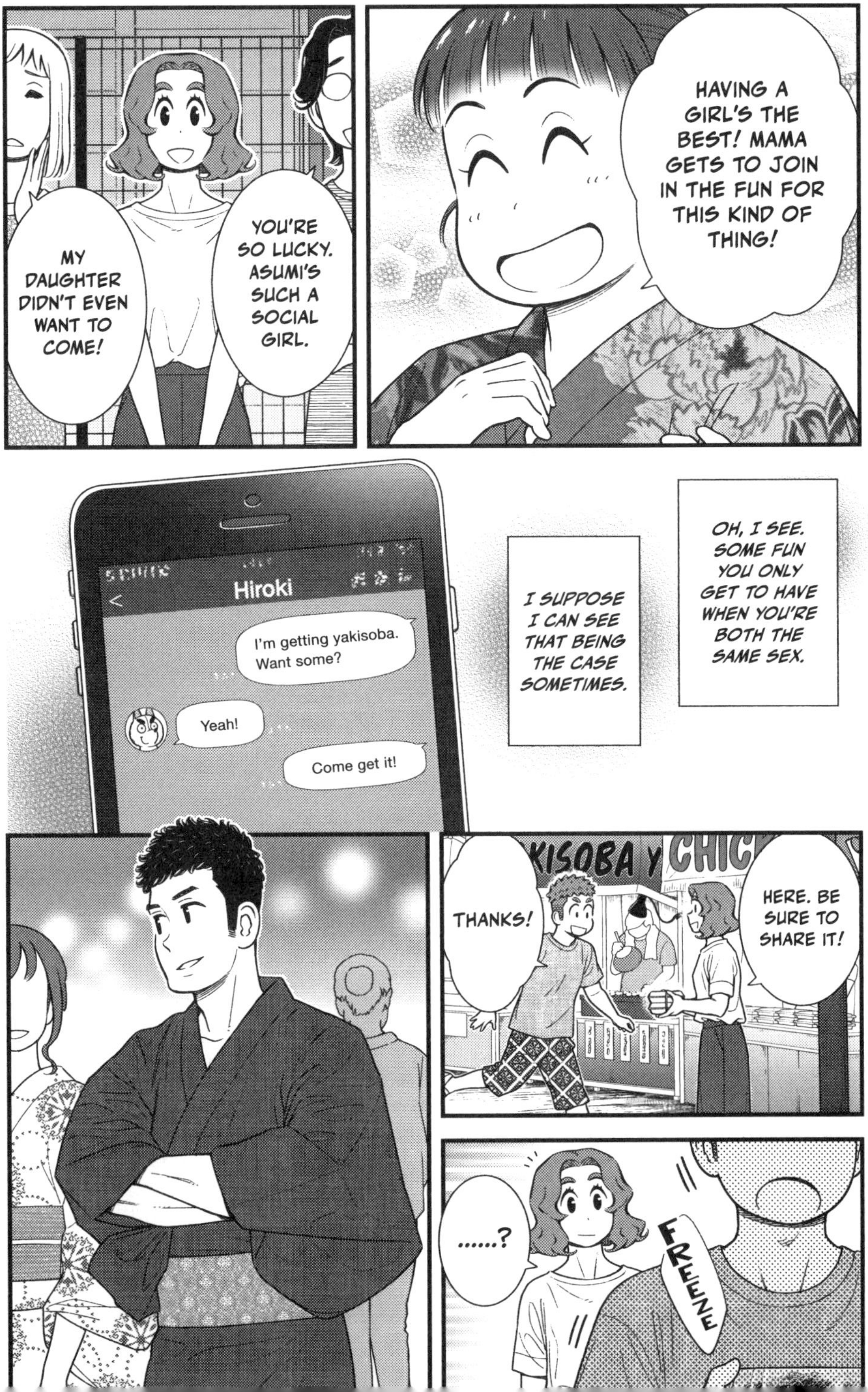
HAVING A GIRL'S THE BEST! MAMA GETS TO JOIN IN THE FUN FOR THIS KIND OF THING!
YOU'RE SO LUCKY. ASUMI'S SUCH A SOCIAL GIRL.
MY DAUGHTER DIDN'T EVEN WANT TO COME!
OH, I SEE. SOME FUN YOU ONLY GET TO HAVE WHEN YOU'RE BOTH THE SAME SEX.
I SUPPOSE I CAN SEE THAT BEING THE CASE SOMETIMES.
Hiroki
I'm getting yakisoba. Want some?
Yeah!
Come get it!
HERE. BE SURE TO SHARE IT!
THANKS!
KISOBA Y CHIC
FREEZE
......?

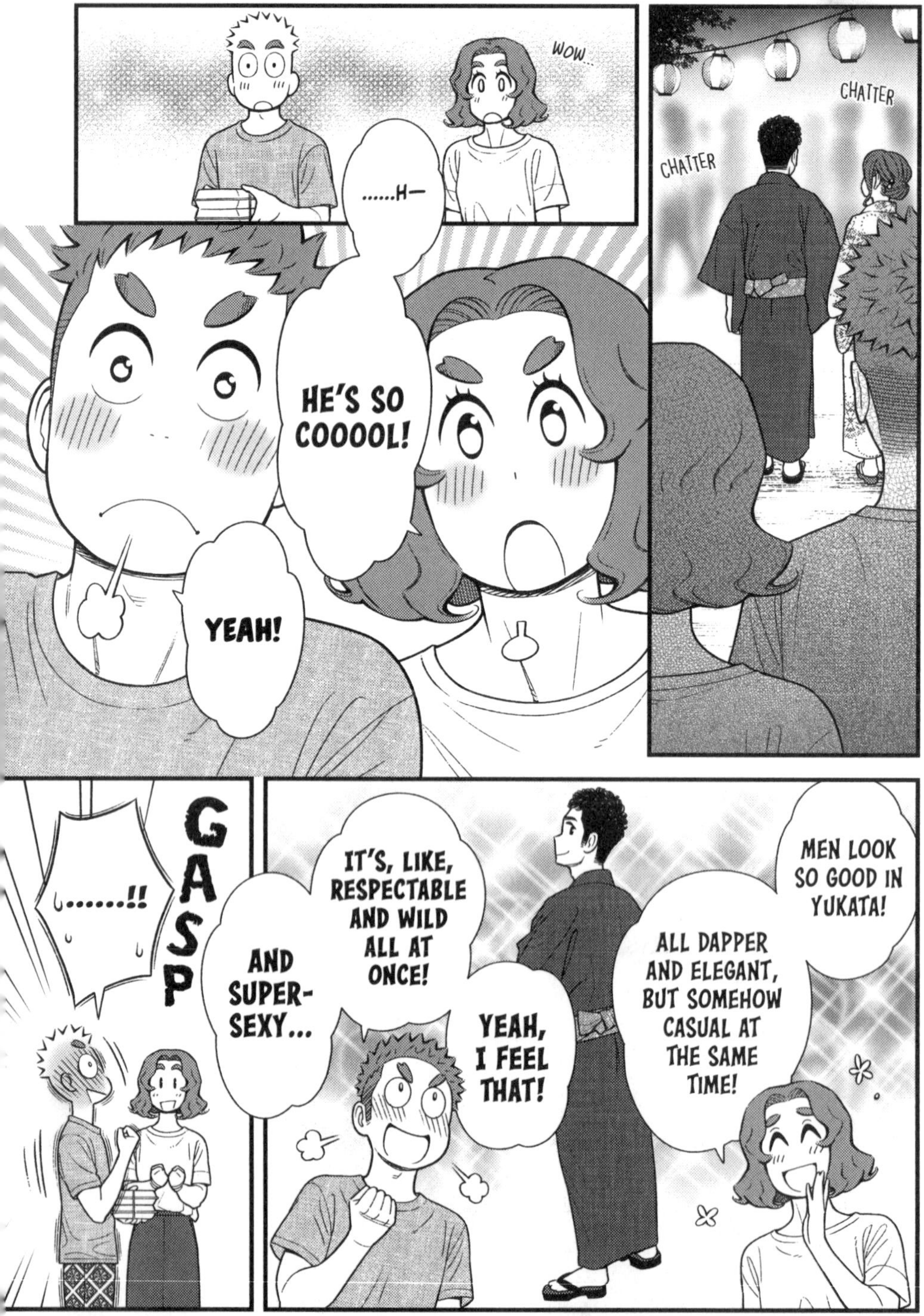
CHATTER
CHATTER
WOW...
......H—
HE'S SO COOOOL!
YEAH!
MEN LOOK SO GOOD IN YUKATA!
ALL DAPPER AND ELEGANT, BUT SOMEHOW CASUAL AT THE SAME TIME!
YEAH, I FEEL THAT!
IT'S, LIKE, RESPECTABLE AND WILD ALL AT ONCE!
AND SUPER-SEXY...
GASP
......!!

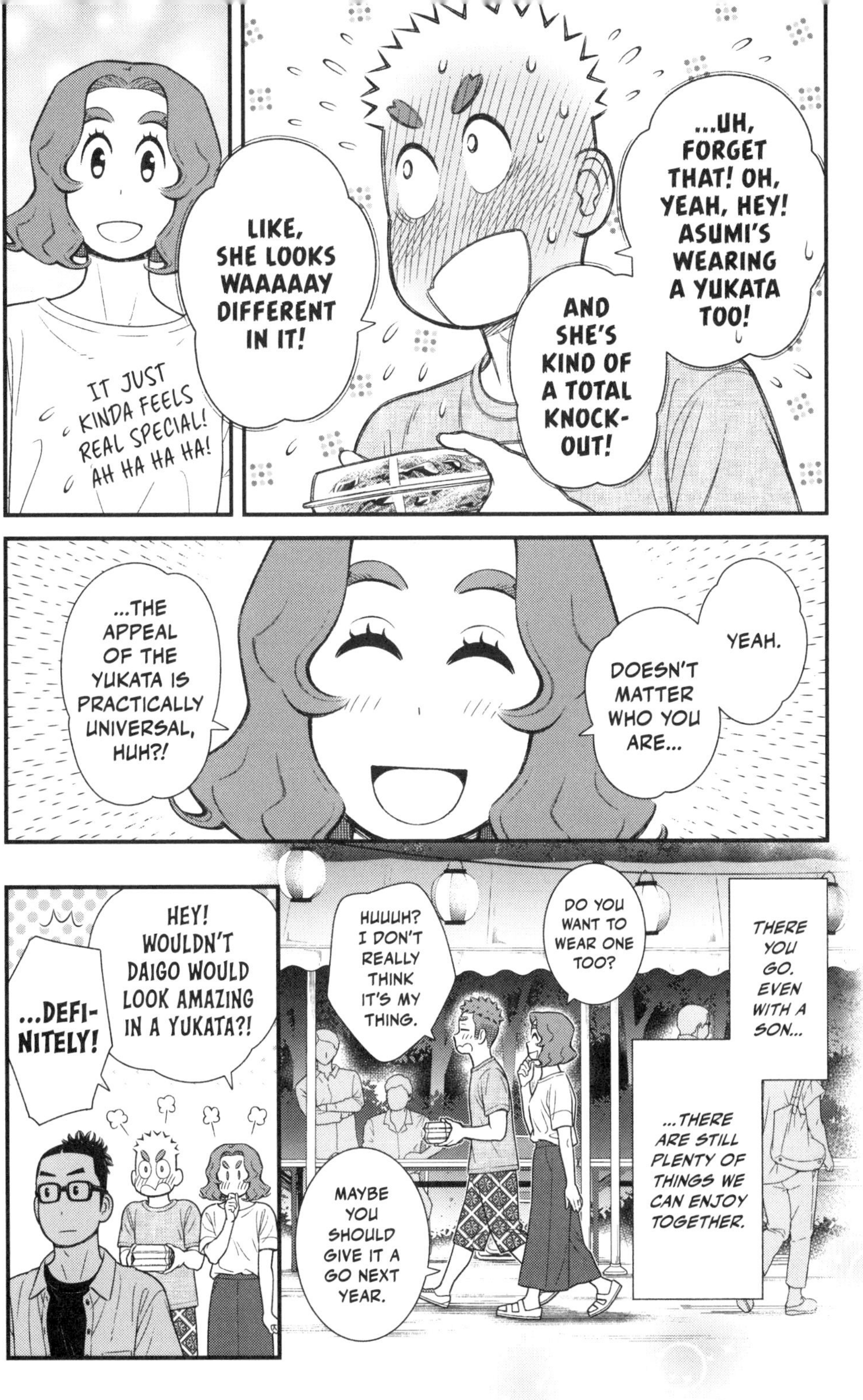
...UH, FORGET THAT! OH, YEAH, HEY! ASUMI'S WEARING A YUKATA TOO!
AND SHE'S KIND OF A TOTAL KNOCK-OUT!
LIKE, SHE LOOKS WAAAAAY DIFFERENT IN IT!
IT JUST KINDA FEELS REAL SPECIAL! AH HA HA HA!
YEAH.
DOESN'T MATTER WHO YOU ARE...
...THE APPEAL OF THE YUKATA IS PRACTICALLY UNIVERSAL, HUH?!
THERE YOU GO. EVEN WITH A SON...
DO YOU WANT TO WEAR ONE TOO?
HUUUH? I DON'T REALLY THINK IT'S MY THING.
MAYBE YOU SHOULD GIVE IT A GO NEXT YEAR.
...THERE ARE STILL PLENTY OF THINGS WE CAN ENJOY TOGETHER.
HEY! WOULDN'T DAIGO WOULD LOOK AMAZING IN A YUKATA?!
...DEFI-NITELY!

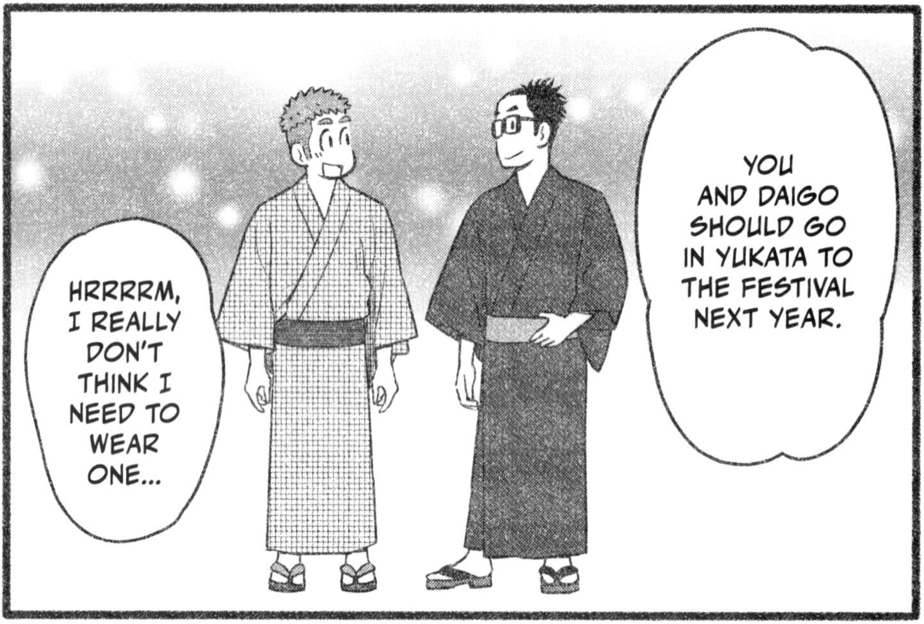
YOU AND DAIGO SHOULD GO IN YUKATA TO THE FESTIVAL NEXT YEAR.
HRRRRM, I REALLY DON'T THINK I NEED TO WEAR ONE...

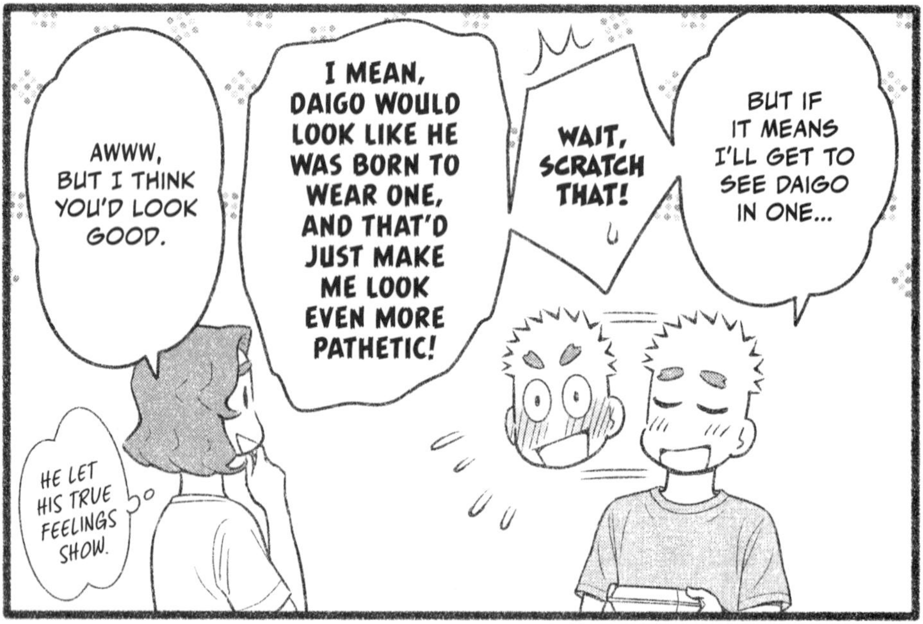
BUT IF IT MEANS I'LL GET TO SEE DAIGO IN ONE...
WAIT, SCRATCH THAT!
I MEAN, DAIGO WOULD LOOK LIKE HE WAS BORN TO WEAR ONE, AND THAT'D JUST MAKE ME LOOK EVEN MORE PATHETIC!
AWWW, BUT I THINK YOU'D LOOK GOOD.
HE LET HIS TRUE FEELINGS SHOW.

I Think
Our Son
Is Gay

CHAPTER 57: A GOOD GUY ①

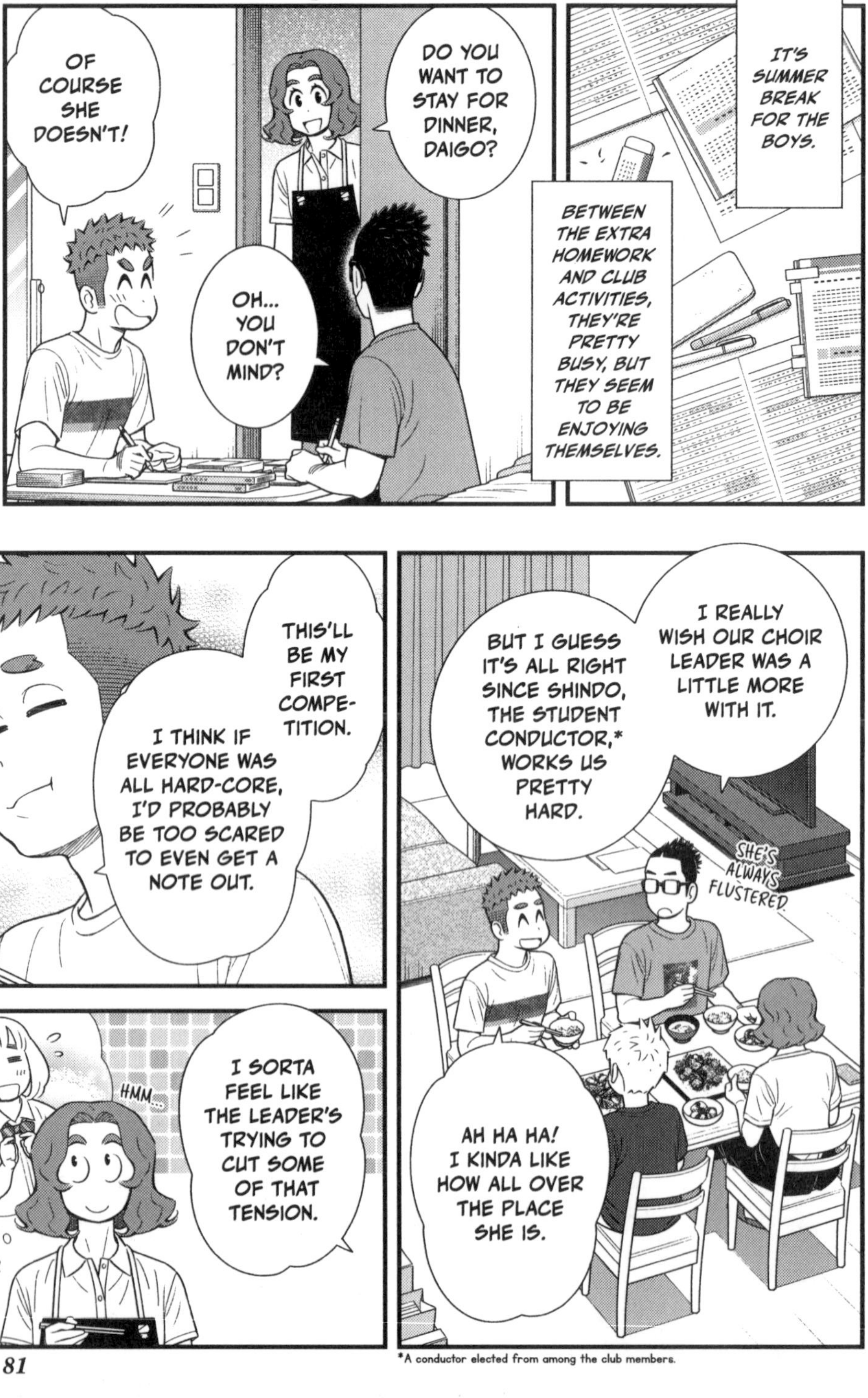
IT'S SUMMER BREAK FOR THE BOYS.
BETWEEN THE EXTRA HOMEWORK AND CLUB ACTIVITIES, THEY'RE PRETTY BUSY, BUT THEY SEEM TO BE ENJOYING THEMSELVES.
DO YOU WANT TO STAY FOR DINNER, DAIGO?
OH... YOU DON'T MIND?
OF COURSE SHE DOESN'T!
I REALLY WISH OUR CHOIR LEADER WAS A LITTLE MORE WITH IT.
BUT I GUESS IT'S ALL RIGHT SINCE SHINDO, THE STUDENT CONDUCTOR,* WORKS US PRETTY HARD.
SHE'S ALWAYS FLUSTERED.
AH HA HA! I KINDA LIKE HOW ALL OVER THE PLACE SHE IS.
THIS'LL BE MY FIRST COMPETITION.
I THINK IF EVERYONE WAS ALL HARD-CORE, I'D PROBABLY BE TOO SCARED TO EVEN GET A NOTE OUT.
I SORTA FEEL LIKE THE LEADER'S TRYING TO CUT SOME OF THAT TENSION.
HMM...
I WONDER WHAT SHE'S LIKE.

*A conductor elected from among the club members.

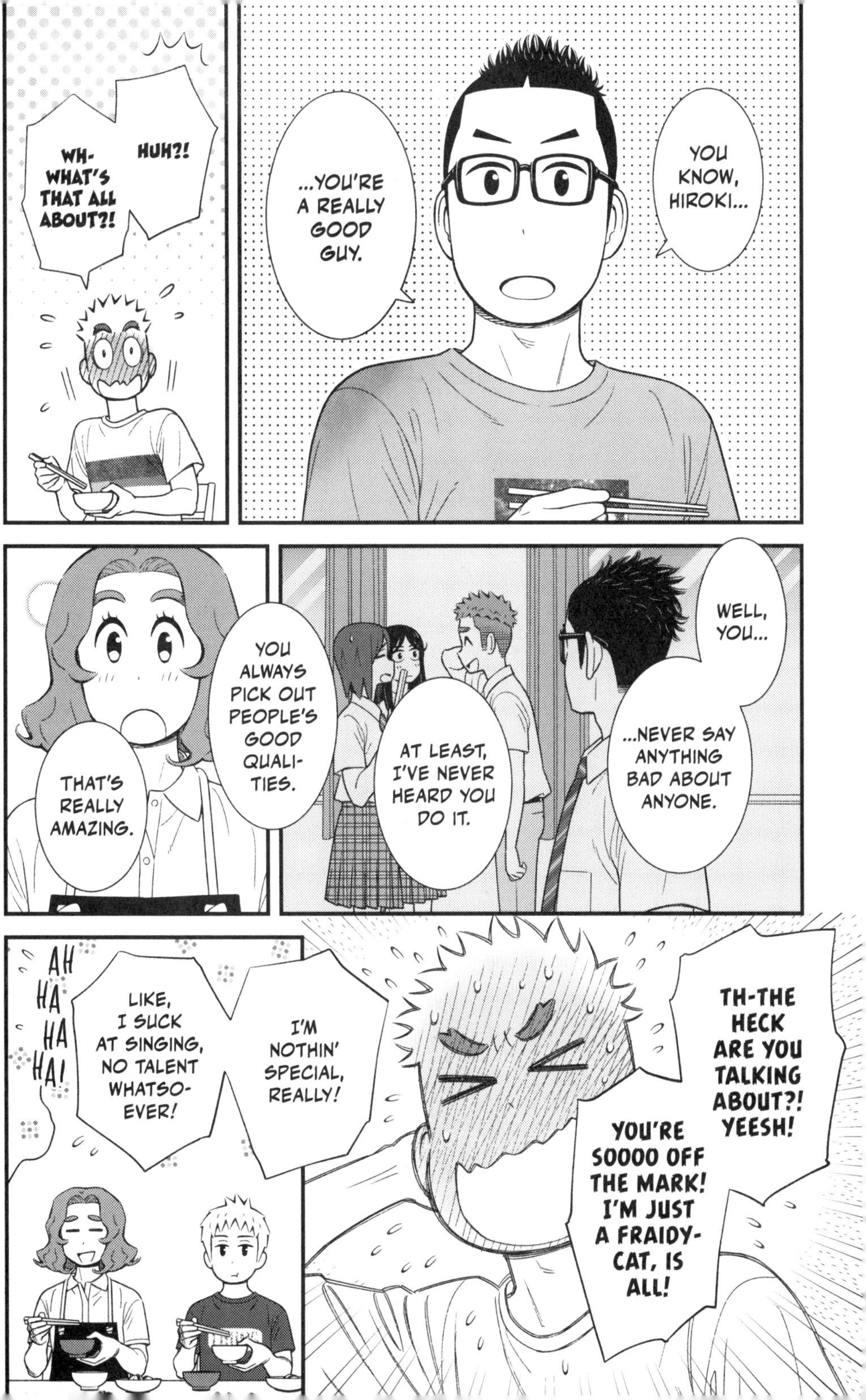

YOU KNOW, HIROKI...
...YOU'RE A REALLY GOOD GUY.
HUH?!
WH- WHAT'S THAT ALL ABOUT?!
WELL, YOU...
...NEVER SAY ANYTHING BAD ABOUT ANYONE.
AT LEAST, I'VE NEVER HEARD YOU DO IT.
YOU ALWAYS PICK OUT PEOPLE'S GOOD QUALI-TIES.
THAT'S REALLY AMAZING.
TH-THE HECK ARE YOU TALKING ABOUT?! YEESH!
YOU'RE SOOOO OFF THE MARK! I'M JUST A FRAIDY-CAT, IS ALL!
I'M NOTHIN' SPECIAL, REALLY!
LIKE, I SUCK AT SINGING, NO TALENT WHATSO-EVER!
AH HA HA HA HA!

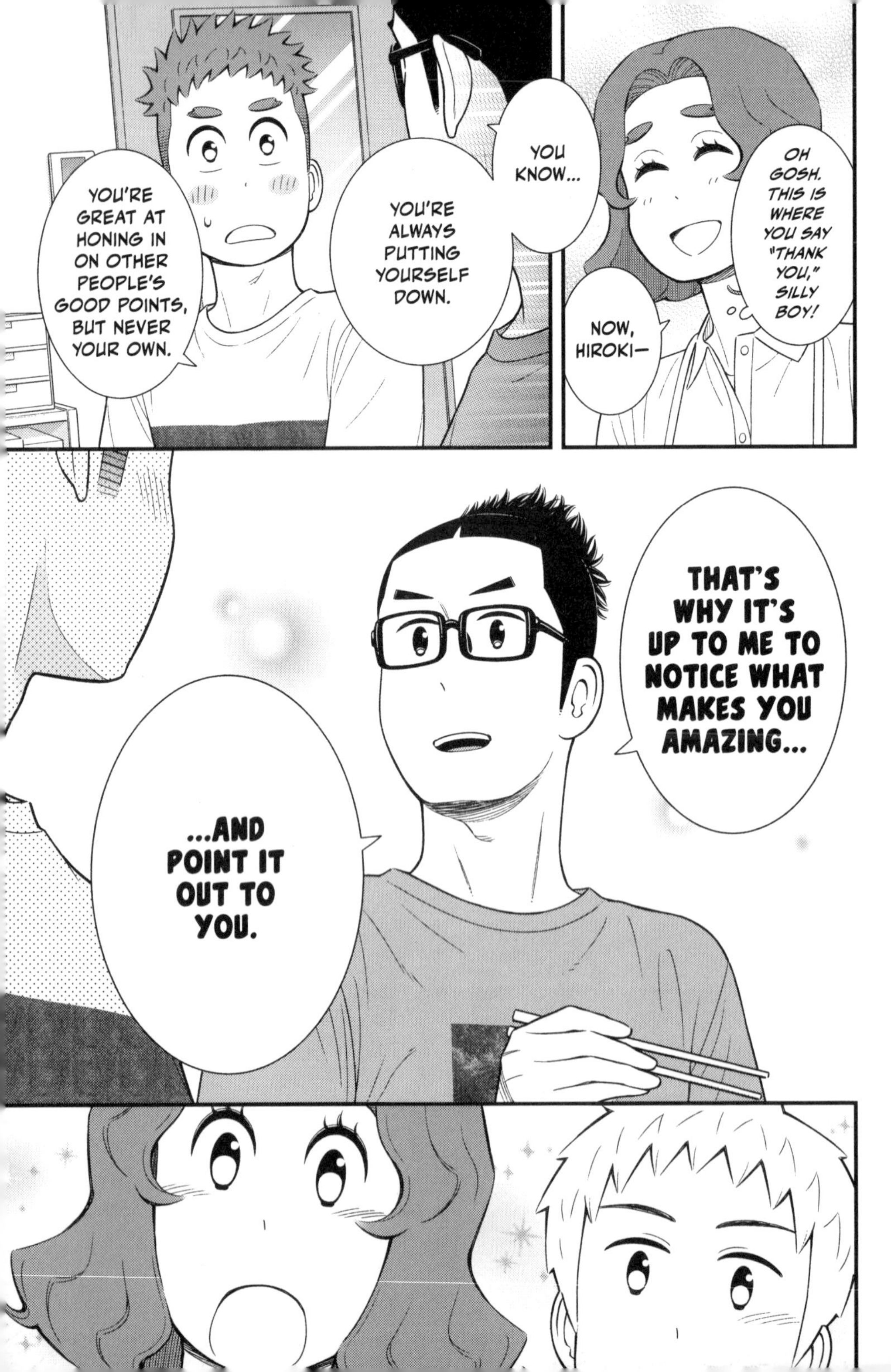
OH GOSH. THIS IS WHERE YOU SAY "THANK YOU," SILLY BOY!
NOW, HIROKI—
YOU KNOW...
YOU'RE ALWAYS PUTTING YOURSELF DOWN.
YOU'RE GREAT AT HONING IN ON OTHER PEOPLE'S GOOD POINTS, BUT NEVER YOUR OWN.
THAT'S WHY IT'S UP TO ME TO NOTICE WHAT MAKES YOU AMAZING...
...AND POINT IT OUT TO YOU.

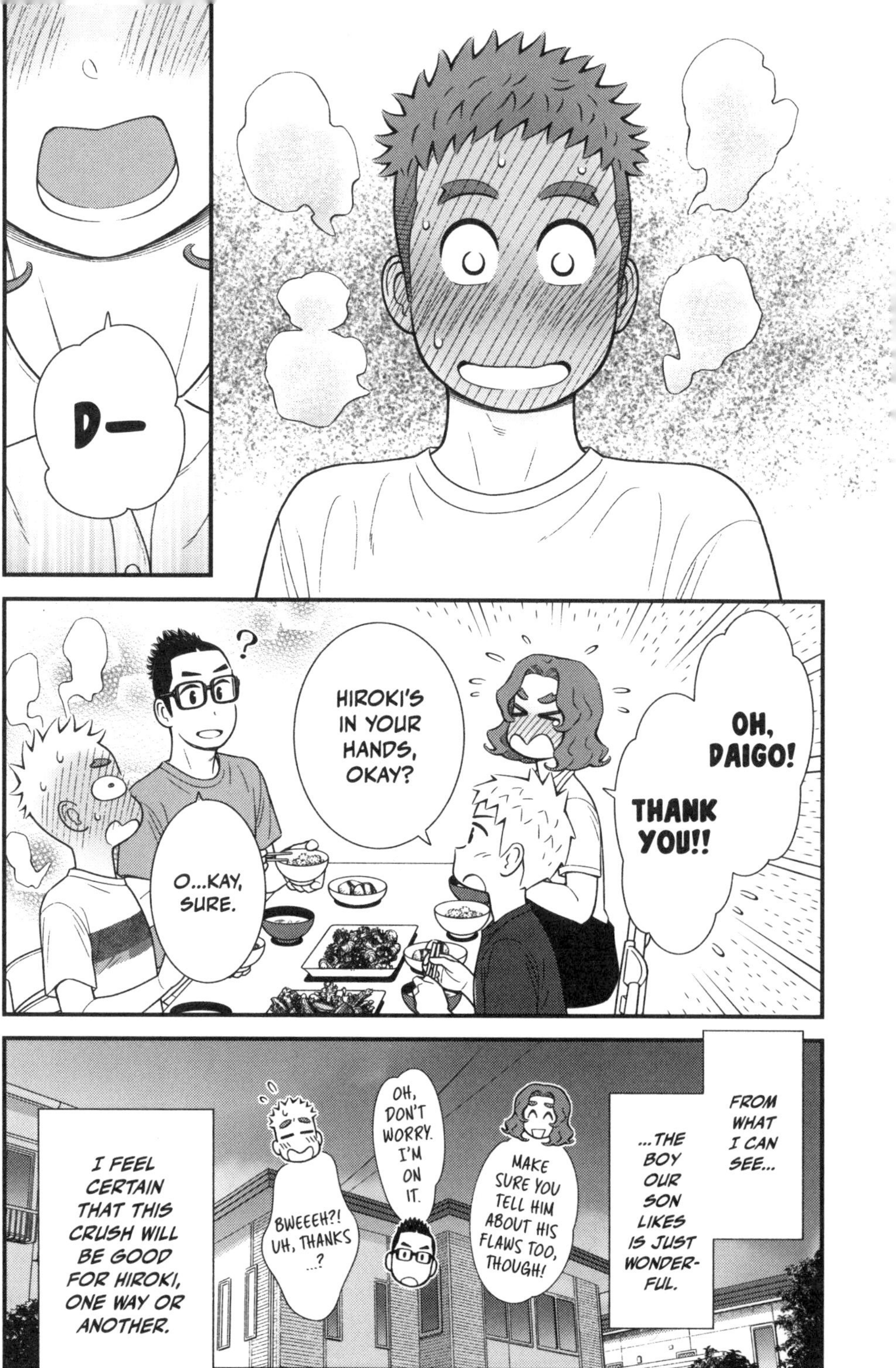
D—
OH, DAIGO! THANK YOU!!
HIROKI'S IN YOUR HANDS, OKAY?
O...KAY, SURE.
FROM WHAT I CAN SEE...
...THE BOY OUR SON LIKES IS JUST WONDER-FUL.
MAKE SURE YOU TELL HIM ABOUT HIS FLAWS TOO, THOUGH!
OH, DON'T WORRY. I'M ON IT.
BWEEEH?! UH, THANKS ...?
I FEEL CERTAIN THAT THIS CRUSH WILL BE GOOD FOR HIROKI, ONE WAY OR ANOTHER.

CHAPTER 58: A GOOD GUY ②

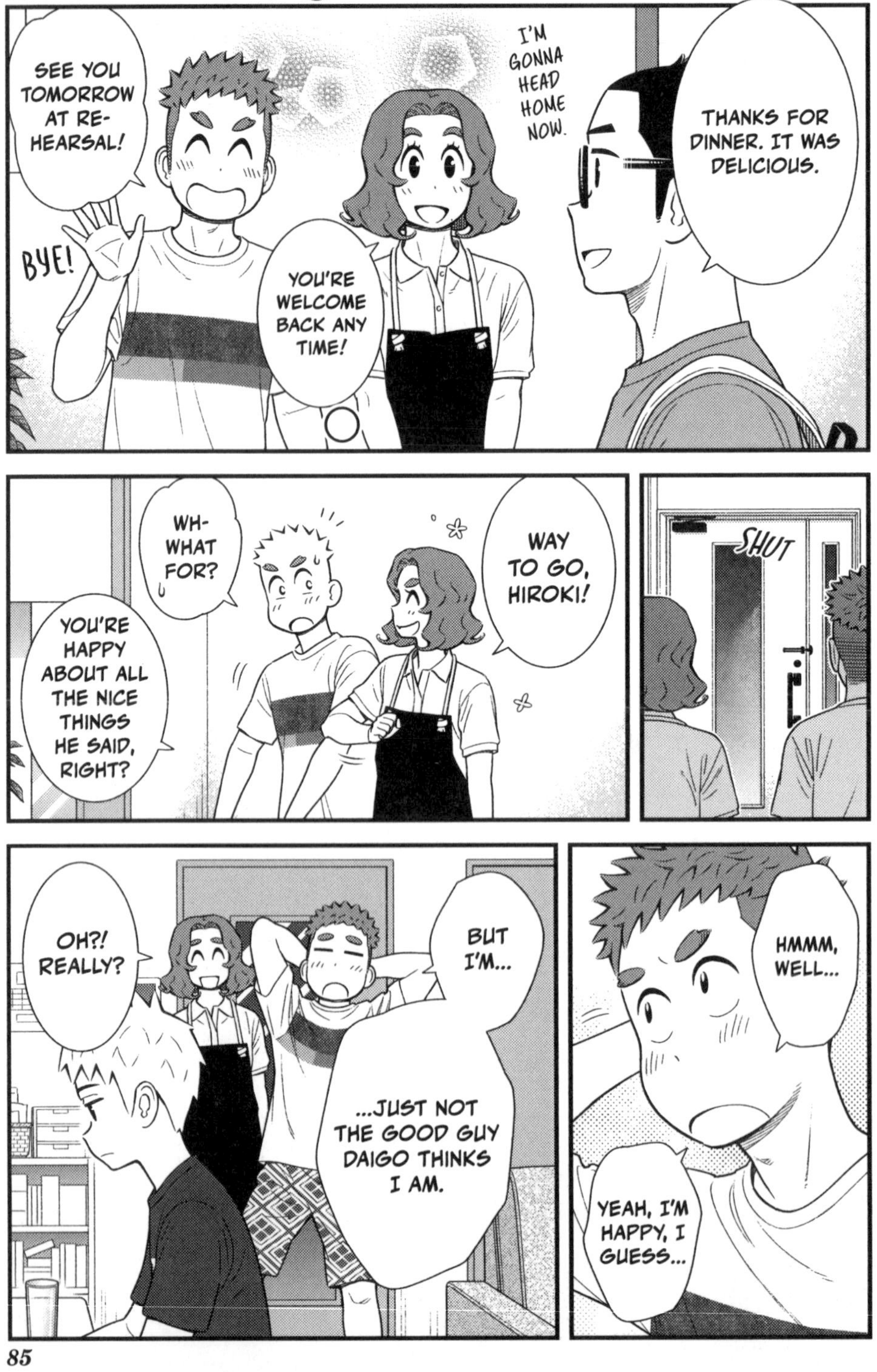
THANKS FOR DINNER. IT WAS DELICIOUS.
I'M GONNA HEAD HOME NOW.
SEE YOU TOMORROW AT RE-HEARSAL!
YOU'RE WELCOME BACK ANY TIME!
BYE!
SHUT
WAY TO GO, HIROKI!
WH- WHAT FOR?
YOU'RE HAPPY ABOUT ALL THE NICE THINGS HE SAID, RIGHT?
HMMM, WELL...
YEAH, I'M HAPPY, I GUESS...
BUT I'M...
...JUST NOT THE GOOD GUY DAIGO THINKS I AM.
OH?! REALLY?

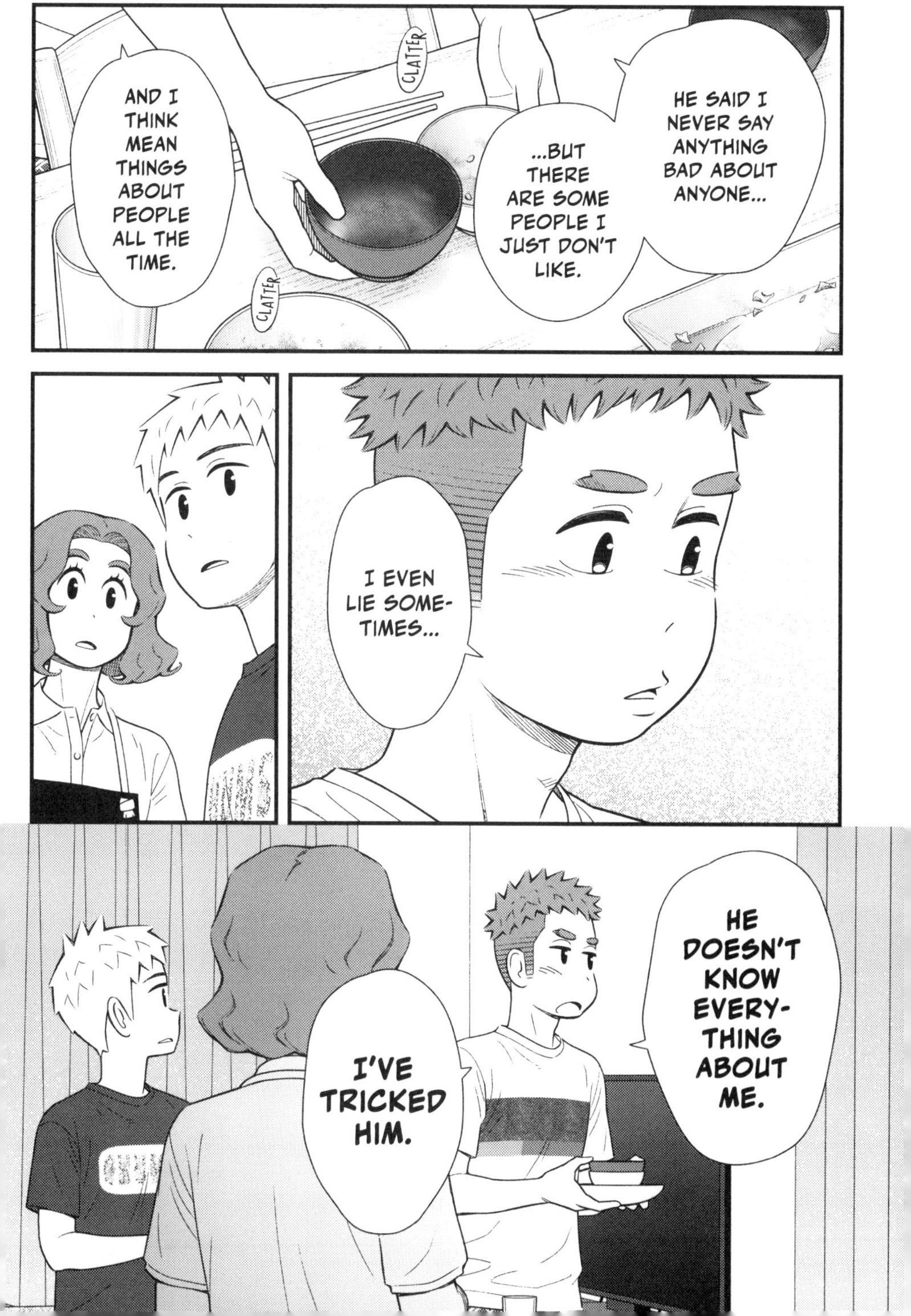
HE SAID I NEVER SAY ANYTHING BAD ABOUT ANYONE...
...BUT THERE ARE SOME PEOPLE I JUST DON'T LIKE.
CLATTER
AND I THINK MEAN THINGS ABOUT PEOPLE ALL THE TIME.
CLATTER
I EVEN LIE SOME-TIMES...
HE DOESN'T KNOW EVERY-THING ABOUT ME.
I'VE TRICKED HIM.

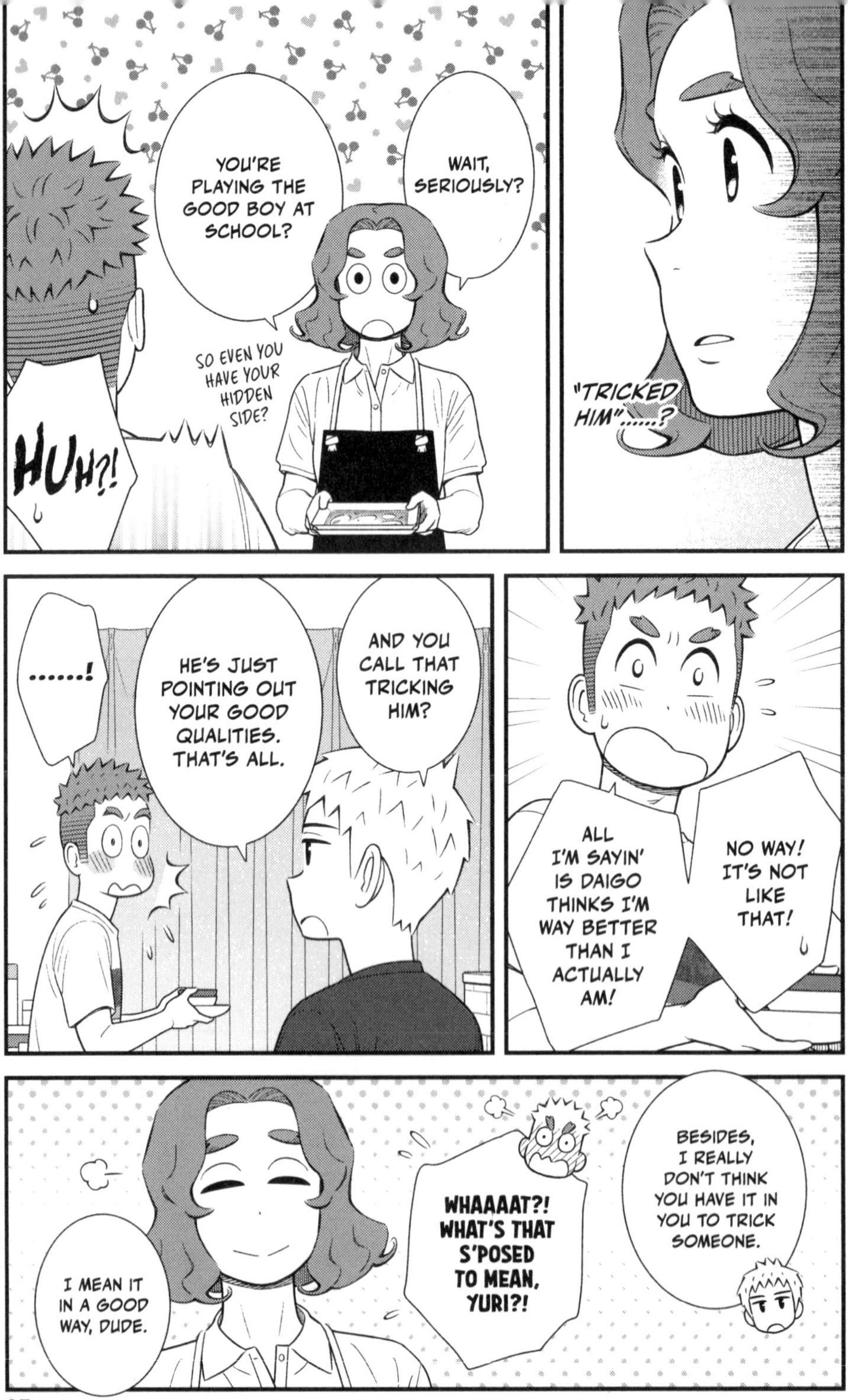
"TRICKED HIM"......?
WAIT, SERIOUSLY?
YOU'RE PLAYING THE GOOD BOY AT SCHOOL?
SO EVEN YOU HAVE YOUR HIDDEN SIDE?
HUH?!
NO WAY! IT'S NOT LIKE THAT!
ALL I'M SAYIN' IS DAIGO THINKS I'M WAY BETTER THAN I ACTUALLY AM!
AND YOU CALL THAT TRICKING HIM?
HE'S JUST POINTING OUT YOUR GOOD QUALITIES. THAT'S ALL.
......!
BESIDES, I REALLY DON'T THINK YOU HAVE IT IN YOU TO TRICK SOMEONE.
WHAAAAT?! WHAT'S THAT S'POSED TO MEAN, YURI?!
I MEAN IT IN A GOOD WAY, DUDE.

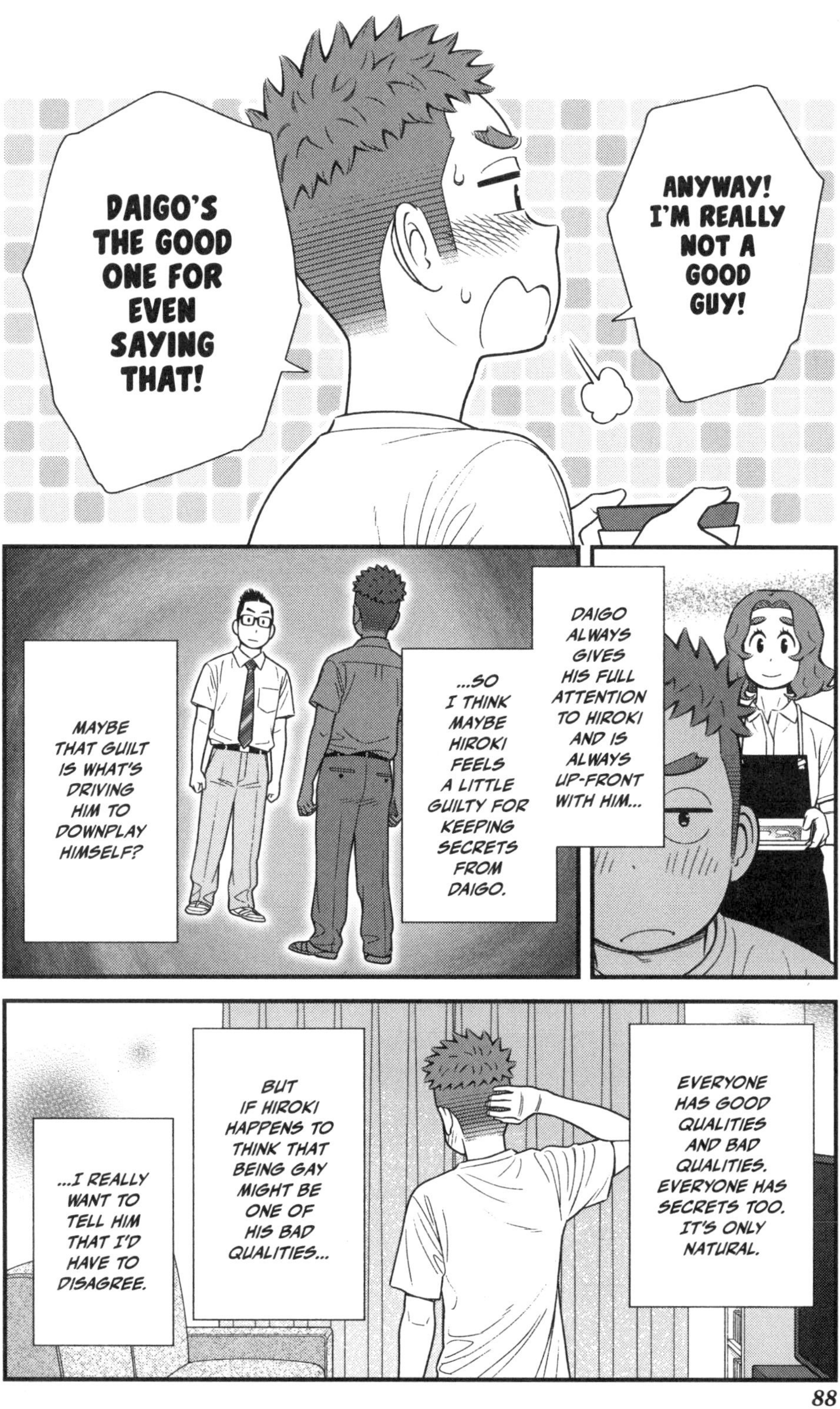
ANYWAY! I'M REALLY NOT A GOOD GUY!
DAIGO'S THE GOOD ONE FOR EVEN SAYING THAT!
DAIGO ALWAYS GIVES HIS FULL ATTENTION TO HIROKI AND IS ALWAYS UP-FRONT WITH HIM...
...SO I THINK MAYBE HIROKI FEELS A LITTLE GUILTY FOR KEEPING SECRETS FROM DAIGO.
MAYBE THAT GUILT IS WHAT'S DRIVING HIM TO DOWNPLAY HIMSELF?
EVERYONE HAS GOOD QUALITIES AND BAD QUALITIES. EVERYONE HAS SECRETS TOO. IT'S ONLY NATURAL.
BUT IF HIROKI HAPPENS TO THINK THAT BEING GAY MIGHT BE ONE OF HIS BAD QUALITIES...
...I REALLY WANT TO TELL HIM THAT I'D HAVE TO DISAGREE.

OUR SON DOESN'T WANT TO HIDE THINGS FROM THE BOY HE LIKES.
BUT BECAUSE IT'S THE BOY HE LIKES...
...I GUESS TELLING THE TRUTH ISN'T EASY EITHER.
LOVE IS ALWAYS SUCH A COMPLI-CATED THING.
YOU KEEP SAYING ALL THIS STUFF, BRO, BUT YOU'RE JUST TRYING TO HIDE HOW EMBARRASSED YOU ARE, AREN'T YOU?
SH-SHUT UP! CAN'T YOU JUST DROP IT?!

I Think
Our Son
Is Gay

Chapter 59: Brothers

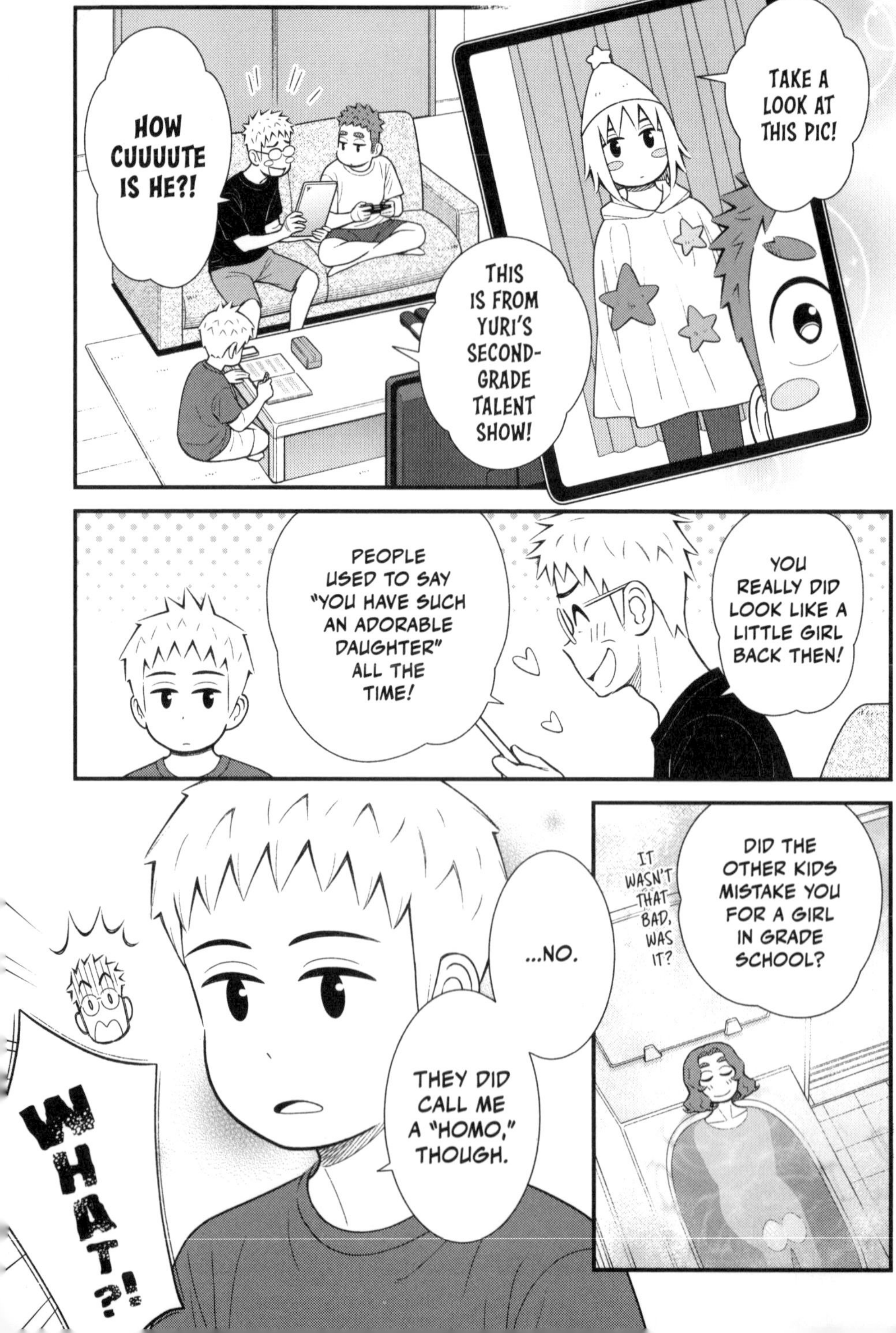

Take a look at this pic!
This is from Yuri's second-grade talent show!
How cuuuute is he?!
You really did look like a little girl back then!
People used to say "You have such an adorable daughter" all the time!
Did the other kids mistake you for a girl in grade school?
It wasn't that bad, was it?
...No.
They did call me a "homo," though.
WHAT?!

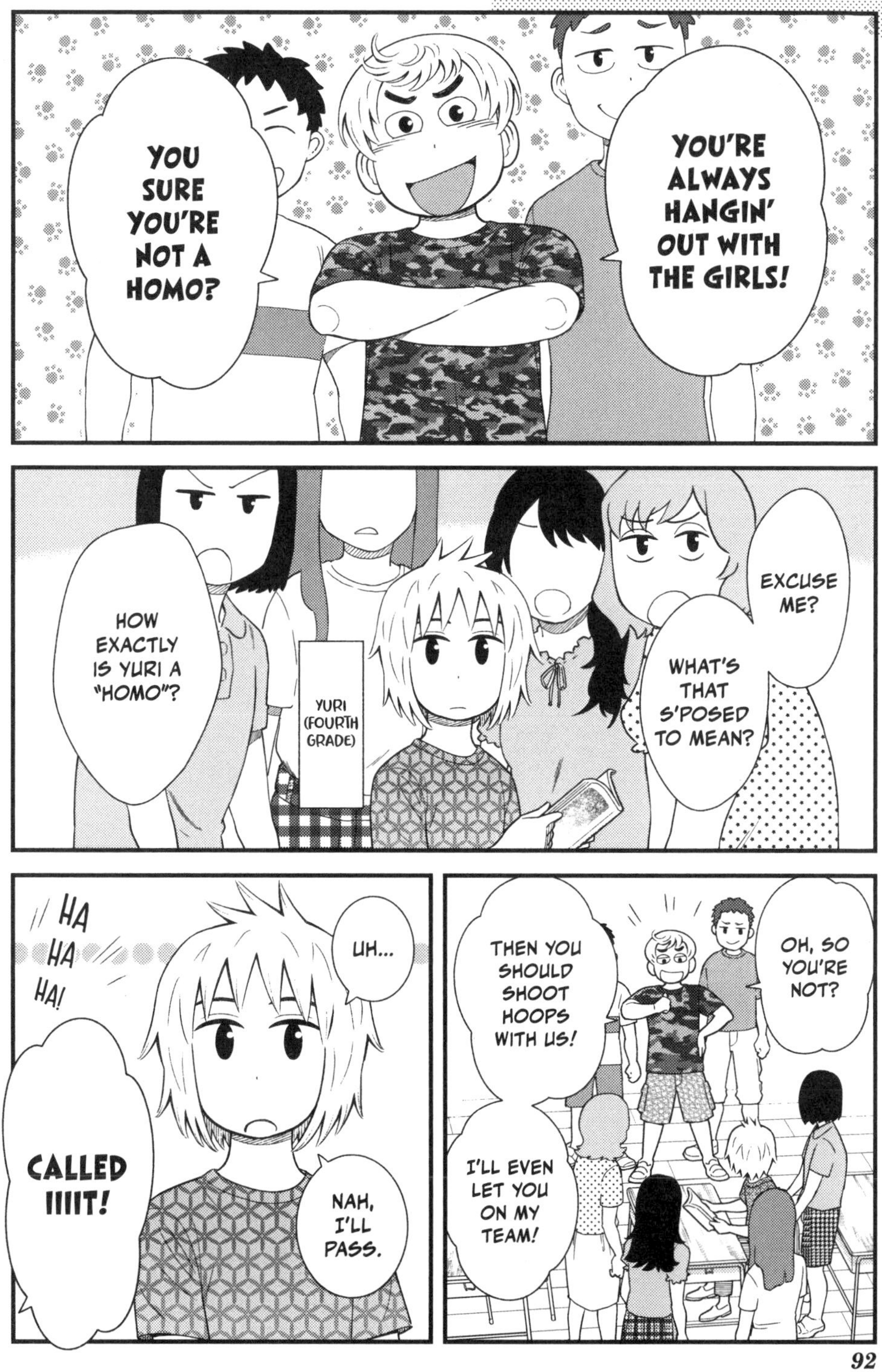
YOU'RE ALWAYS HANGIN' OUT WITH THE GIRLS!
YOU SURE YOU'RE NOT A HOMO?
EXCUSE ME?
WHAT'S THAT S'POSED TO MEAN?
YURI (FOURTH GRADE)
HOW EXACTLY IS YURI A "HOMO"?
OH, SO YOU'RE NOT?
THEN YOU SHOULD SHOOT HOOPS WITH US!
I'LL EVEN LET YOU ON MY TEAM!
UH...
NAH, I'LL PASS.
HA HA HA!
CALLED IIIIT!

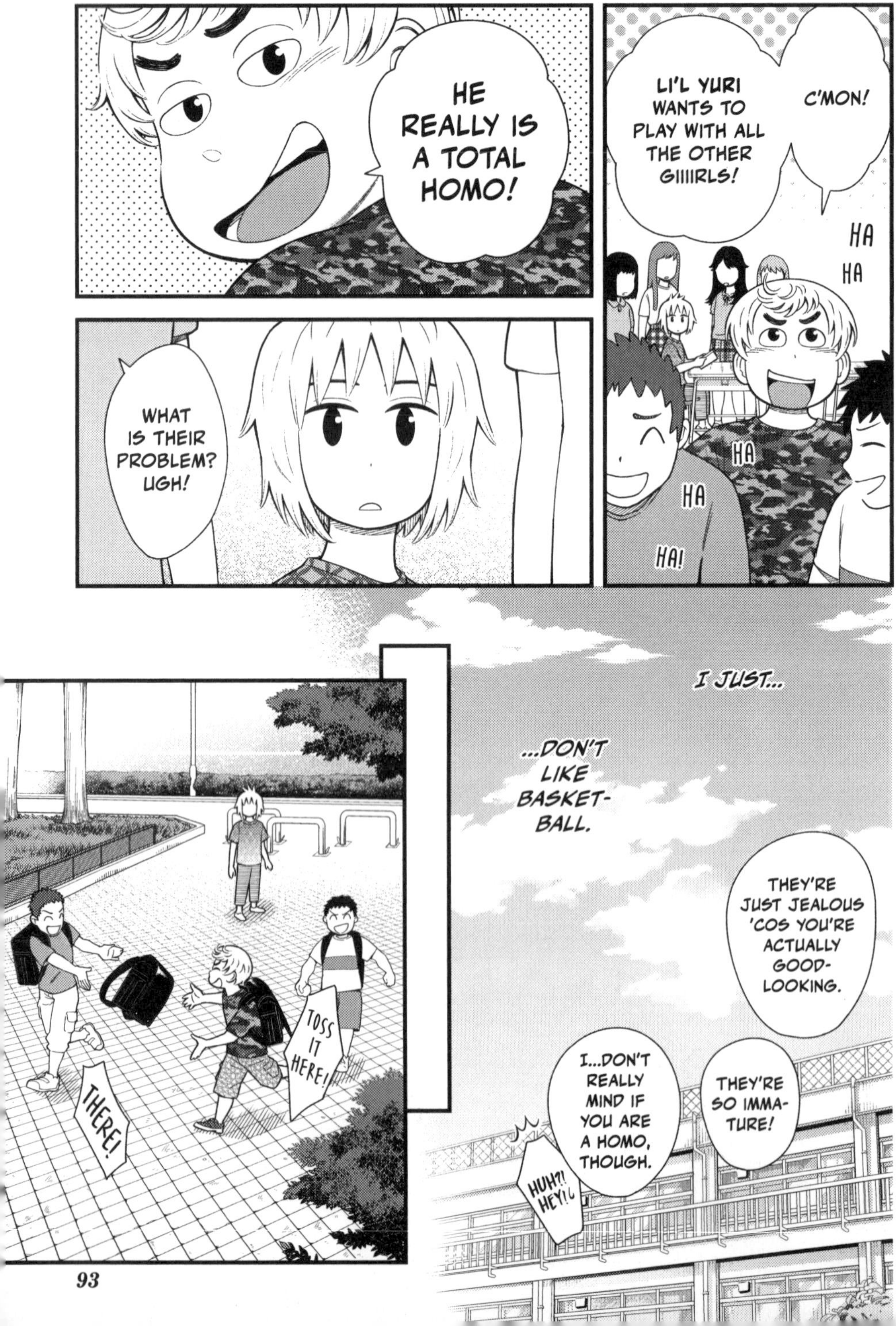

C'MON!
LI'L YURI WANTS TO PLAY WITH ALL THE OTHER GIIIIRLS!
HA HA
HA HA HA!
HE REALLY IS A TOTAL HOMO!
WHAT IS THEIR PROBLEM? UGH!
I JUST...
...DON'T LIKE BASKET-BALL.
THEY'RE JUST JEALOUS 'COS YOU'RE ACTUALLY GOOD-LOOKING.
THEY'RE SO IMMA-TURE!
I...DON'T REALLY MIND IF YOU ARE A HOMO, THOUGH.
HUH?! HEY!
TOSS IT HERE!
THERE!

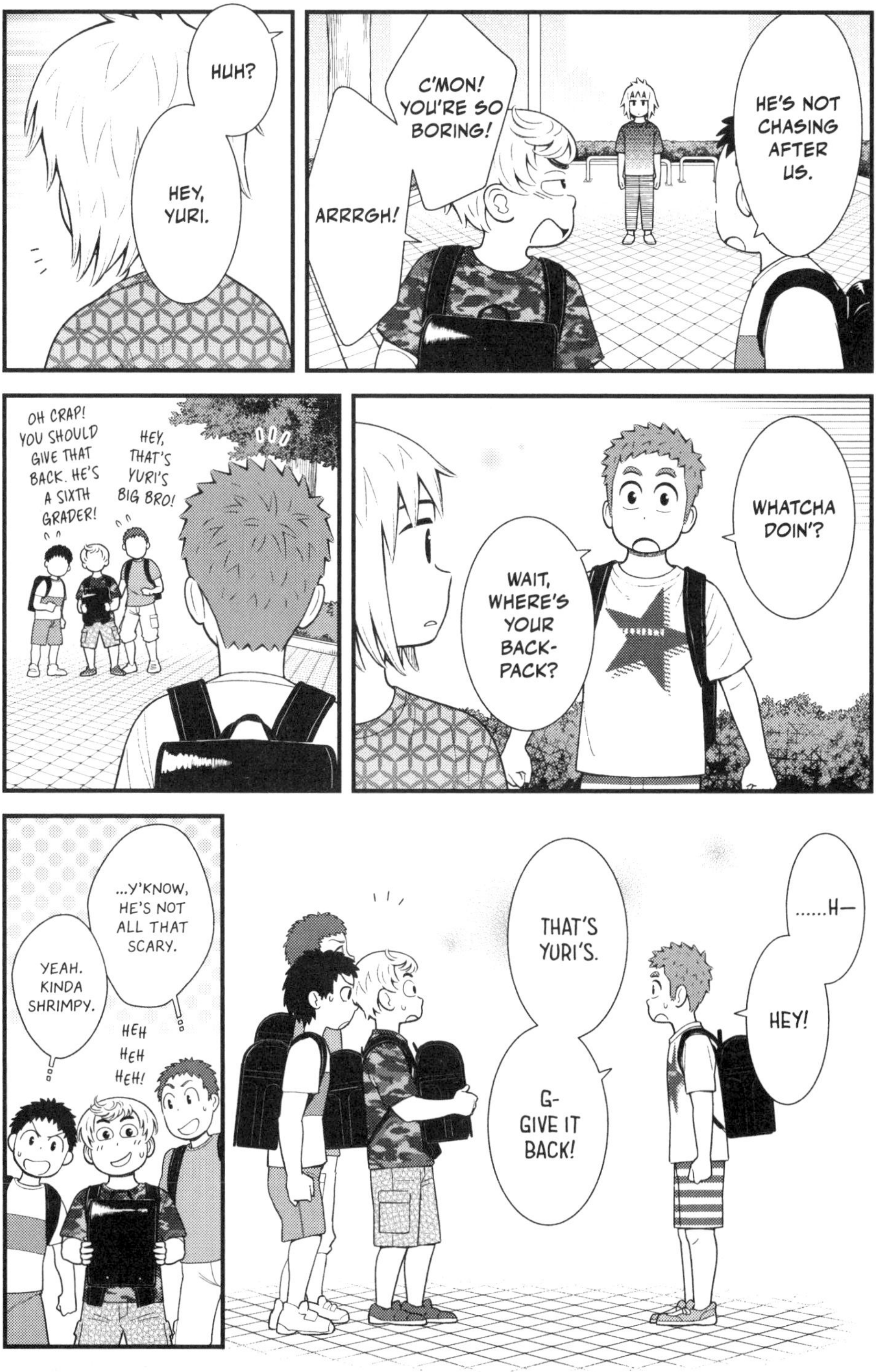
HE'S NOT CHASING AFTER US.
C'MON! YOU'RE SO BORING!
ARRRGH!
HUH?
HEY, YURI.
WHATCHA DOIN'?
WAIT, WHERE'S YOUR BACK-PACK?
HEY, THAT'S YURI'S BIG BRO!
OH CRAP! YOU SHOULD GIVE THAT BACK. HE'S A SIXTH GRADER!
......H—
HEY!
THAT'S YURI'S.
G-GIVE IT BACK!
...Y'KNOW, HE'S NOT ALL THAT SCARY.
YEAH. KINDA SHRIMPY.
HEH HEH HEH!

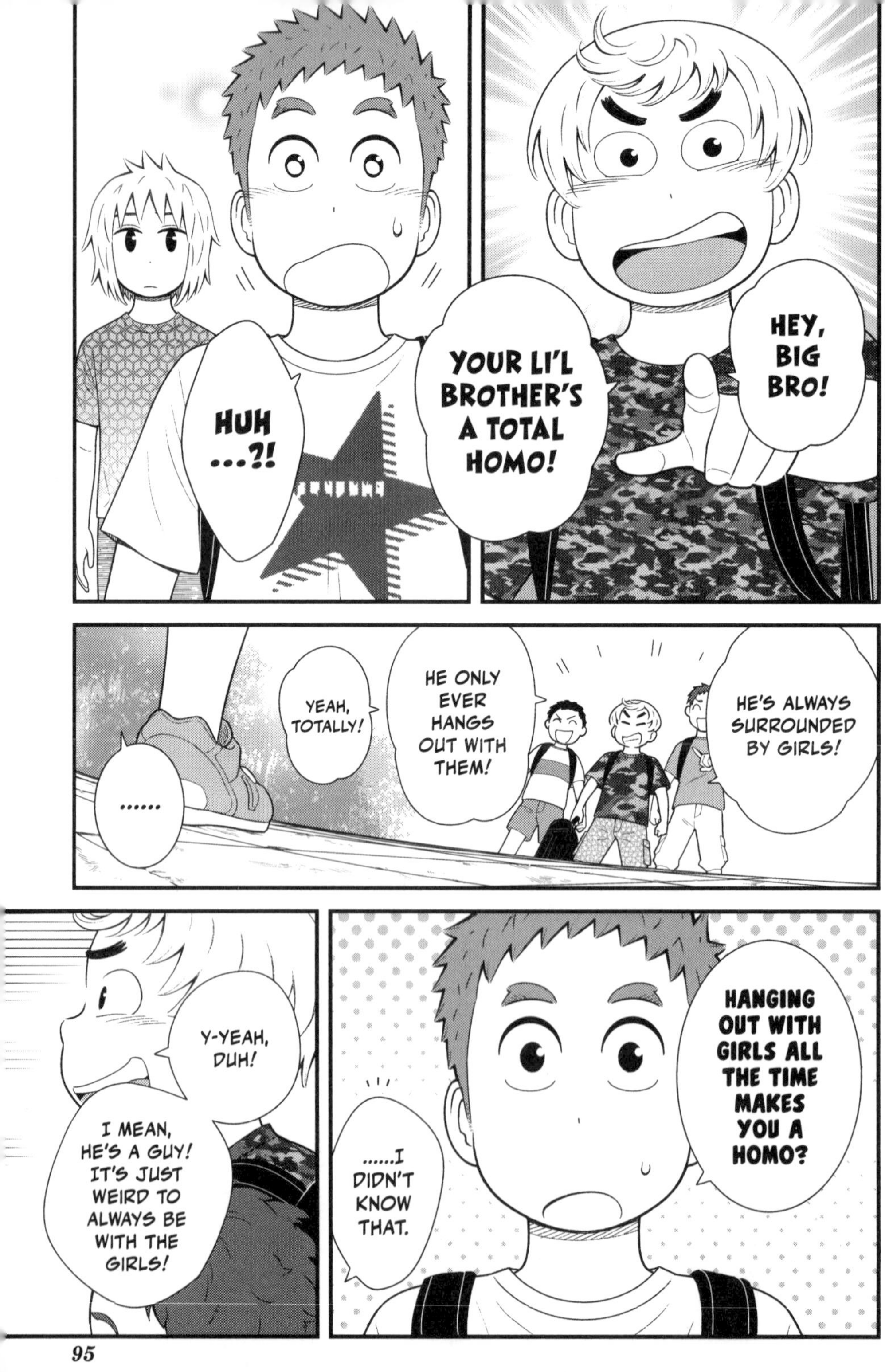
HEY, BIG BRO!
YOUR LI'L BROTHER'S A TOTAL HOMO!
HUH ...?!
HE'S ALWAYS SURROUNDED BY GIRLS!
HE ONLY EVER HANGS OUT WITH THEM!
YEAH, TOTALLY!
......
HANGING OUT WITH GIRLS ALL THE TIME MAKES YOU A HOMO?
......I DIDN'T KNOW THAT.
Y-YEAH, DUH!
I MEAN, HE'S A GUY! IT'S JUST WEIRD TO ALWAYS BE WITH THE GIRLS!

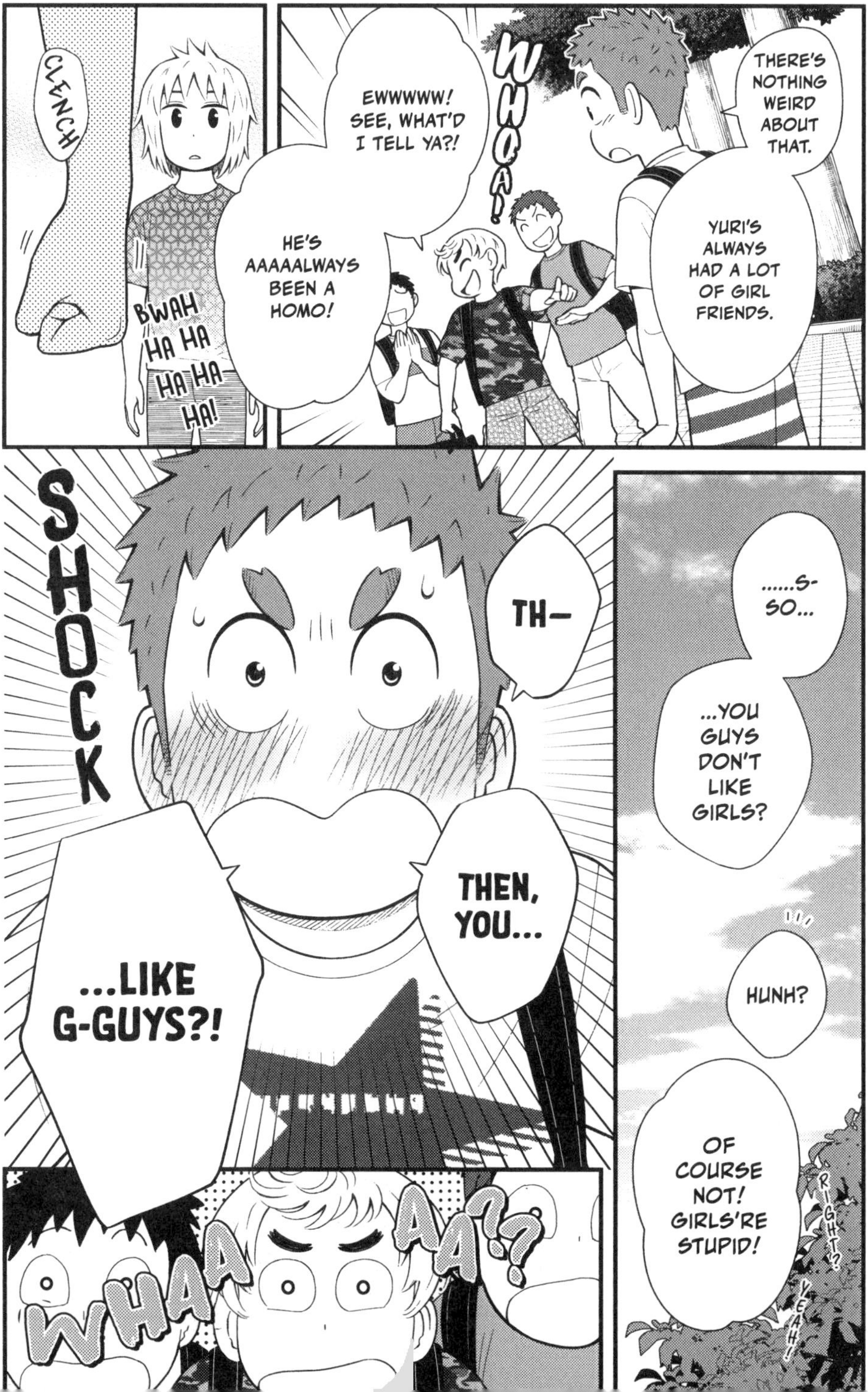
THERE'S NOTHING WEIRD ABOUT THAT.
YURI'S ALWAYS HAD A LOT OF GIRL FRIENDS.
WHOA!
EWWWWW! SEE, WHAT'D I TELL YA?!
HE'S AAAAALWAYS BEEN A HOMO!
CLENCH
BWAH HA HA HA HA HA!
......S-SO...
...YOU GUYS DON'T LIKE GIRLS?
HUNH?
OF COURSE NOT! GIRLS'RE STUPID!
RIGHT?
YEAH!
SHOCK
TH—
THEN, YOU...
...LIKE G-GUYS?!
WHAAAA?!

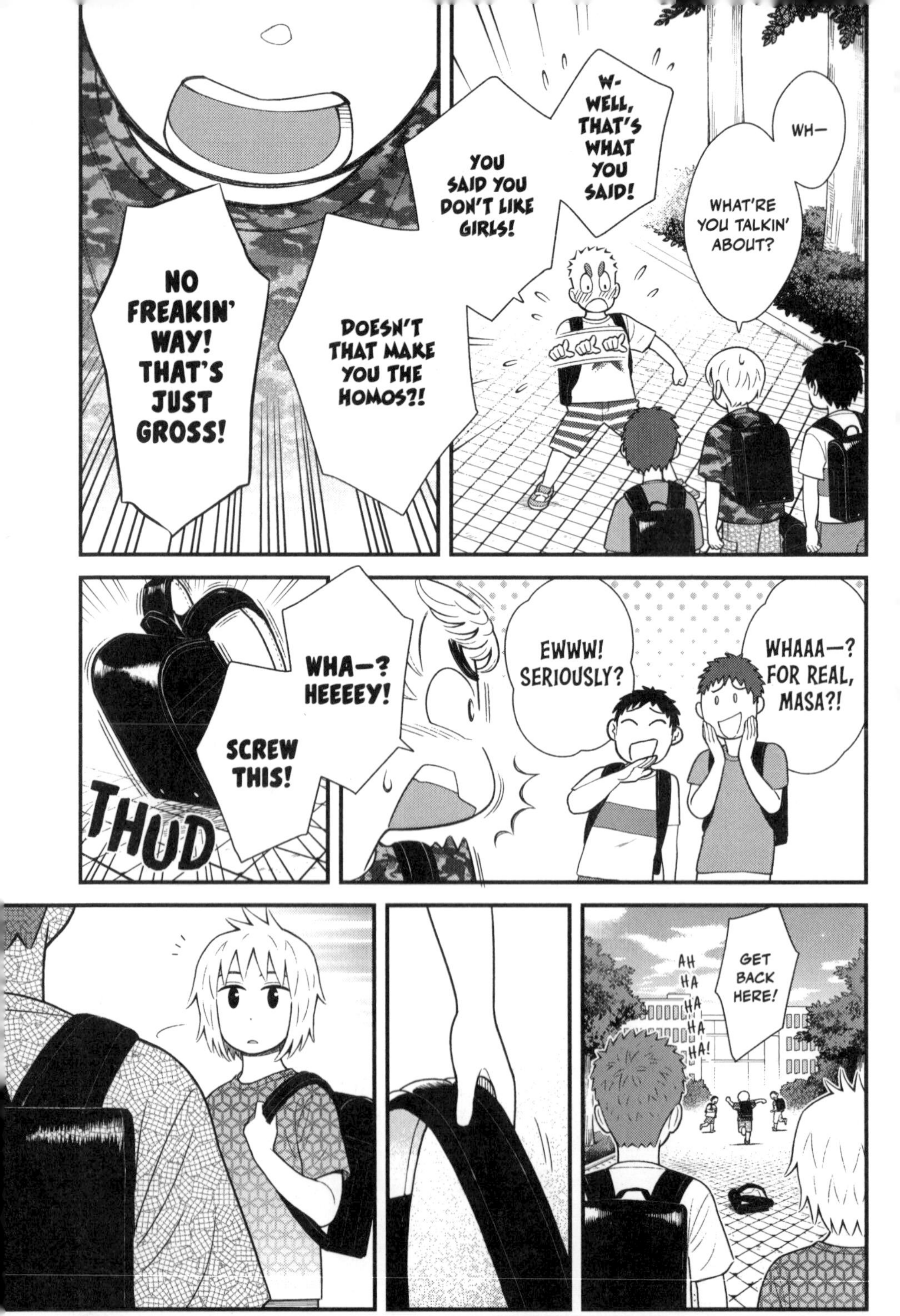
WH—
WHAT'RE YOU TALKIN' ABOUT?
W- WELL, THAT'S WHAT YOU SAID!
YOU SAID YOU DON'T LIKE GIRLS!
DOESN'T THAT MAKE YOU THE HOMOS?!
NO FREAKIN' WAY! THAT'S JUST GROSS!
WHAAA—? FOR REAL, MASA?!
EWWW! SERIOUSLY?
WHA—? HEEEEY!
SCREW THIS!
THUD
GET BACK HERE!
AH HA HA HA HA!

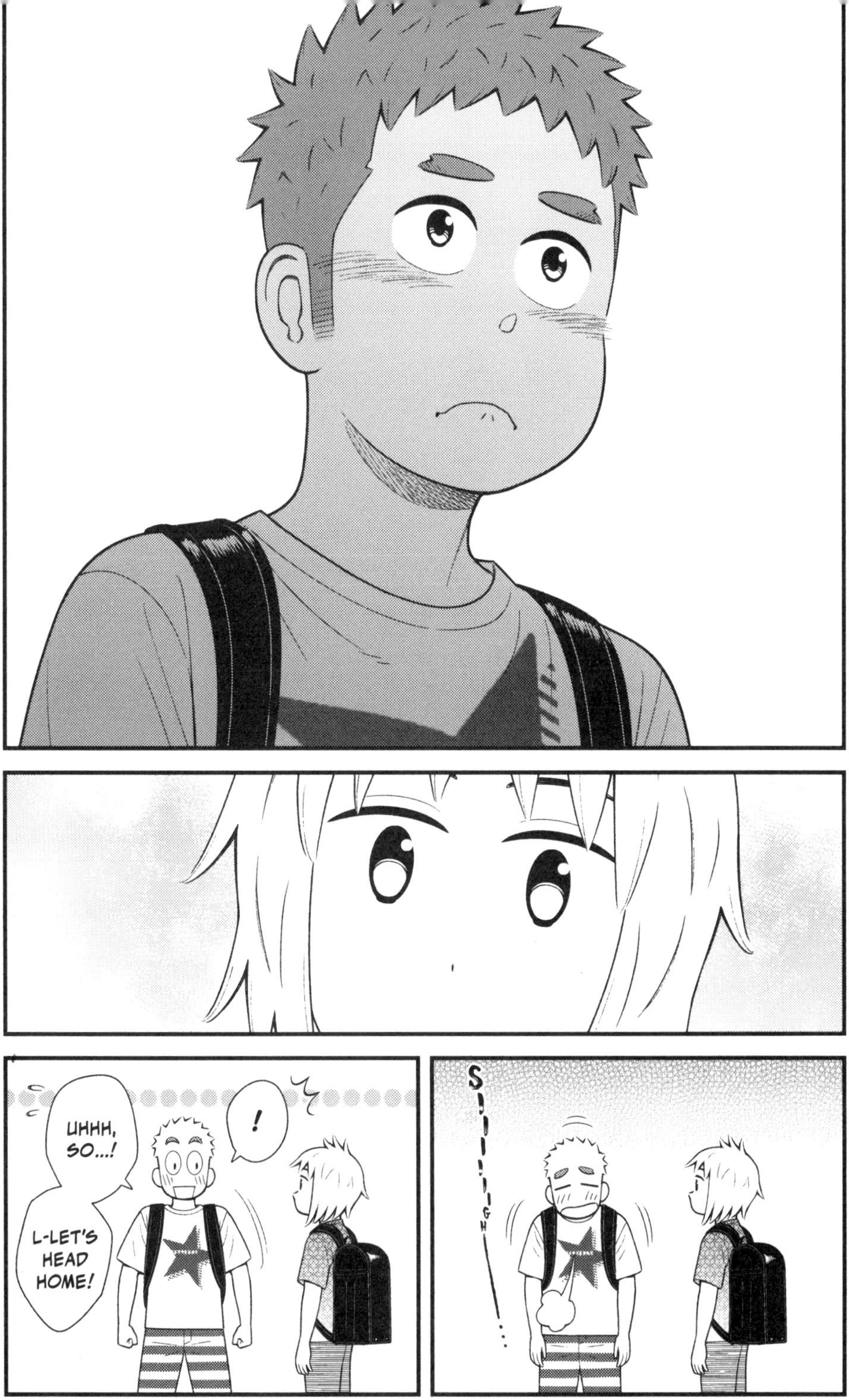
SIIIIIIGH...
!
UHHH, SO...!
L-LET'S HEAD HOME!

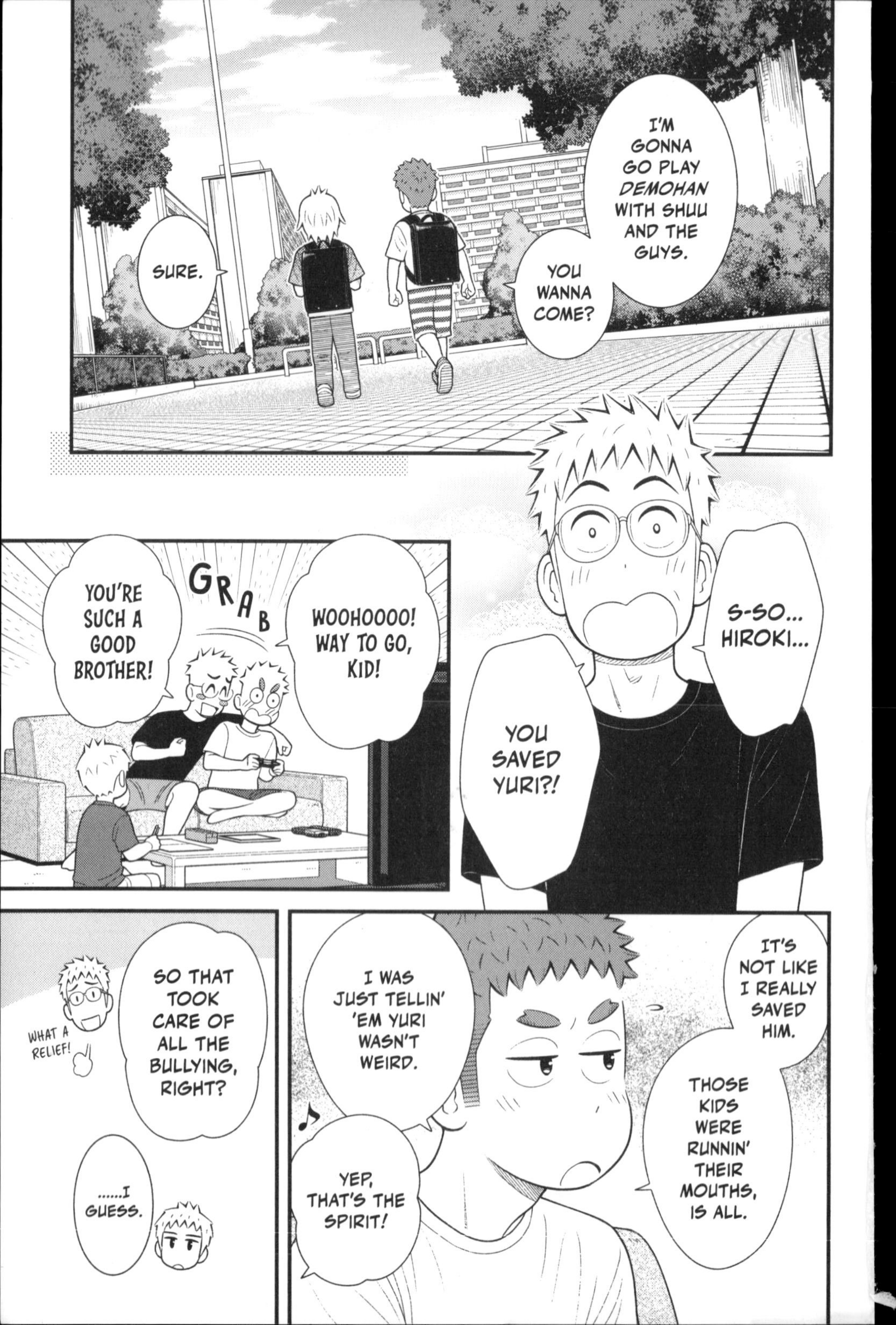
I'M GONNA GO PLAY *DEMOHAN* WITH SHUU AND THE GUYS.
YOU WANNA COME?
SURE.
S-SO... HIROKI...
YOU SAVED YURI?!
WOOHOOOO! WAY TO GO, KID!
GRAB
YOU'RE SUCH A GOOD BROTHER!
IT'S NOT LIKE I REALLY SAVED HIM.
THOSE KIDS WERE RUNNIN' THEIR MOUTHS, IS ALL.
I WAS JUST TELLIN' 'EM YURI WASN'T WEIRD.
YEP, THAT'S THE SPIRIT!
SO THAT TOOK CARE OF ALL THE BULLYING, RIGHT?
WHAT A RELIEF!
......I GUESS.

OH, TOMOKO!
YOU WON'T BELIEVE WHAT I JUST HEARD!
HUH? WHAT?
WAIT, DID YOU KNOW ABOUT THIS ALREADY?
THAT WASN'T REALLY THE END OF IT, THOUGH.
THEY KEPT PICKING ON ME AFTER THAT...
...BUT I JUST DIDN'T CARE.
I HAD MY FRIENDS.
I HAD HIROKI AND HIS FRIENDS.
I WAS HAVING FUN.
BUT THAT DOESN'T CHANGE THE FACT THAT HIROKI PUSHED HIMSELF TO STAND UP FOR ME...
...AND I'M GRATEFUL FOR THAT.
......WAIT, DID I EVER THANK HIM?
THANKS, BRO.
HUH?
WHAT FOR?

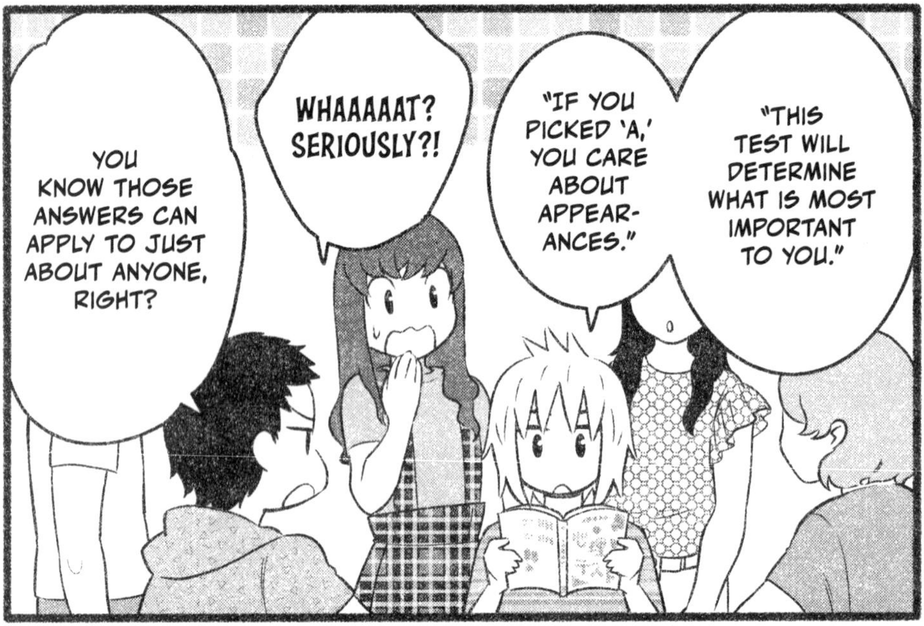
"THIS TEST WILL DETERMINE WHAT IS MOST IMPORTANT TO YOU."
"IF YOU PICKED 'A,' YOU CARE ABOUT APPEAR-ANCES."
WHAAAAAT? SERIOUSLY?!
YOU KNOW THOSE ANSWERS CAN APPLY TO JUST ABOUT ANYONE, RIGHT?

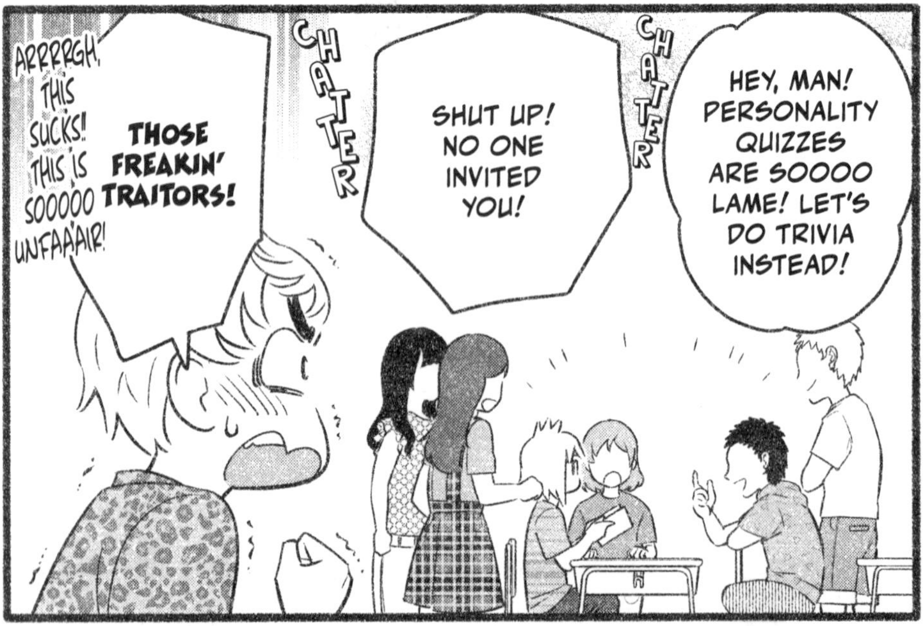
HEY, MAN! PERSONALITY QUIZZES ARE SOOOO LAME! LET'S DO TRIVIA INSTEAD!
CHATTER
SHUT UP! NO ONE INVITED YOU!
CHATTER
THOSE FREAKIN' TRAITORS!
ARRRRGH, THIS SUCKS!! THIS IS SOOOOO UNFAAAIR!

I Think
Our Son
Is Gay

Chapter 60: Father and Son

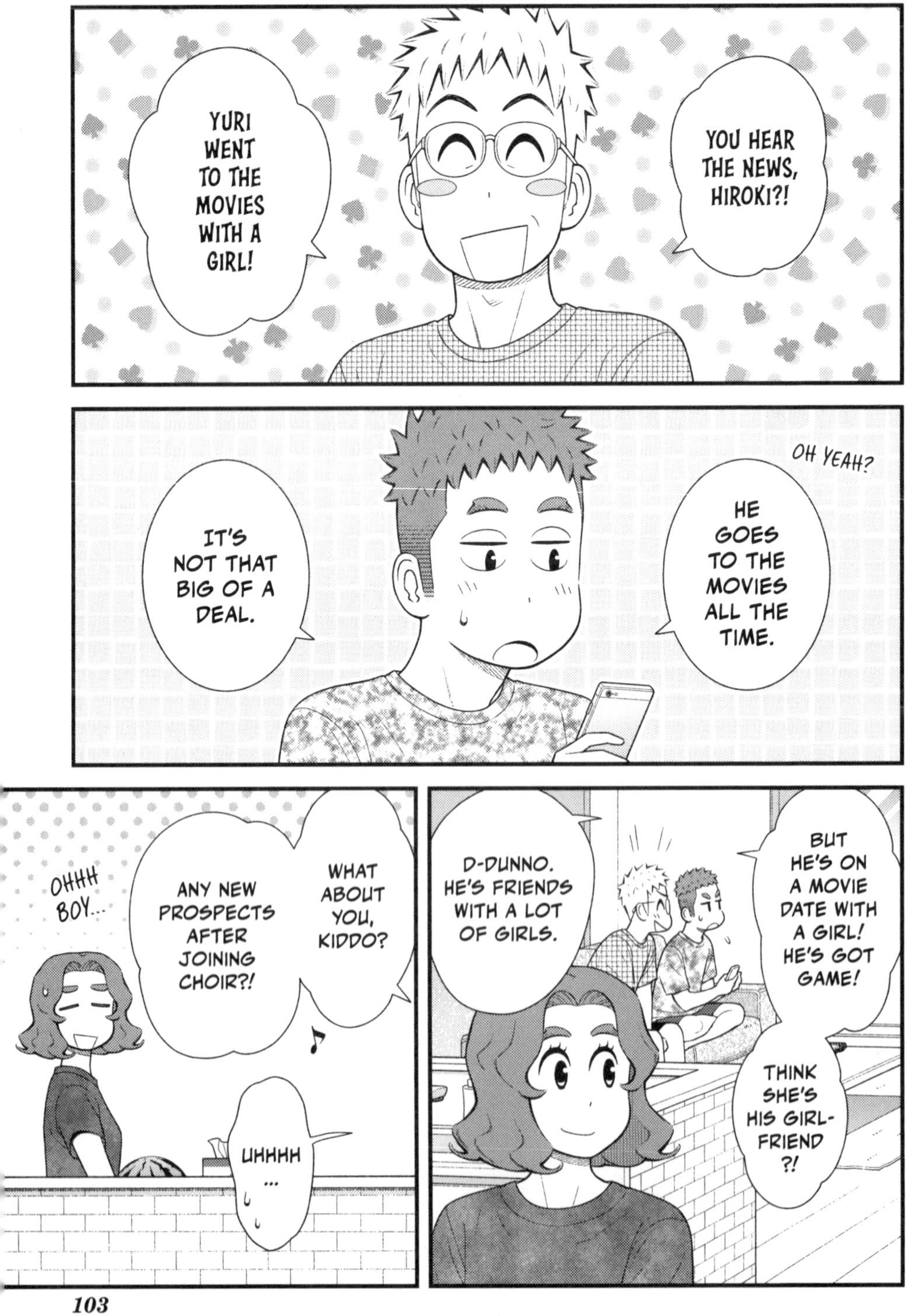
YOU HEAR THE NEWS, HIROKI?!
YURI WENT TO THE MOVIES WITH A GIRL!
OH YEAH?
HE GOES TO THE MOVIES ALL THE TIME.
IT'S NOT THAT BIG OF A DEAL.
BUT HE'S ON A MOVIE DATE WITH A GIRL! HE'S GOT GAME!
THINK SHE'S HIS GIRL-FRIEND ?!
D-DUNNO. HE'S FRIENDS WITH A LOT OF GIRLS.
WHAT ABOUT YOU, KIDDO?
ANY NEW PROSPECTS AFTER JOINING CHOIR?!
OHHH BOY...
UHHHH ...

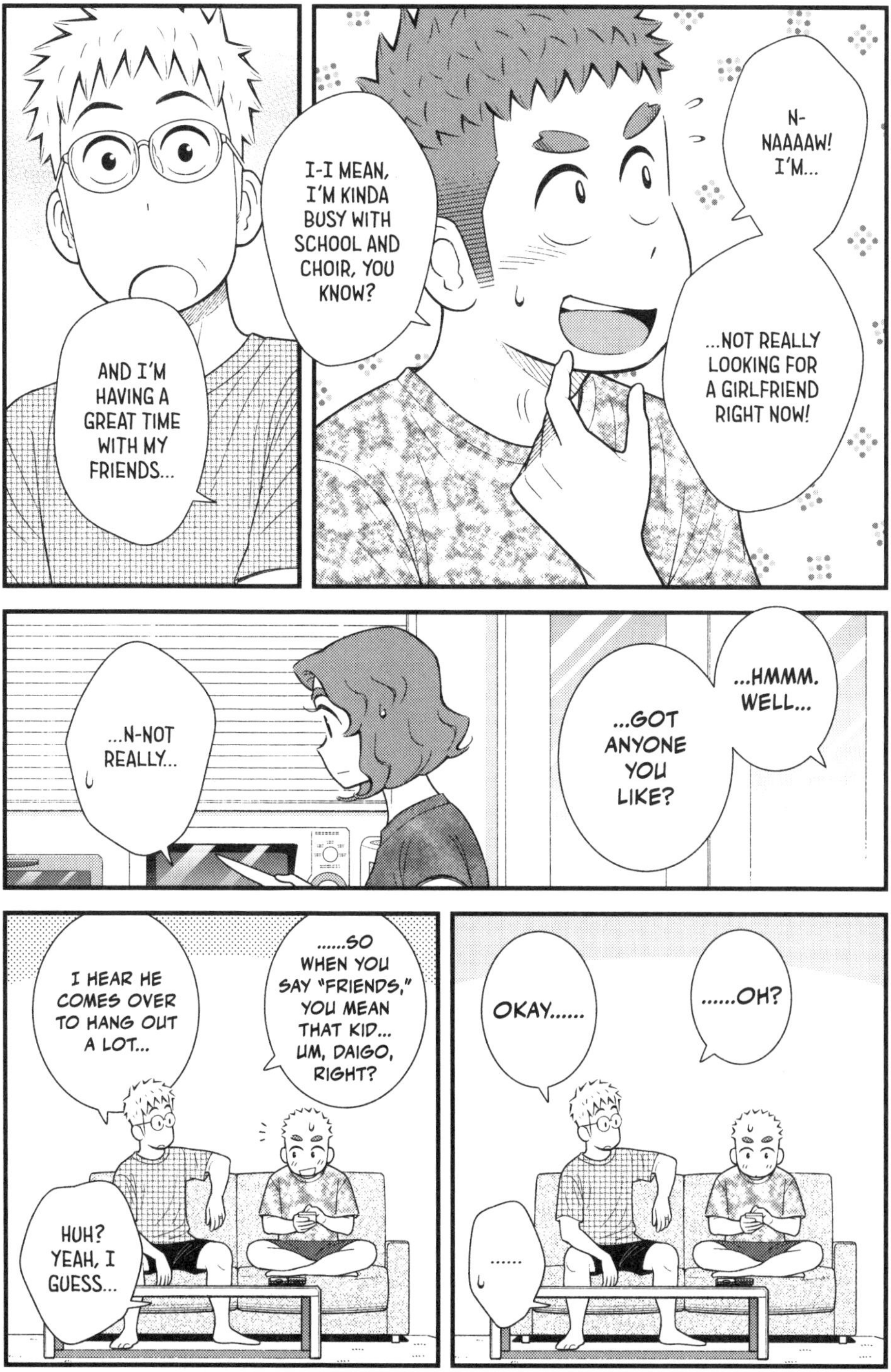
N-NAAAAW! I'M...
...NOT REALLY LOOKING FOR A GIRLFRIEND RIGHT NOW!
I-I MEAN, I'M KINDA BUSY WITH SCHOOL AND CHOIR, YOU KNOW?
AND I'M HAVING A GREAT TIME WITH MY FRIENDS...
...HMMM. WELL...
...GOT ANYONE YOU LIKE?
...N-NOT REALLY...
......OH?
OKAY......
......
......SO WHEN YOU SAY "FRIENDS," YOU MEAN THAT KID... UM, DAIGO, RIGHT?
I HEAR HE COMES OVER TO HANG OUT A LOT...
HUH? YEAH, I GUESS...

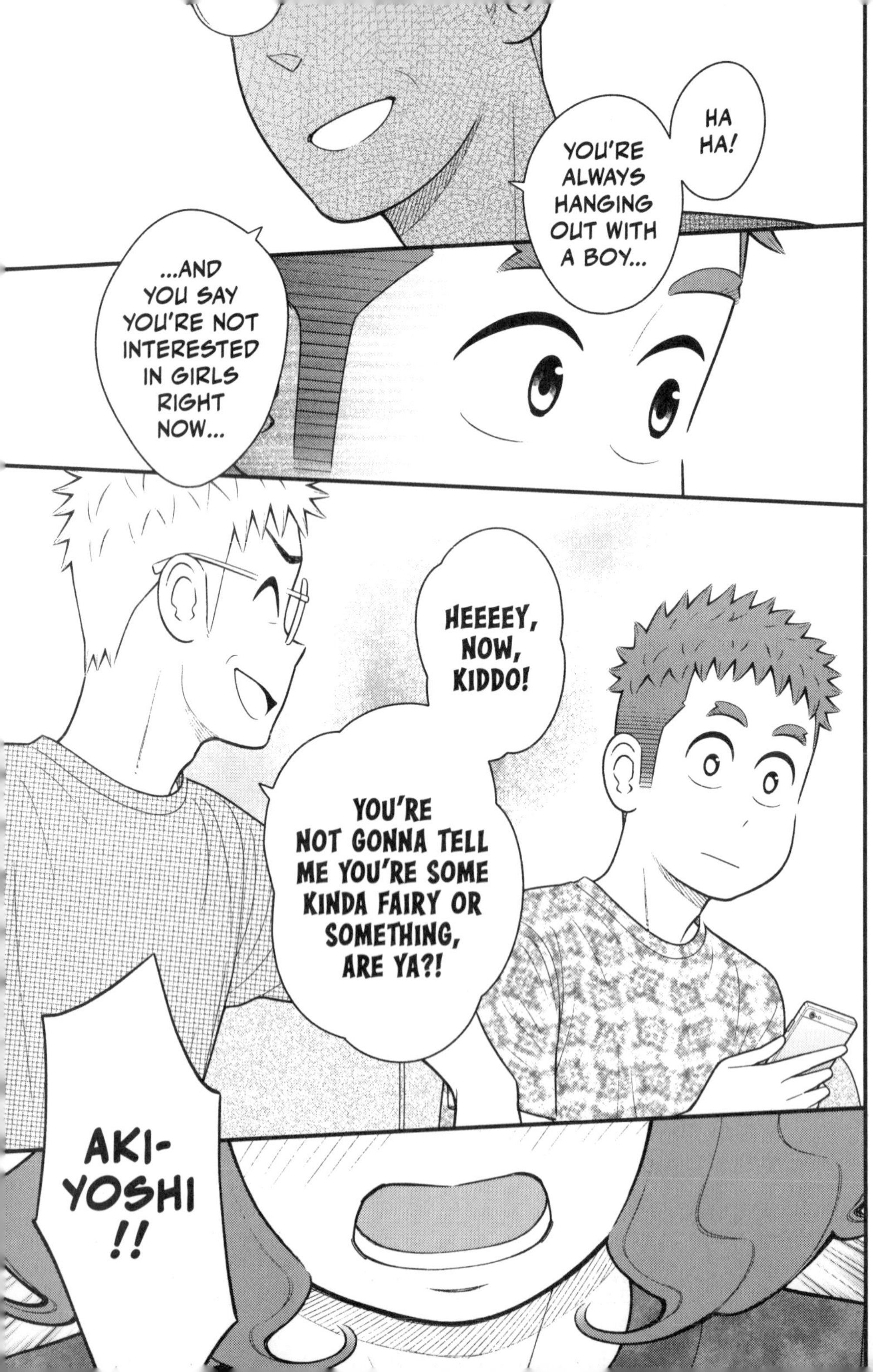
HA HA!
YOU'RE ALWAYS HANGING OUT WITH A BOY...
...AND YOU SAY YOU'RE NOT INTERESTED IN GIRLS RIGHT NOW...
HEEEEY, NOW, KIDDO!
YOU'RE NOT GONNA TELL ME YOU'RE SOME KINDA FAIRY OR SOMETHING, ARE YA?!
AKI-YOSHI!!

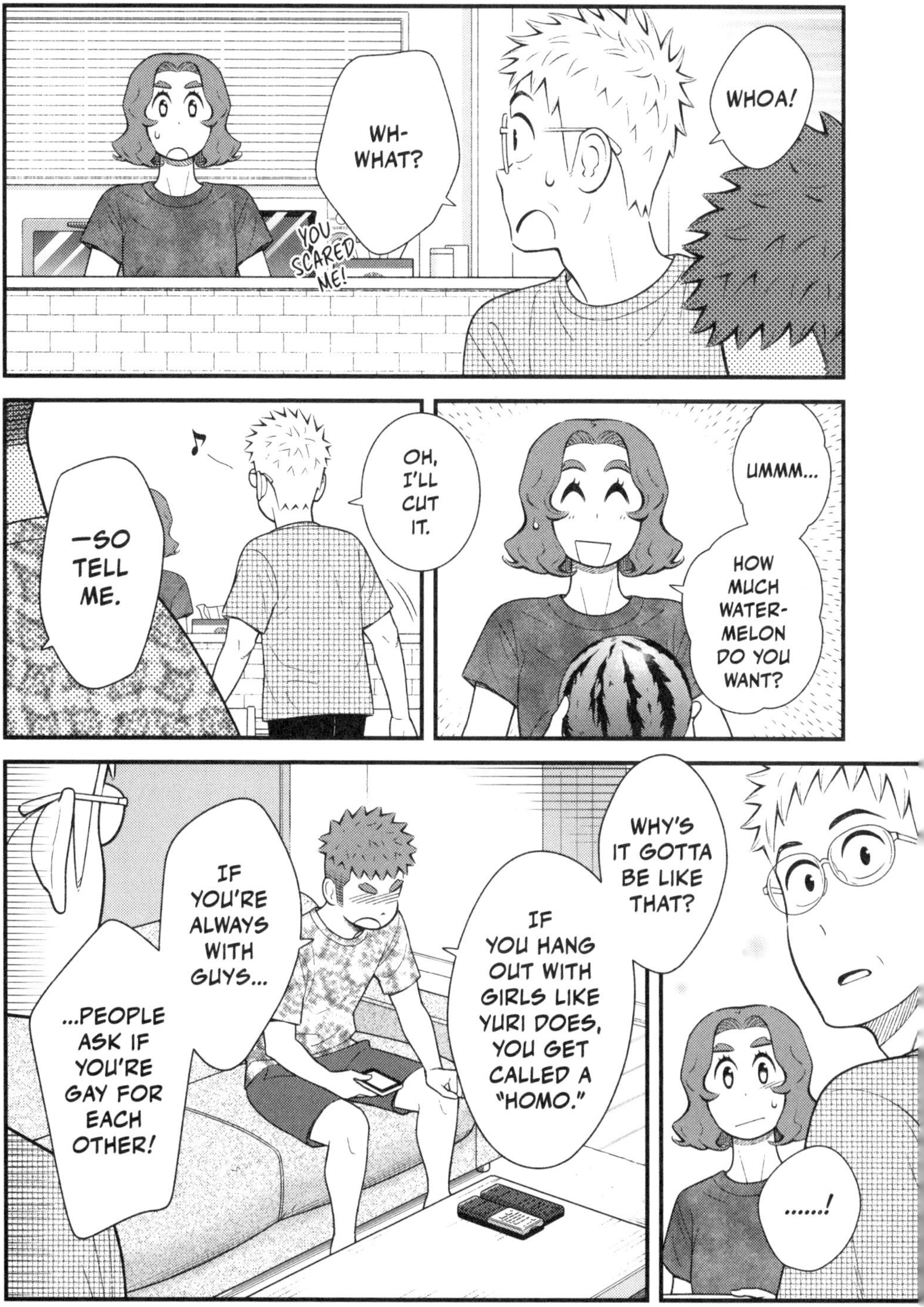
WHOA!
WH- WHAT?
YOU SCARED ME!
UMMM...
HOW MUCH WATER- MELON DO YOU WANT?
OH, I'LL CUT IT.
—SO TELL ME.
......!
WHY'S IT GOTTA BE LIKE THAT?
IF YOU HANG OUT WITH GIRLS LIKE YURI DOES, YOU GET CALLED A "HOMO."
IF YOU'RE ALWAYS WITH GUYS...
...PEOPLE ASK IF YOU'RE GAY FOR EACH OTHER!

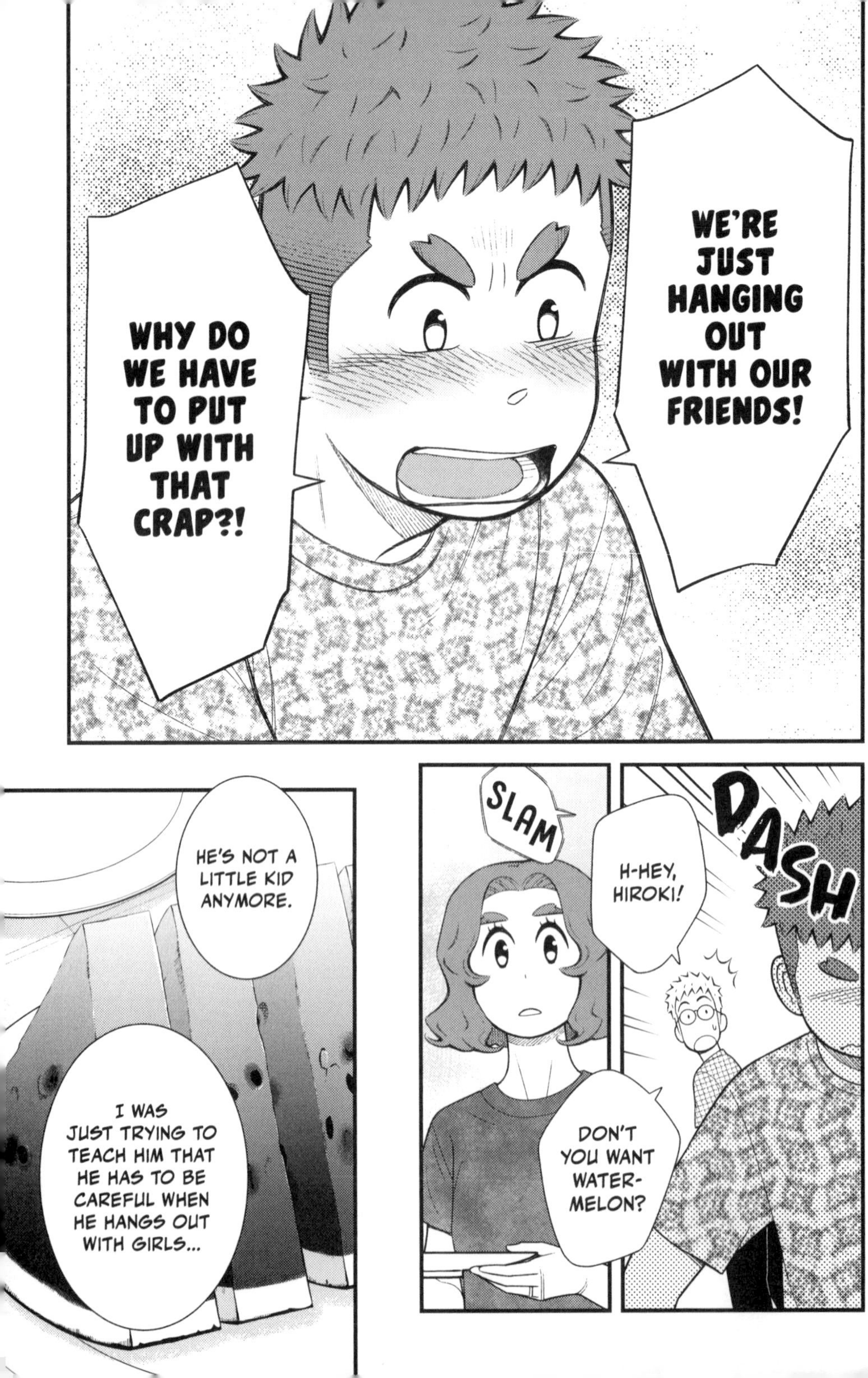
WE'RE JUST HANGING OUT WITH OUR FRIENDS!
WHY DO WE HAVE TO PUT UP WITH THAT CRAP?!
DASH
H-HEY, HIROKI!
SLAM
DON'T YOU WANT WATER-MELON?
HE'S NOT A LITTLE KID ANYMORE.
I WAS JUST TRYING TO TEACH HIM THAT HE HAS TO BE CAREFUL WHEN HE HANGS OUT WITH GIRLS...

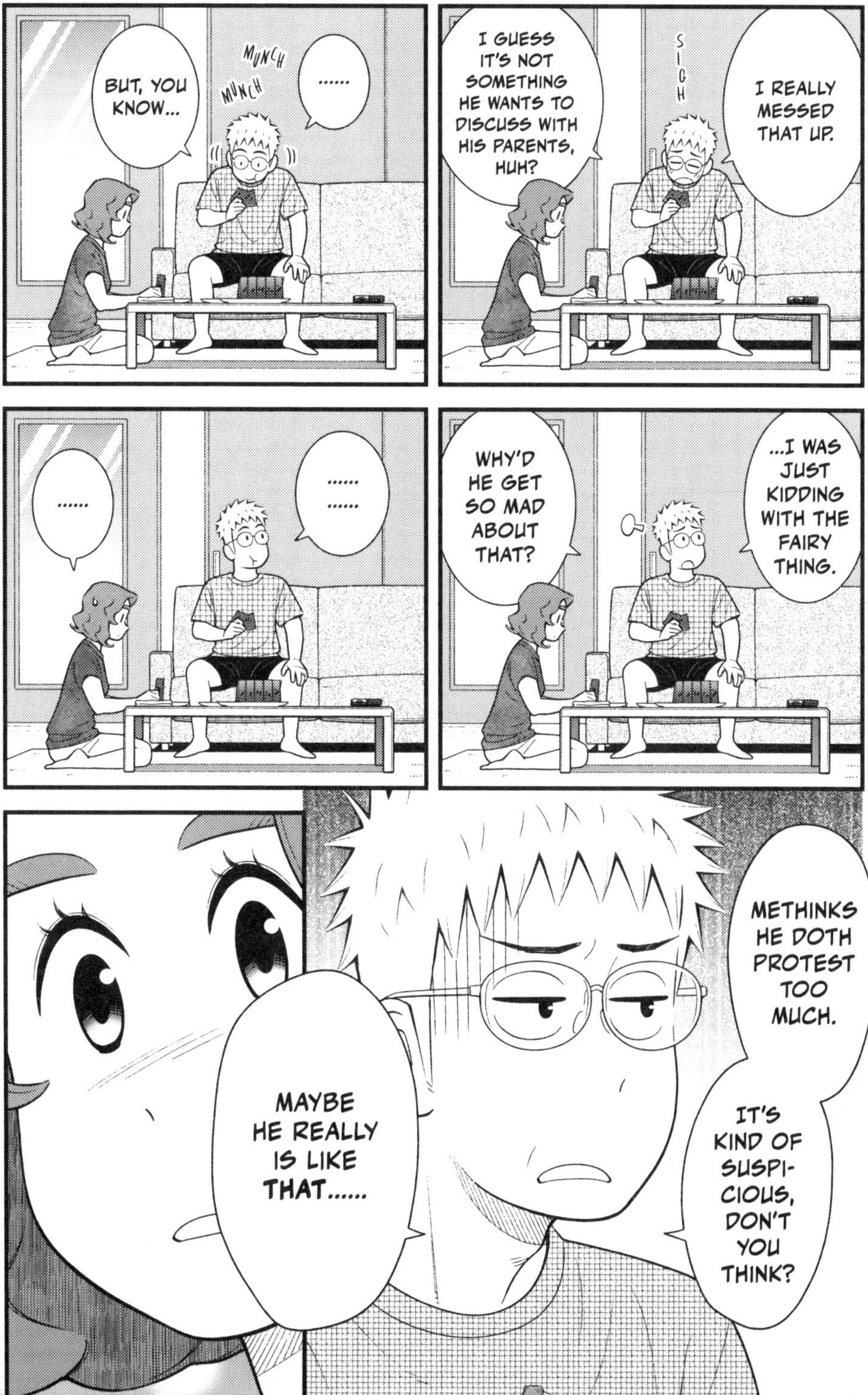
I REALLY MESSED THAT UP.
SIGH
I GUESS IT'S NOT SOMETHING HE WANTS TO DISCUSS WITH HIS PARENTS, HUH?
......
MUNCH
MUNCH
BUT, YOU KNOW...
...I WAS JUST KIDDING WITH THE FAIRY THING.
WHY'D HE GET SO MAD ABOUT THAT?
....
......
METHINKS HE DOTH PROTEST TOO MUCH.
IT'S KIND OF SUSPICIOUS, DON'T YOU THINK?
MAYBE HE REALLY IS LIKE THAT......

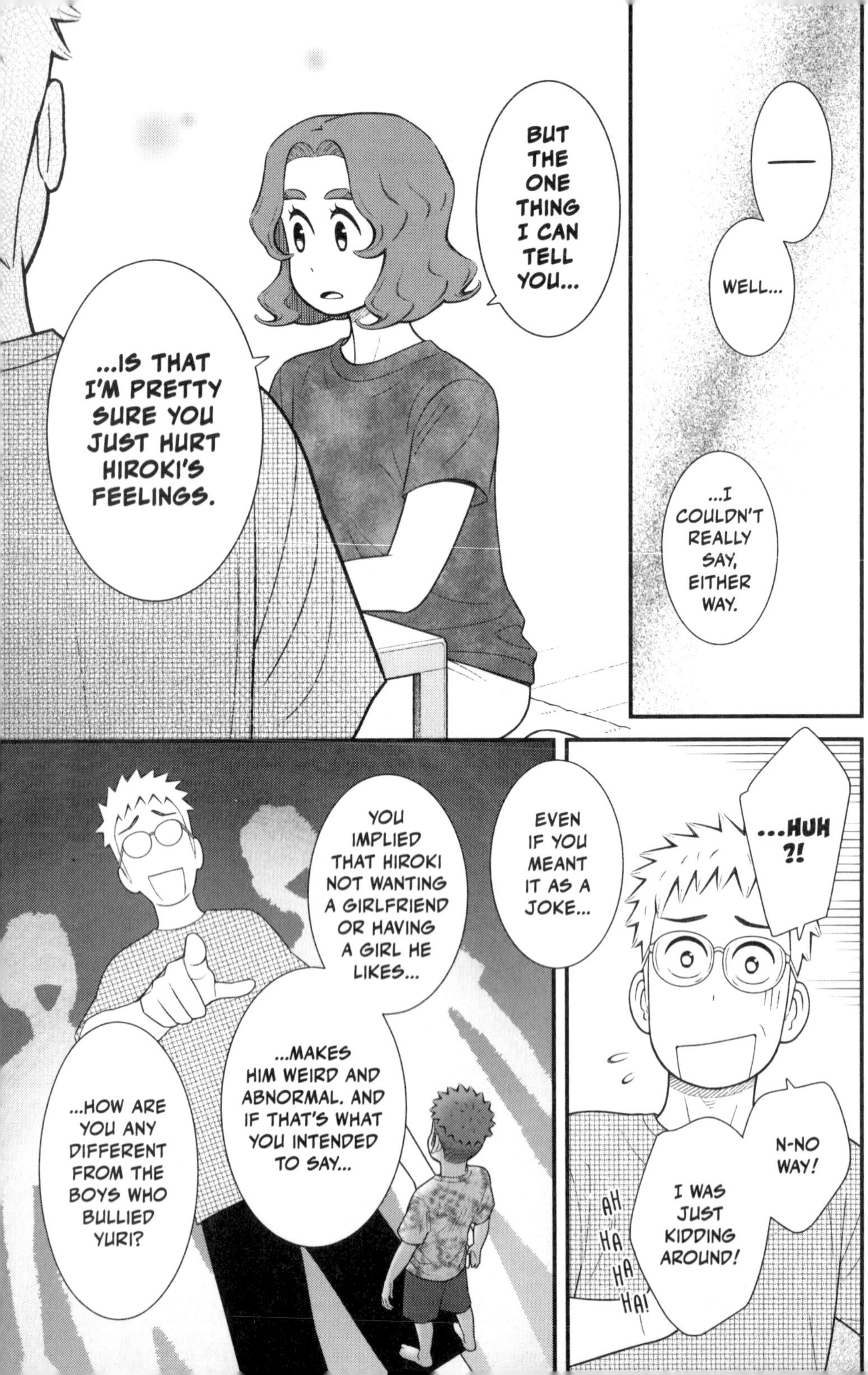
—
WELL...
...I COULDN'T REALLY SAY, EITHER WAY.
BUT THE ONE THING I CAN TELL YOU...
...IS THAT I'M PRETTY SURE YOU JUST HURT HIROKI'S FEELINGS.
...HUH ?!
N-NO WAY!
I WAS JUST KIDDING AROUND!
AH HA HA HA!
EVEN IF YOU MEANT IT AS A JOKE...
YOU IMPLIED THAT HIROKI NOT WANTING A GIRLFRIEND OR HAVING A GIRL HE LIKES...
...MAKES HIM WEIRD AND ABNORMAL. AND IF THAT'S WHAT YOU INTENDED TO SAY...
...HOW ARE YOU ANY DIFFERENT FROM THE BOYS WHO BULLIED YURI?

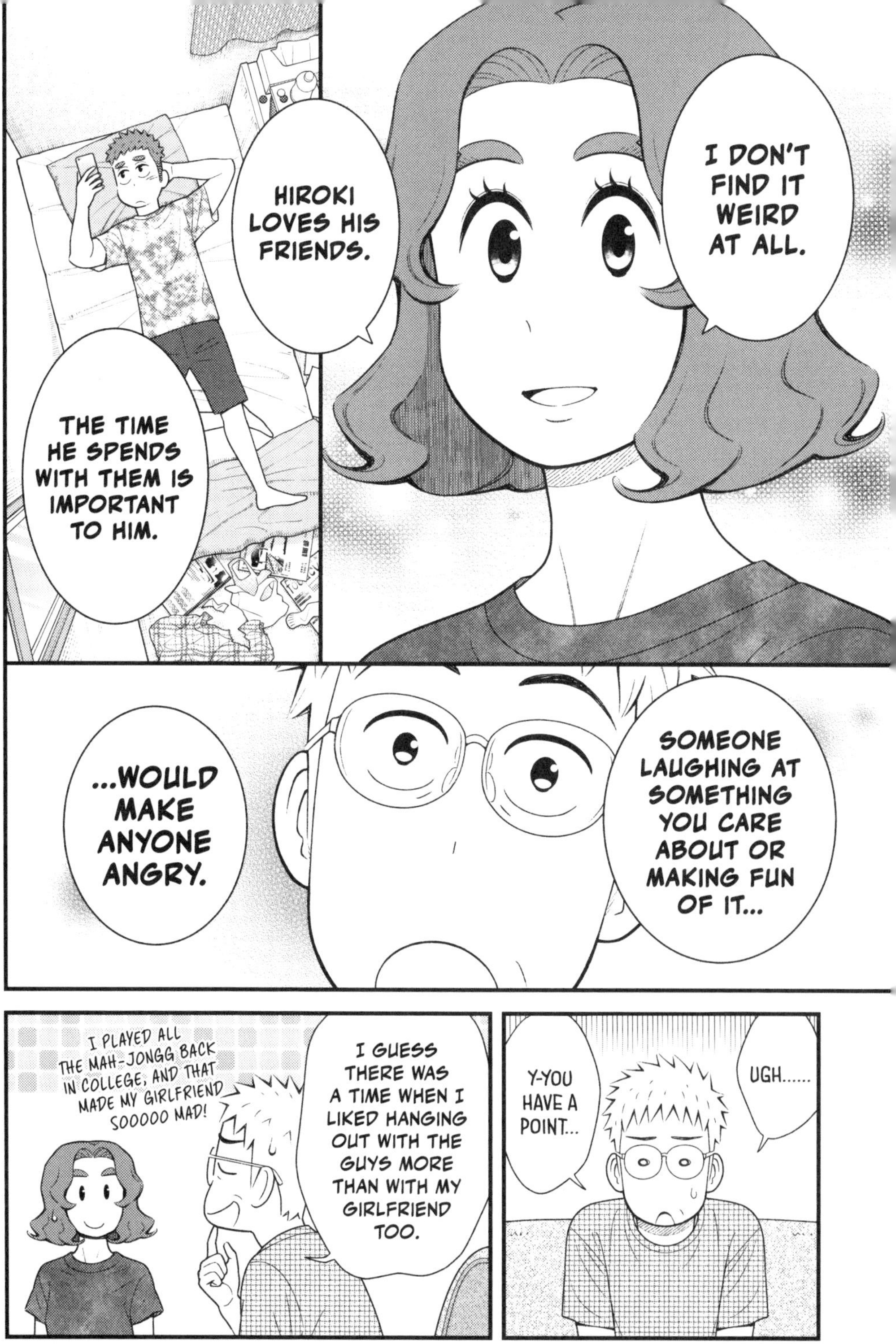
I DON'T FIND IT WEIRD AT ALL.
HIROKI LOVES HIS FRIENDS.
THE TIME HE SPENDS WITH THEM IS IMPORTANT TO HIM.
SOMEONE LAUGHING AT SOMETHING YOU CARE ABOUT OR MAKING FUN OF IT...
...WOULD MAKE ANYONE ANGRY.
UGH......
Y-YOU HAVE A POINT...
I GUESS THERE WAS A TIME WHEN I LIKED HANGING OUT WITH THE GUYS MORE THAN WITH MY GIRLFRIEND TOO.
I PLAYED ALL THE MAH-JONGG BACK IN COLLEGE, AND THAT MADE MY GIRLFRIEND SOOOOO MAD!

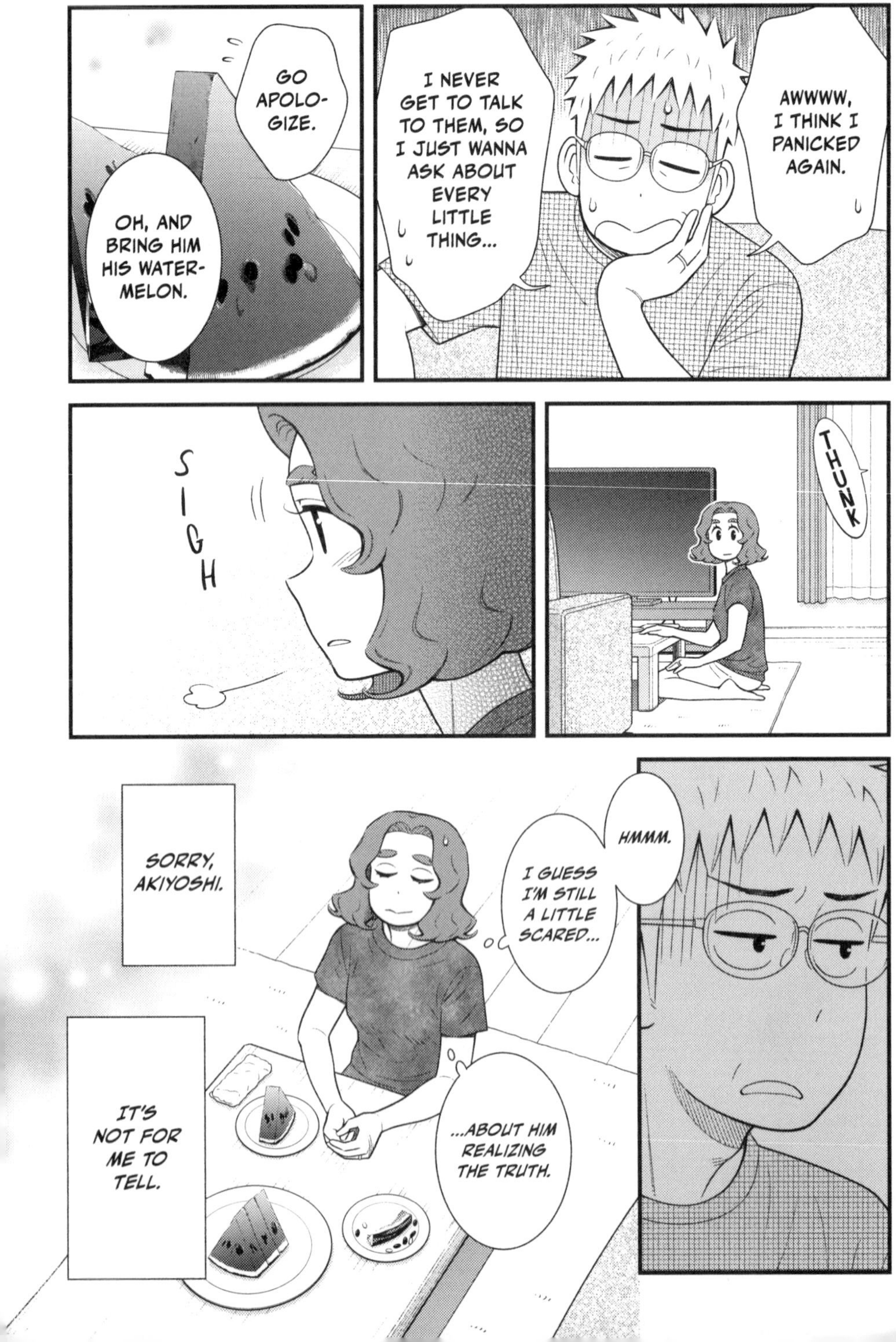
AWWWW, I THINK I PANICKED AGAIN.
I NEVER GET TO TALK TO THEM, SO I JUST WANNA ASK ABOUT EVERY LITTLE THING...
GO APOLOGIZE.
OH, AND BRING HIM HIS WATER-MELON.
THUNK
SIGH
HMMM.
I GUESS I'M STILL A LITTLE SCARED...
...ABOUT HIM REALIZING THE TRUTH.
SORRY, AKIYOSHI.
IT'S NOT FOR ME TO TELL.

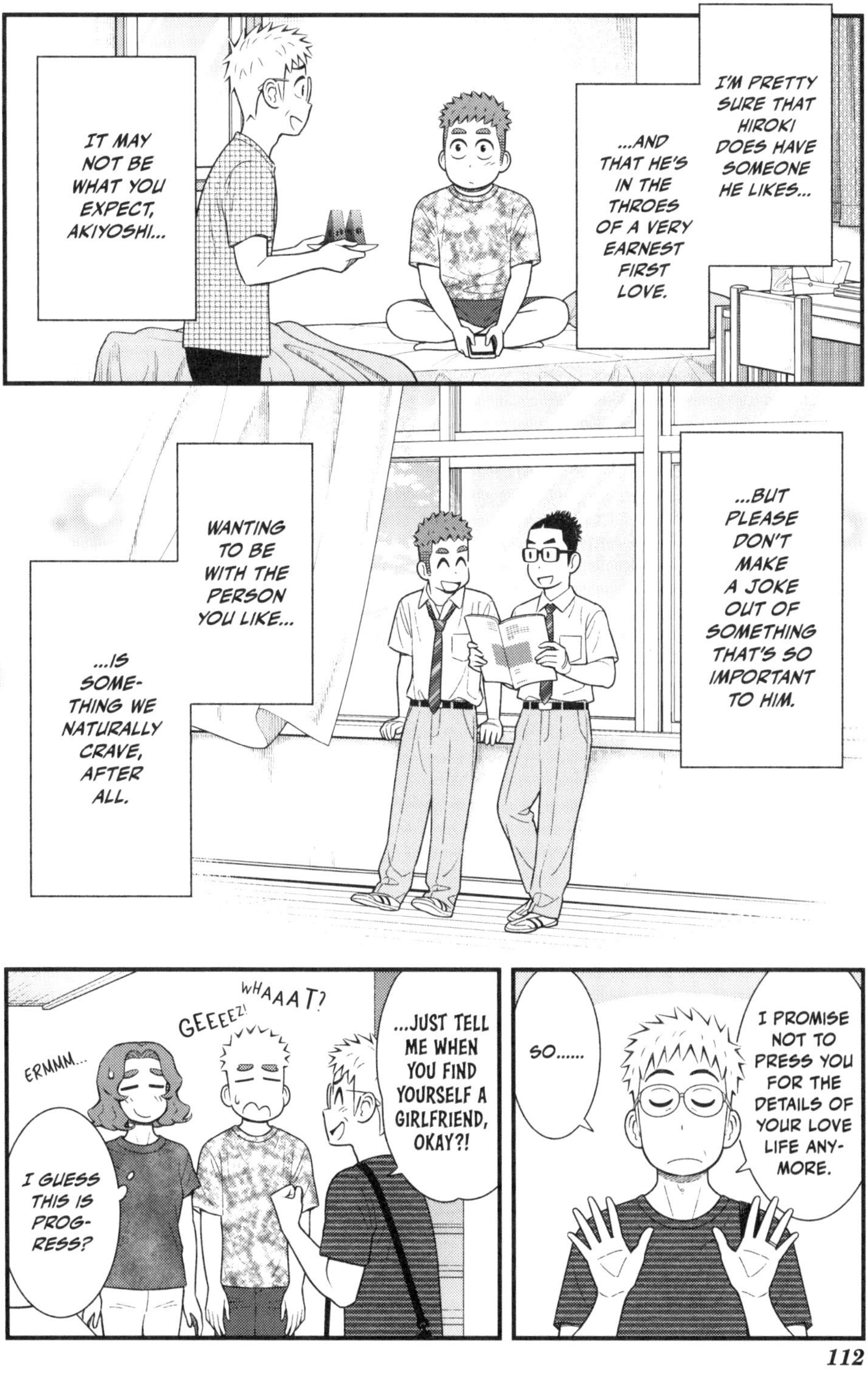

I'M PRETTY SURE THAT HIROKI DOES HAVE SOMEONE HE LIKES...
...AND THAT HE'S IN THE THROES OF A VERY EARNEST FIRST LOVE.
IT MAY NOT BE WHAT YOU EXPECT, AKIYOSHI...
...BUT PLEASE DON'T MAKE A JOKE OUT OF SOMETHING THAT'S SO IMPORTANT TO HIM.
WANTING TO BE WITH THE PERSON YOU LIKE...
...IS SOME-THING WE NATURALLY CRAVE, AFTER ALL.
I PROMISE NOT TO PRESS YOU FOR THE DETAILS OF YOUR LOVE LIFE ANY-MORE.
SO......
...JUST TELL ME WHEN YOU FIND YOURSELF A GIRLFRIEND, OKAY?!
WHAAAT?
GEEEEZ!
ERMMM...
I GUESS THIS IS PROG-RESS?

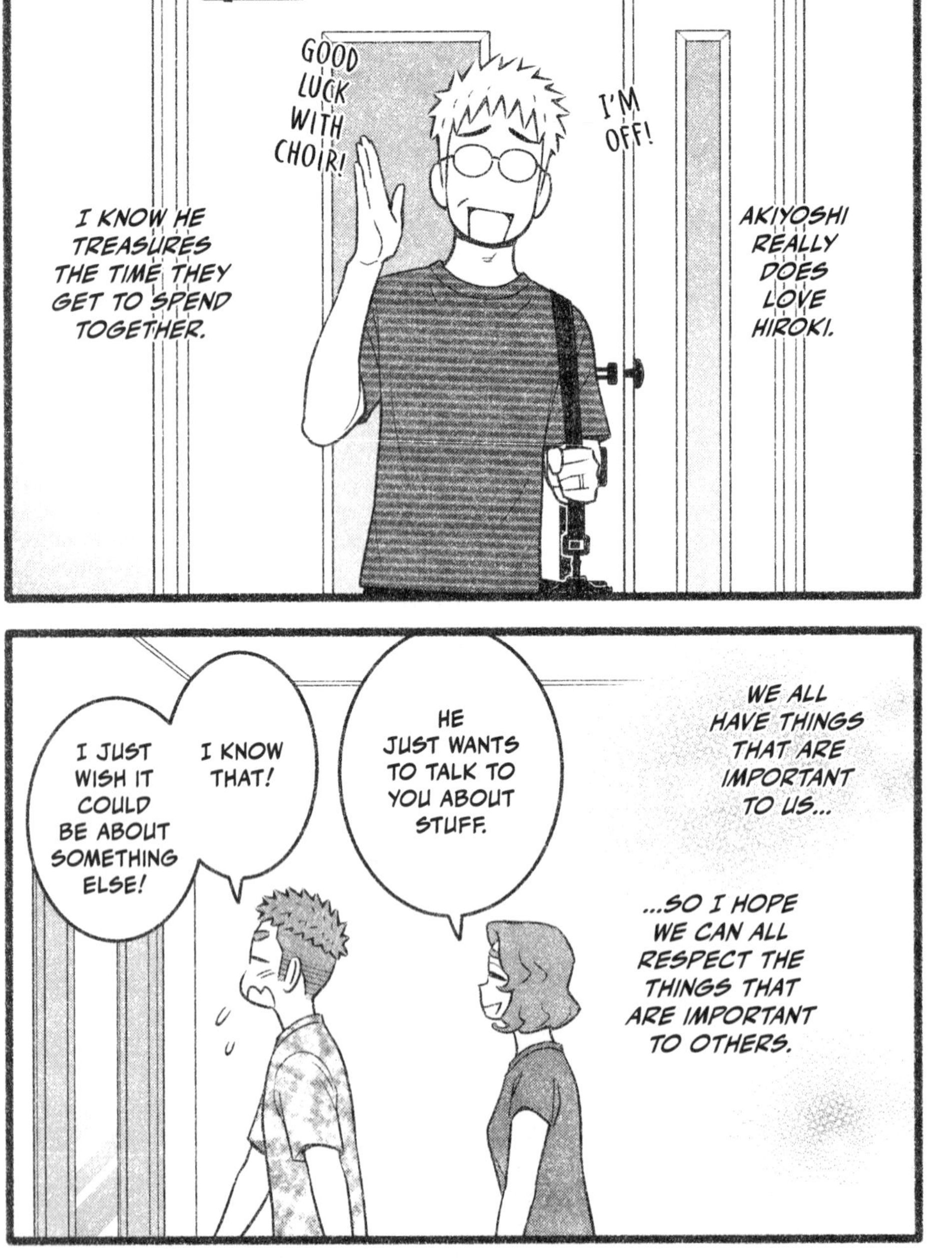
I'M OFF!
GOOD LUCK WITH CHOIR!
AKIYOSHI REALLY DOES LOVE HIROKI.
I KNOW HE TREASURES THE TIME THEY GET TO SPEND TOGETHER.
WE ALL HAVE THINGS THAT ARE IMPORTANT TO US...
HE JUST WANTS TO TALK TO YOU ABOUT STUFF.
I KNOW THAT!
I JUST WISH IT COULD BE ABOUT SOMETHING ELSE!
...SO I HOPE WE CAN ALL RESPECT THE THINGS THAT ARE IMPORTANT TO OTHERS.

I Think
Our Son
Is Gay

Chapter 61: What Do You Think?

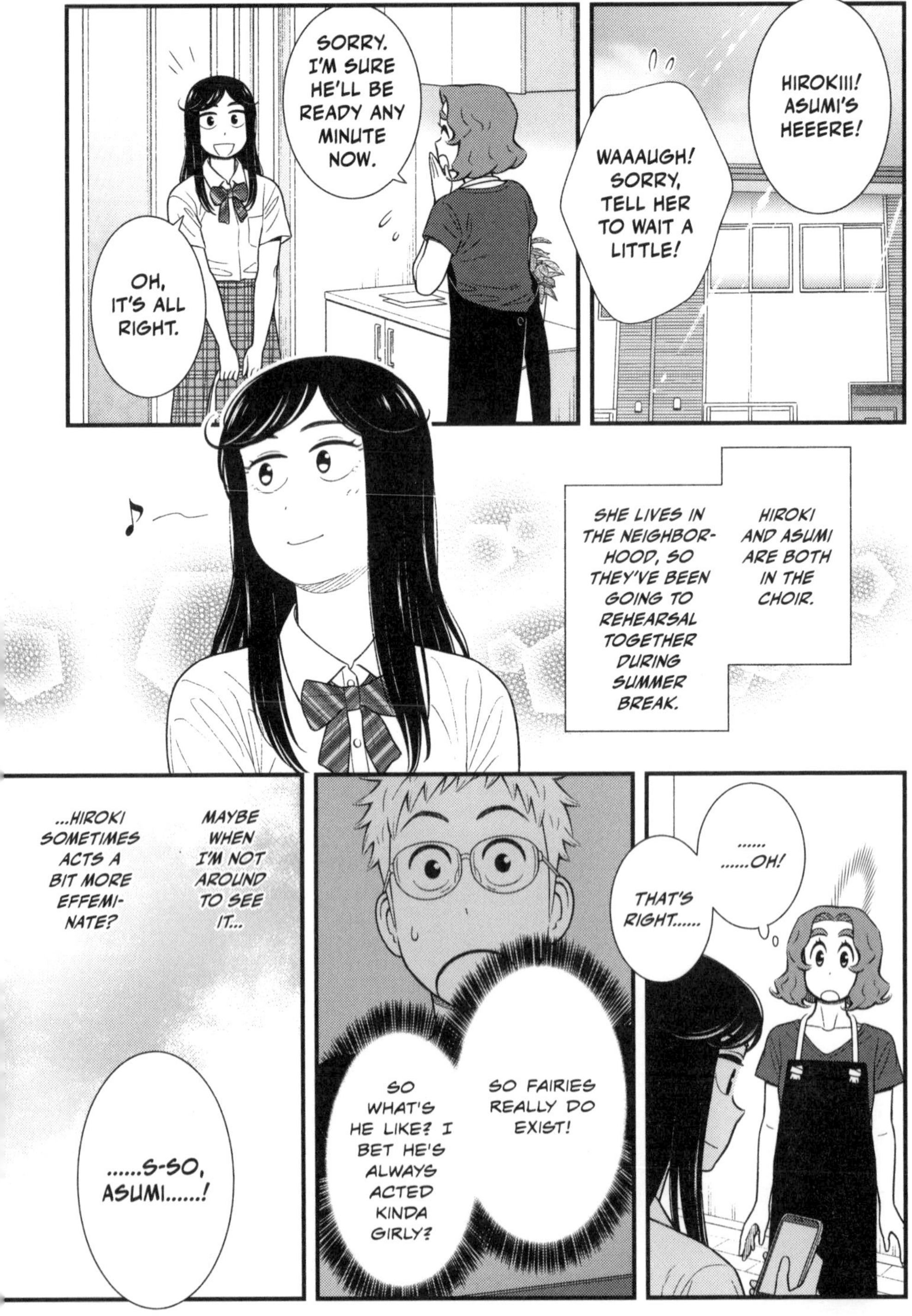
HIROKIII! ASUMI'S HEEERE!
WAAAUGH! SORRY, TELL HER TO WAIT A LITTLE!
SORRY. I'M SURE HE'LL BE READY ANY MINUTE NOW.
OH, IT'S ALL RIGHT.
HIROKI AND ASUMI ARE BOTH IN THE CHOIR.
SHE LIVES IN THE NEIGHBORHOOD, SO THEY'VE BEEN GOING TO REHEARSAL TOGETHER DURING SUMMER BREAK.
....OH!
THAT'S RIGHT......
SO FAIRIES REALLY DO EXIST!
SO WHAT'S HE LIKE? I BET HE'S ALWAYS ACTED KINDA GIRLY?
MAYBE WHEN I'M NOT AROUND TO SEE IT...
...HIROKI SOMETIMES ACTS A BIT MORE EFFEMINATE?
......S-SO, ASUMI......!

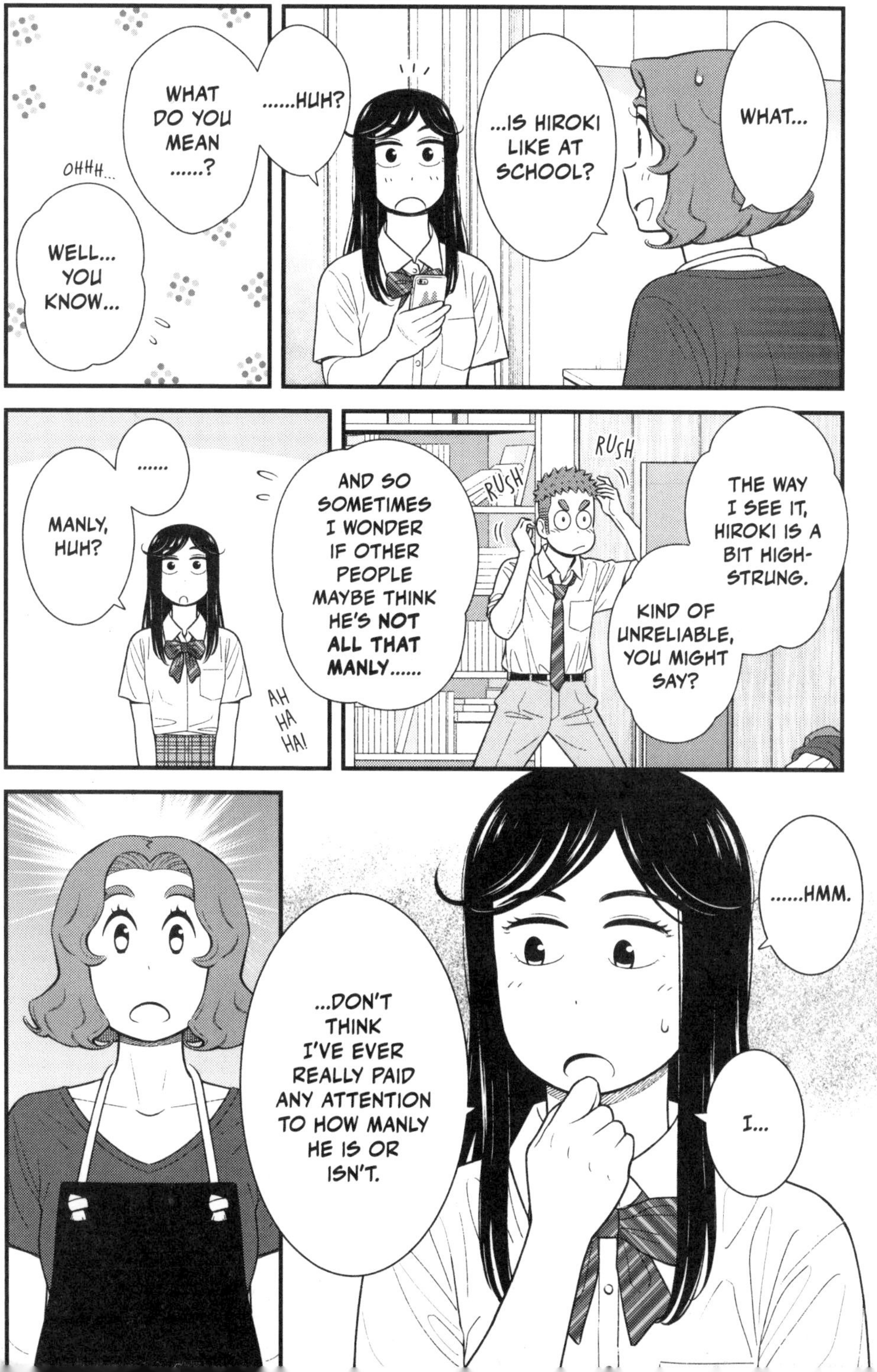
WHAT...
...IS HIROKI LIKE AT SCHOOL?
......HUH?
WHAT DO YOU MEAN ......?
OHHH...
WELL... YOU KNOW...
THE WAY I SEE IT, HIROKI IS A BIT HIGH-STRUNG.
KIND OF UNRELIABLE, YOU MIGHT SAY?
RUSH
RUSH
AND SO SOMETIMES I WONDER IF OTHER PEOPLE MAYBE THINK HE'S **NOT ALL THAT MANLY**......
......
MANLY, HUH?
AH HA HA!
......HMM.
I...
...DON'T THINK I'VE EVER REALLY PAID ANY ATTENTION TO HOW MANLY HE IS OR ISN'T.

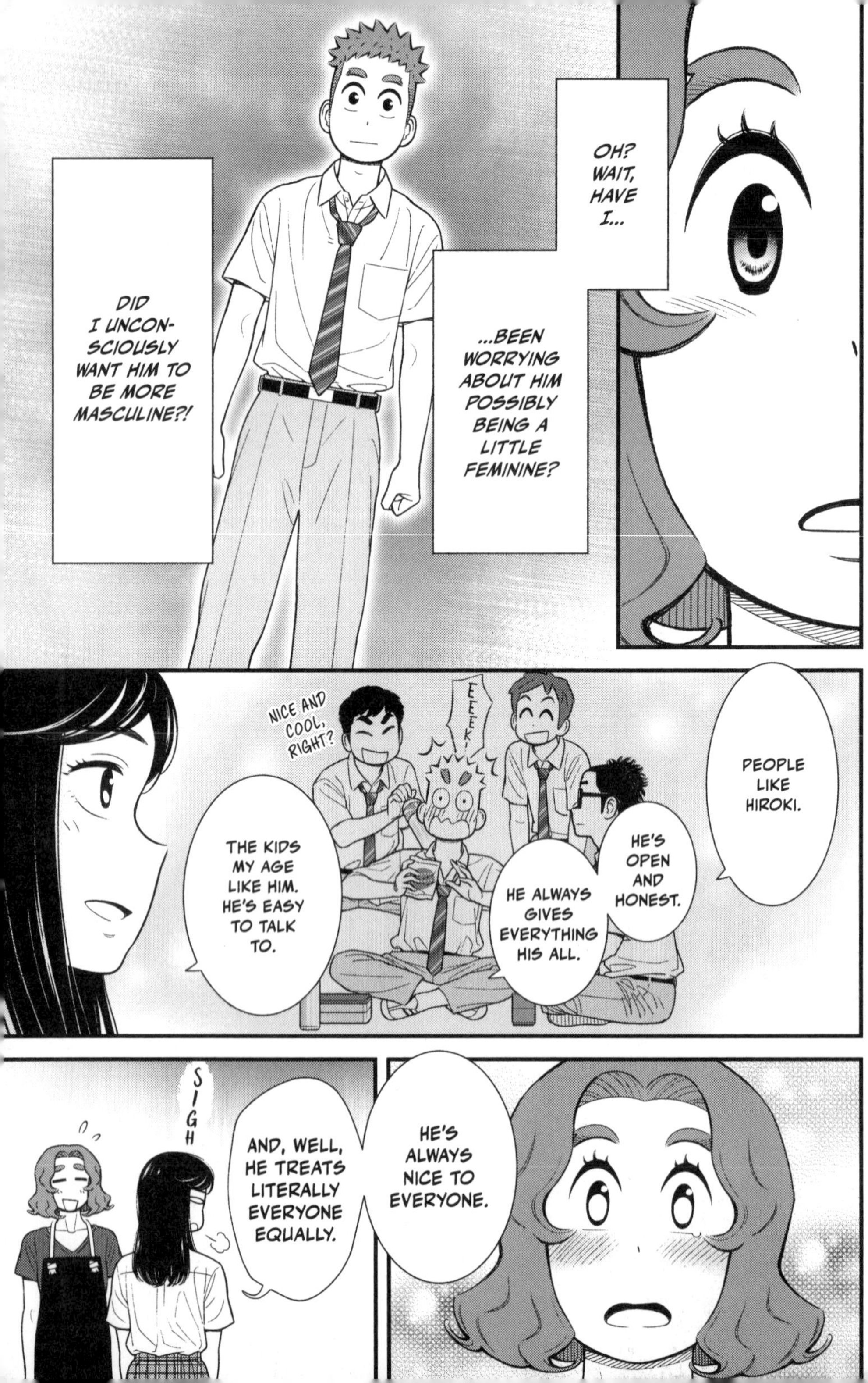
OH? WAIT, HAVE I...
...BEEN WORRYING ABOUT HIM POSSIBLY BEING A LITTLE FEMININE?
DID I UNCON-SCIOUSLY WANT HIM TO BE MORE MASCULINE?!
PEOPLE LIKE HIROKI.
HE'S OPEN AND HONEST.
HE ALWAYS GIVES EVERYTHING HIS ALL.
EEEK!
NICE AND COOL, RIGHT?
THE KIDS MY AGE LIKE HIM. HE'S EASY TO TALK TO.
HE'S ALWAYS NICE TO EVERYONE.
AND, WELL, HE TREATS LITERALLY EVERYONE EQUALLY.
SIGH

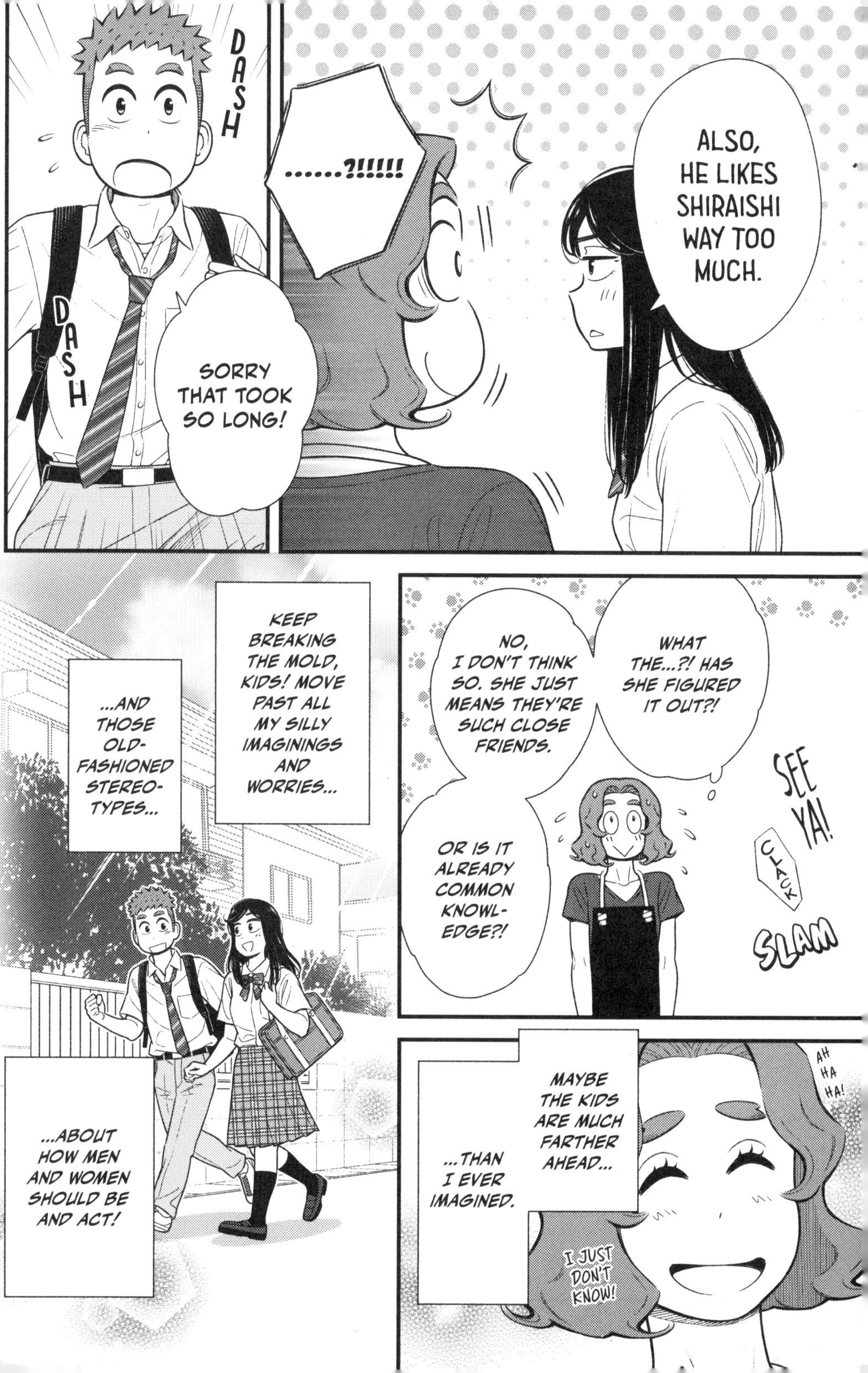
ALSO, HE LIKES SHIRAISHI WAY TOO MUCH.
......?!!!!!
DASH
DASH
SORRY THAT TOOK SO LONG!
WHAT THE...?! HAS SHE FIGURED IT OUT?!
NO, I DON'T THINK SO. SHE JUST MEANS THEY'RE SUCH CLOSE FRIENDS.
OR IS IT ALREADY COMMON KNOWL-EDGE?!
SEE YA!
CLACK
SLAM
MAYBE THE KIDS ARE MUCH FARTHER AHEAD...
...THAN I EVER IMAGINED.
AH HA HA!
I JUST DON'T KNOW!
KEEP BREAKING THE MOLD, KIDS! MOVE PAST ALL MY SILLY IMAGININGS AND WORRIES...
...AND THOSE OLD-FASHIONED STEREO-TYPES...
...ABOUT HOW MEN AND WOMEN SHOULD BE AND ACT!

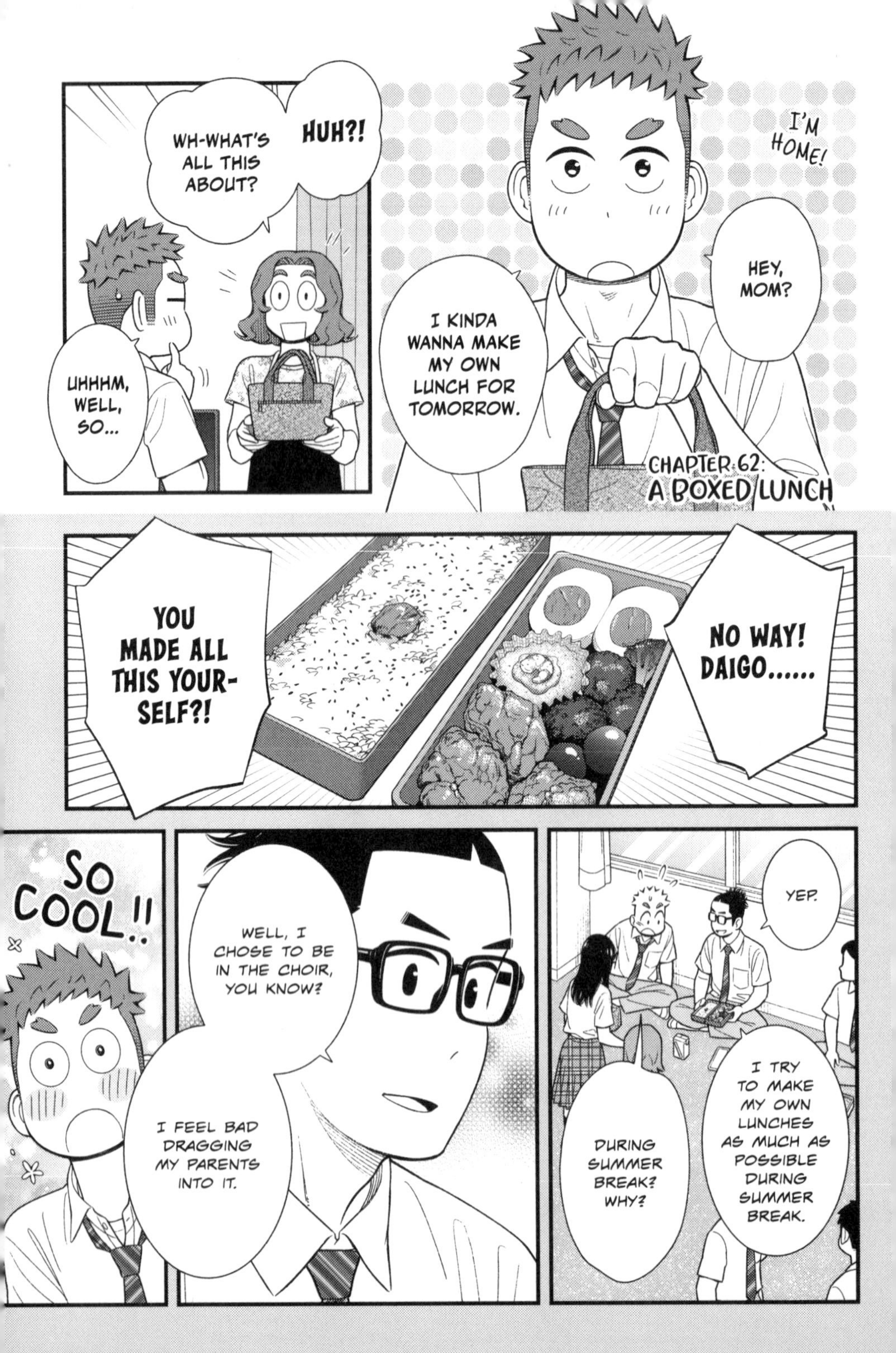
I'M HOME!
HEY, MOM?
I KINDA WANNA MAKE MY OWN LUNCH FOR TOMORROW.
CHAPTER 62: A BOXED LUNCH
HUH?!
WH-WHAT'S ALL THIS ABOUT?
UHHHM, WELL, SO...
NO WAY! DAIGO......
YOU MADE ALL THIS YOUR-SELF?!
YEP.
I TRY TO MAKE MY OWN LUNCHES AS MUCH AS POSSIBLE DURING SUMMER BREAK.
DURING SUMMER BREAK? WHY?
WELL, I CHOSE TO BE IN THE CHOIR, YOU KNOW?
I FEEL BAD DRAGGING MY PARENTS INTO IT.
SO COOL!!

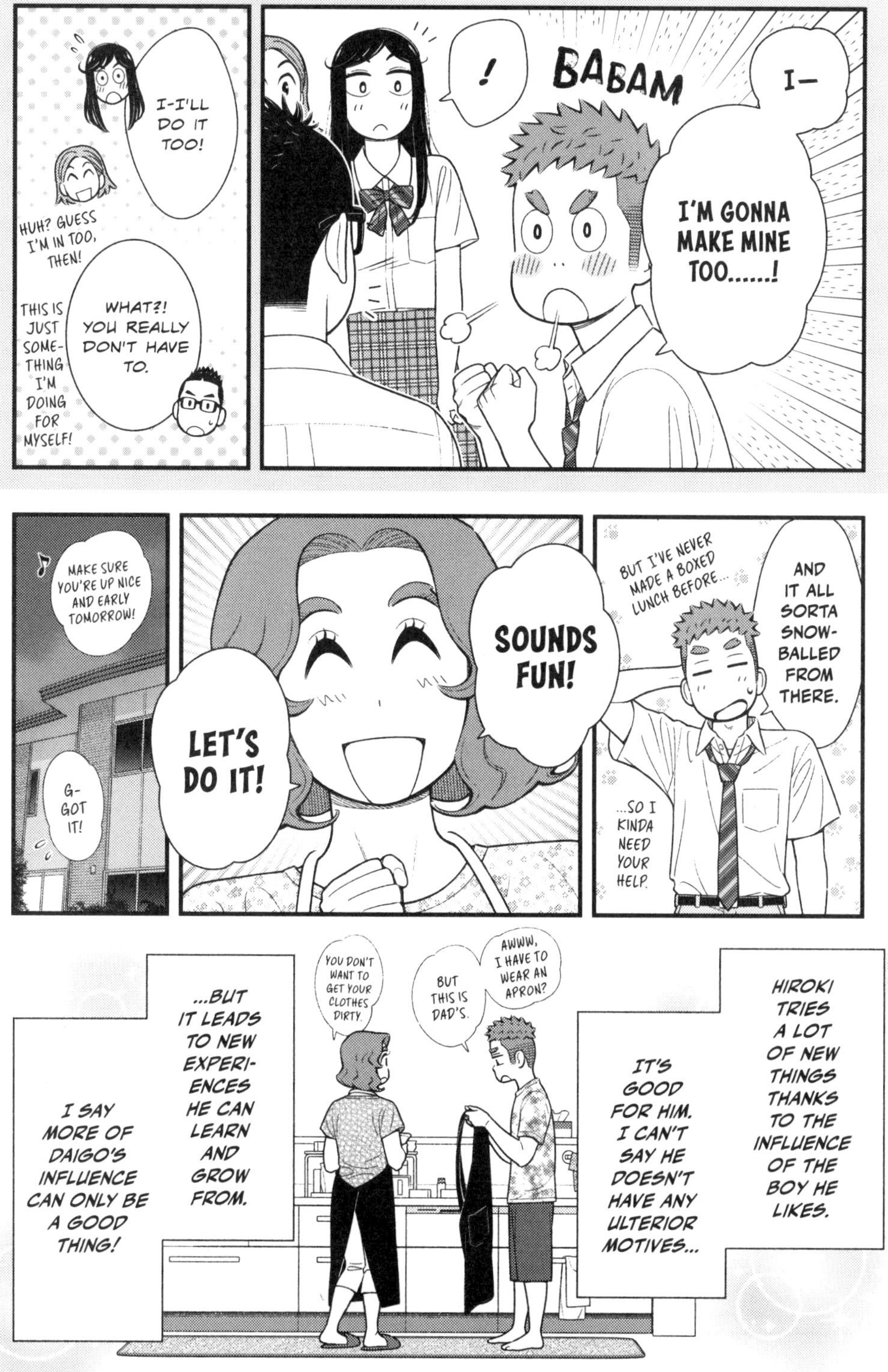

I—
I'M GONNA MAKE MINE TOO......!
BABAM
!
I-I'LL DO IT TOO!
HUH? GUESS I'M IN TOO, THEN!
WHAT?! YOU REALLY DON'T HAVE TO.
THIS IS JUST SOME-THING I'M DOING FOR MYSELF!
AND IT ALL SORTA SNOW-BALLED FROM THERE.
BUT I'VE NEVER MADE A BOXED LUNCH BEFORE...
...SO I KINDA NEED YOUR HELP.
SOUNDS FUN!
LET'S DO IT!
MAKE SURE YOU'RE UP NICE AND EARLY TOMORROW!
G-GOT IT!
HIROKI TRIES A LOT OF NEW THINGS THANKS TO THE INFLUENCE OF THE BOY HE LIKES.
IT'S GOOD FOR HIM. I CAN'T SAY HE DOESN'T HAVE ANY ULTERIOR MOTIVES...
AWWW, I HAVE TO WEAR AN APRON?
BUT THIS IS DAD'S.
YOU DON'T WANT TO GET YOUR CLOTHES DIRTY.
...BUT IT LEADS TO NEW EXPERI-ENCES HE CAN LEARN AND GROW FROM.
I SAY MORE OF DAIGO'S INFLUENCE CAN ONLY BE A GOOD THING!

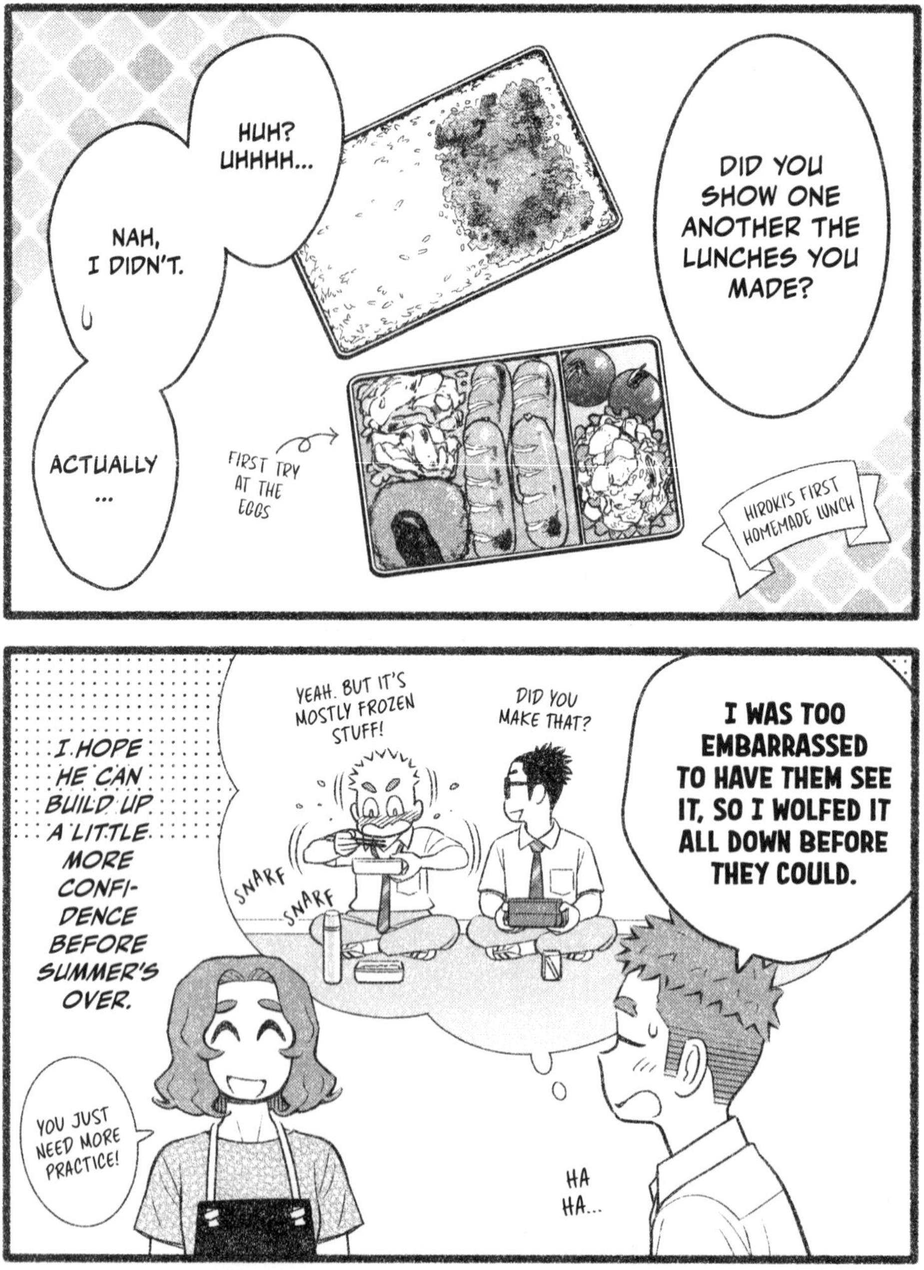
DID YOU SHOW ONE ANOTHER THE LUNCHES YOU MADE?
HUH? UHHHH...
NAH, I DIDN'T.
ACTUALLY ...
HIROKI'S FIRST HOMEMADE LUNCH
FIRST TRY AT THE EGGS
I WAS TOO EMBARRASSED TO HAVE THEM SEE IT, SO I WOLFED IT ALL DOWN BEFORE THEY COULD.
DID YOU MAKE THAT?
YEAH. BUT IT'S MOSTLY FROZEN STUFF!
SNARF SNARF
I HOPE HE CAN BUILD UP A LITTLE MORE CONFI-DENCE BEFORE SUMMER'S OVER.
HA HA...
YOU JUST NEED MORE PRACTICE!

I Think Our Son Is Gay

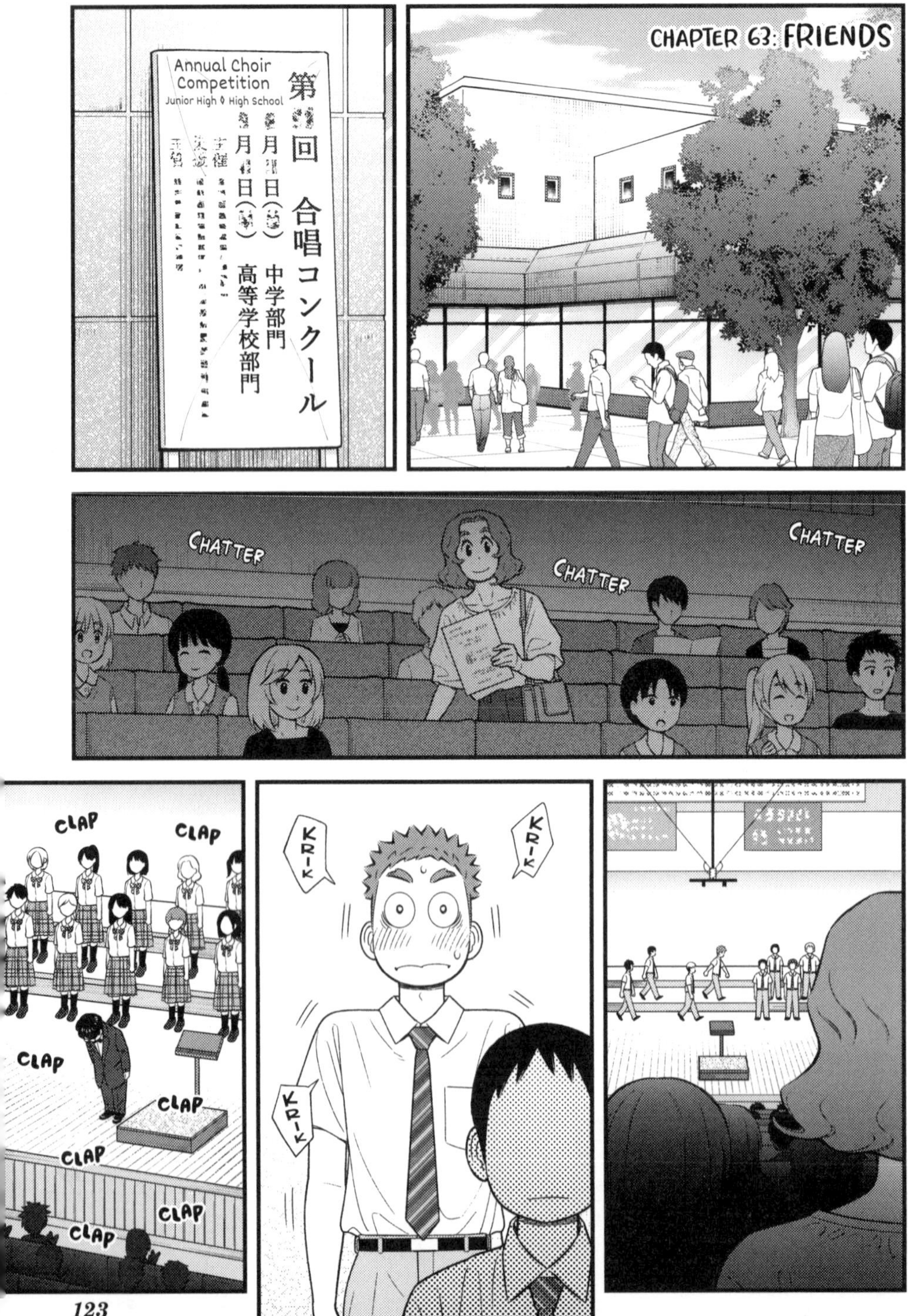
Chapter 63: Friends
Annual Choir Competition
Junior High & High School
第 回 合唱コンクール
中学部門
高等学校部門
Chatter
Chatter
Chatter
Krik
Krik
Krik
Clap
Clap
Clap
Clap
Clap
Clap
Clap

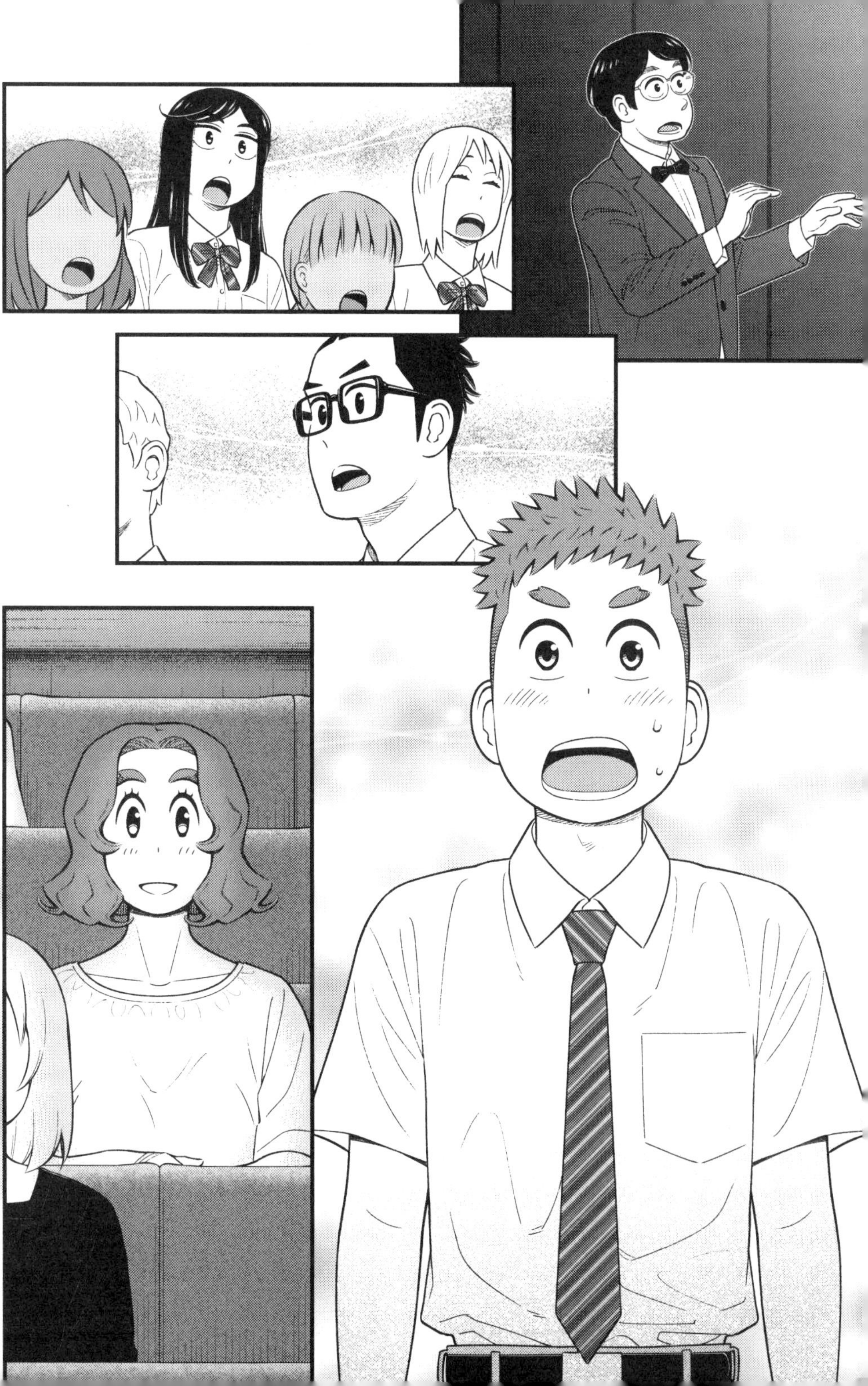

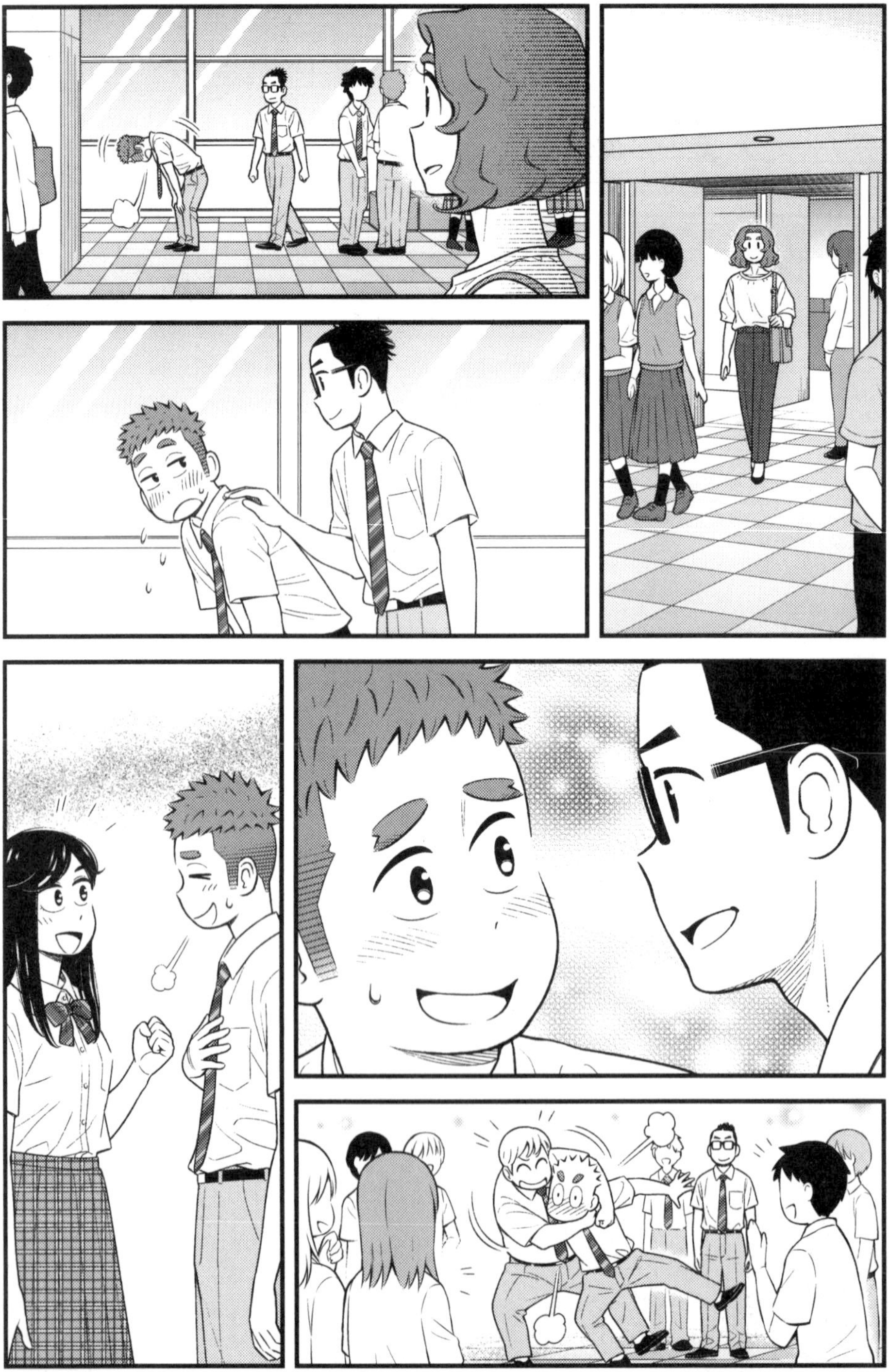

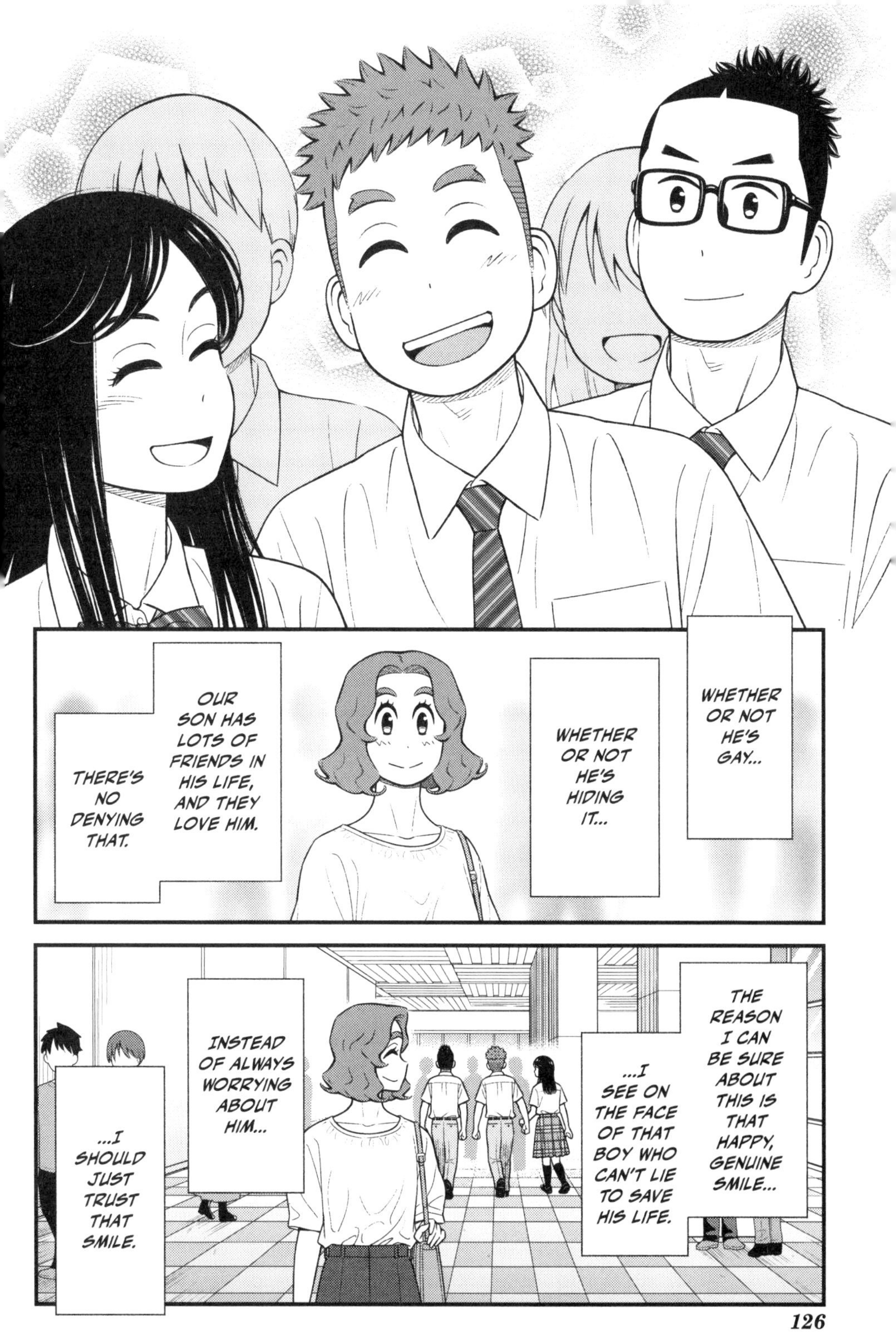
WHETHER OR NOT HE'S GAY...
WHETHER OR NOT HE'S HIDING IT...
OUR SON HAS LOTS OF FRIENDS IN HIS LIFE, AND THEY LOVE HIM.
THERE'S NO DENYING THAT.
THE REASON I CAN BE SURE ABOUT THIS IS THAT HAPPY, GENUINE SMILE...
...I SEE ON THE FACE OF THAT BOY WHO CAN'T LIE TO SAVE HIS LIFE.
INSTEAD OF ALWAYS WORRYING ABOUT HIM...
...I SHOULD JUST TRUST THAT SMILE.

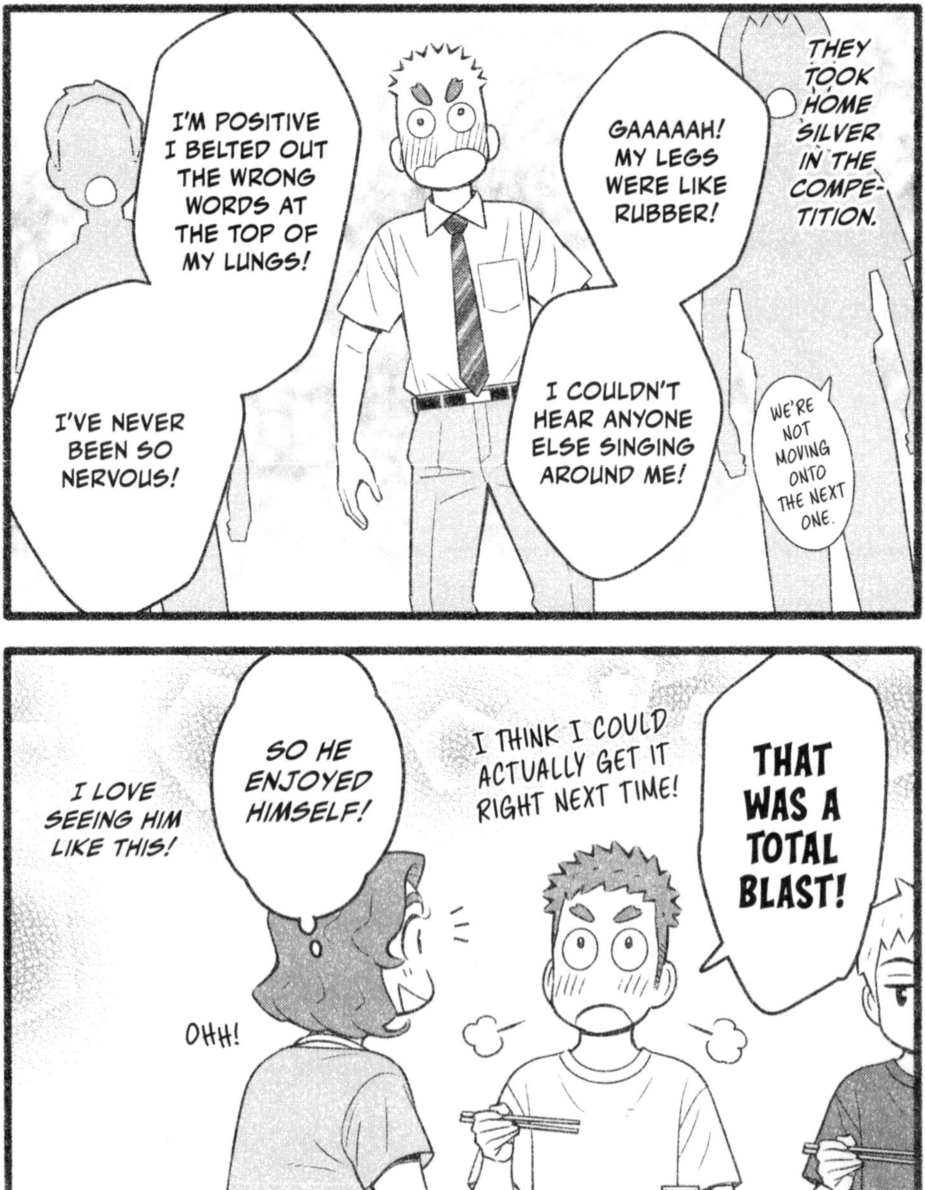
THEY TOOK HOME SILVER IN THE COMPETITION.
WE'RE NOT MOVING ONTO THE NEXT ONE.
GAAAAAH! MY LEGS WERE LIKE RUBBER!
I COULDN'T HEAR ANYONE ELSE SINGING AROUND ME!
I'M POSITIVE I BELTED OUT THE WRONG WORDS AT THE TOP OF MY LUNGS!
I'VE NEVER BEEN SO NERVOUS!
THAT WAS A TOTAL BLAST!
I THINK I COULD ACTUALLY GET IT RIGHT NEXT TIME!
SO HE ENJOYED HIMSELF!
I LOVE SEEING HIM LIKE THIS!
OHH!

I Think
Our Son
Is Gay

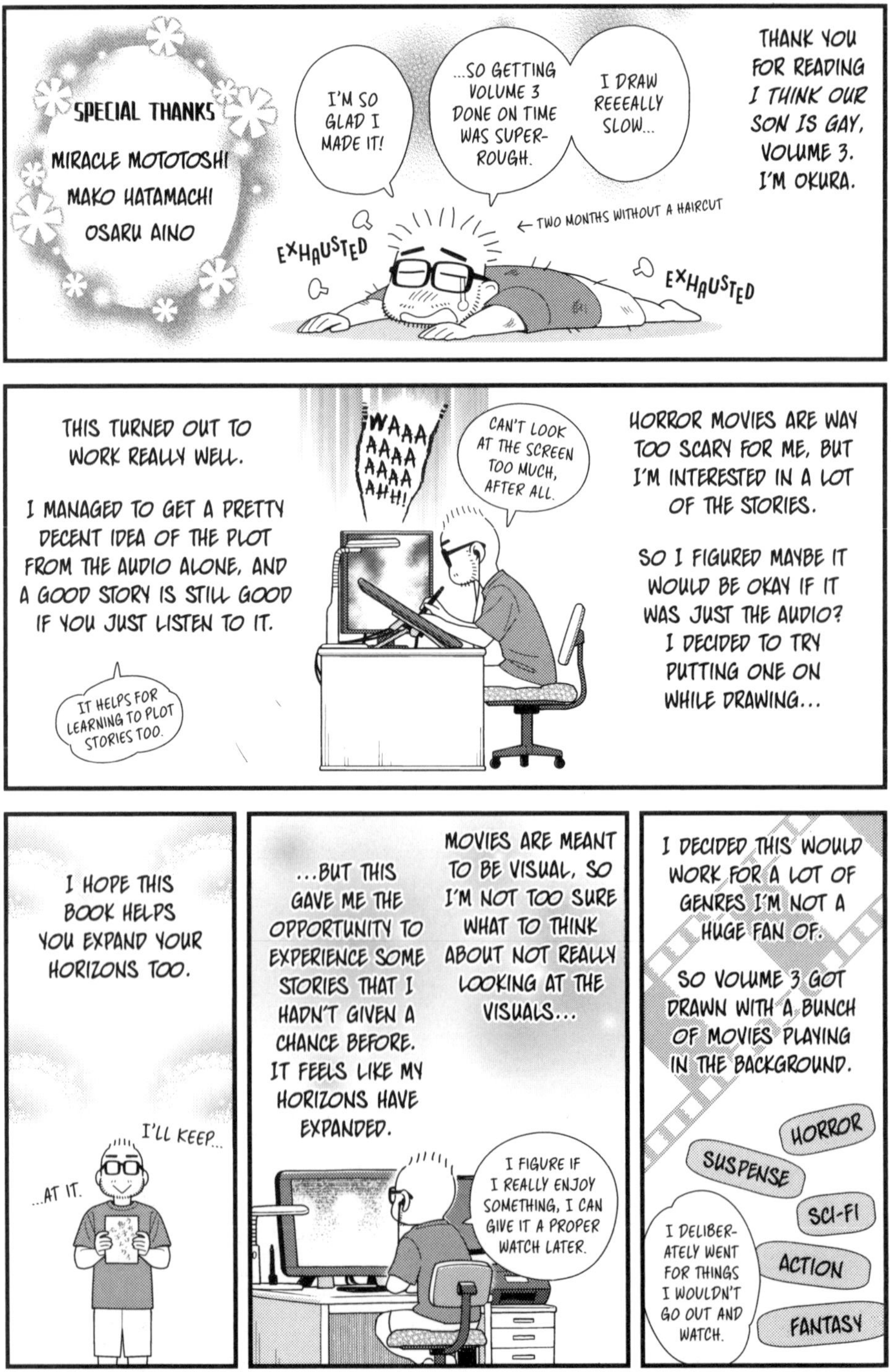
THANK YOU FOR READING *I THINK OUR SON IS GAY*, VOLUME 3. I'M OKURA.
I DRAW REEEALLY SLOW...
...SO GETTING VOLUME 3 DONE ON TIME WAS SUPER-ROUGH.
I'M SO GLAD I MADE IT!
← TWO MONTHS WITHOUT A HAIRCUT
EXHAUSTED
EXHAUSTED
SPECIAL THANKS
MIRACLE MOTOTOSHI
MAKO HATAMACHI
OSARU AINO
HORROR MOVIES ARE WAY TOO SCARY FOR ME, BUT I'M INTERESTED IN A LOT OF THE STORIES.
SO I FIGURED MAYBE IT WOULD BE OKAY IF IT WAS JUST THE AUDIO? I DECIDED TO TRY PUTTING ONE ON WHILE DRAWING...
CAN'T LOOK AT THE SCREEN TOO MUCH, AFTER ALL.
WAAAAAAAAAAAAAAHH!
THIS TURNED OUT TO WORK REALLY WELL.
I MANAGED TO GET A PRETTY DECENT IDEA OF THE PLOT FROM THE AUDIO ALONE, AND A GOOD STORY IS STILL GOOD IF YOU JUST LISTEN TO IT.
IT HELPS FOR LEARNING TO PLOT STORIES TOO.
I DECIDED THIS WOULD WORK FOR A LOT OF GENRES I'M NOT A HUGE FAN OF.
SO VOLUME 3 GOT DRAWN WITH A BUNCH OF MOVIES PLAYING IN THE BACKGROUND.
HORROR
SUSPENSE
SCI-FI
ACTION
FANTASY
I DELIBERATELY WENT FOR THINGS I WOULDN'T GO OUT AND WATCH.
MOVIES ARE MEANT TO BE VISUAL, SO I'M NOT TOO SURE WHAT TO THINK ABOUT NOT REALLY LOOKING AT THE VISUALS...
...BUT THIS GAVE ME THE OPPORTUNITY TO EXPERIENCE SOME STORIES THAT I HADN'T GIVEN A CHANCE BEFORE. IT FEELS LIKE MY HORIZONS HAVE EXPANDED.
I FIGURE IF I REALLY ENJOY SOMETHING, I CAN GIVE IT A PROPER WATCH LATER.
I HOPE THIS BOOK HELPS YOU EXPAND YOUR HORIZONS TOO.
I'LL KEEP...
...AT IT.

2020.10. OKURA

I Think Our Son Is Gay

YO-AGU-478

3

OKURA

Translation: Leighann Harvey
Lettering: Lor Prescott
Cover Design: Andrea Miller
Editor: Tania Biswas

I THINK OUR SON IS GAY Volume 3
© 2020 Okura/SQUARE ENIX CO., LTD.
First published in Japan in 2020 by SQUARE ENIX CO., LTD.
English translation rights arranged with
SQUARE ENIX CO., LTD. and SQUARE ENIX, INC.
English translation © 2022 by SQUARE ENIX CO., LTD.

ISBN: 978-1-64609-126-3

Library of Congress Cataloging-in-Publication
Data is on file with the publisher.

Printed in Canada
First printing, May 2022
10 9 8 7 6 5 4 3 2 1

SQUARE ENIX
MANGA & BOOKS
www.square-enix-books.com